FRAGMENTS OF HOME

Fragments of Home

Refugee Housing and the Politics of Shelter

TOM SCOTT-SMITH

STANFORD UNIVERSITY PRESS
Stanford, California

Stanford University Press
Stanford, California

© 2024 by Tom Alastair Scott-Smith. All rights reserved.

No part of this book may be reproduced or transmitted in any form or by any means, electronic or mechanical, including photocopying and recording, or in any information storage or retrieval system, without the prior written permission of Stanford University Press.

Printed in the United States of America on acid-free, archival-quality paper

Epigraph is copyright © John Berger and John Berger Estate, 2005, *And Our Faces, My Heart, Brief as Photos*, Bloomsbury Publishing Plc.

Library of Congress Cataloging-in-Publication Data

Names: Scott-Smith, Tom, 1980– author.

Title: Fragments of home : refugee housing and the politics of shelter / Tom Scott-Smith.

Description: Stanford, California : Stanford University Press, 2024. | Includes bibliographical references and index.

Identifiers: LCCN 2023058087 (print) | LCCN 2023058088 (ebook) | ISBN 9781503639782 (cloth) | ISBN 9781503640283 (paperback) | ISBN 9781503640290 (epub)

Subjects: LCSH: Refugees—Housing. | Refuge (Humanitarian assistance) | Emigration and immigration—Social aspects.

Classification: LCC HV640 .S367 2024 (print) | LCC HV640 (ebook) | DDC 362.87—dc23/eng/20240313

LC record available at https://lccn.loc.gov/2023058087

LC ebook record available at https://lccn.loc.gov/2023058088

Cover design: Lindy Kasler

Cover photograph: Temporary shelters in the *Camp de la Lande*. Calais, France. © University of Oxford / Mark E. Breeze, 2016

For Rosa and Thea

Without a home everything was fragmentation

John Berger

Contents

Illustrations

Acknowledgments

My last book was something of a solitary pursuit, but this one has been helped along from the very start by the kindness and support of hundreds of people. First, and most crucially, I would like to thank Mark E. Breeze, who was absolutely pivotal throughout the research. For simplicity, I wrote this book in the first person, but I was rarely alone: Mark was often there with humor, wisdom, and sensibility. He helped me develop the research plan, he was closely involved with the fieldwork, he organized many of the visits, and he took the photographs and led on the film that accompanies this book. I hope readers will watch the film, which brings many of these examples to life through Mark's beautiful and poised images (it is freely available at https://www.rsc.ox.ac.uk/shelter-without-shelter). This book delves into these issues analytically (and not necessarily in a way that Mark would agree with), but he has influenced the text in many respects—and of course, he ultimately prevailed in wearing down my skepticism about the value of humanitarian architecture. Criticisms? What criticisms? Mark, you are a great friend, a brilliant collaborator, and I'm truly indebted to you.

The grant for this project was written with the help of Dan Hicks, who lodged the idea in my head that shelter might exist in objects as well as structures while we were driving a car around freezing Calais. His work on conflict and contemporary archaeology has been edifying from the beginning. The project also relied on the enthusiasm and perception of Rachael Kiddey, with her remarkable ability to connect with people, and I am particularly grateful for her help with fieldwork in Greece. I could not have done this research without Zoey Poll, whose assistance was absolutely critical in Paris. Her writings taught me a lot, and they always crackled with ideas. For background research and help on the ground, I am especially grateful to Evan Easton-Calabria and Francesco Bosso in Berlin and Sarah Mallet, Cannelle Gueugen–Teil, and Rosanna O'Keefe in Calais. For help with translation and transcription, many thanks indeed to Nancy Naser Al Deen, Amani Awad, Nora Bardelli, Zoey Poll again, and Dimitra Dantsiou.

The Architectures of Displacement project was funded through a partnership between the Arts and Humanities Research Council and the Economic and Social Research Council of the United Kingdom. Additional funding came from the Oxford Department of International Development (ODID), the Refugee Studies Centre/Swiss FDFA Seed Fund, and the Fell Fund at the University of Oxford. I'm grateful to everyone who helped manage these grants, especially to Emma Rundall for being such a calm presence. I have been lucky to work with so many fantastic colleagues at the Refugee Studies Centre over the years, and even if they were not directly involved in this project, I would like to thank them all. Particular thanks must go to Matthew Gibney for his kind mentorship alongside drinks in the Kidneys and to Catherine Briddick for providing coffee and a calm empathetic presence at the Refugee Studies Centre. Thanks also to Dawn Chatty and Roger Zetter for their wisdom and to Alex Betts for his thoughts on autonomy. I'm grateful to Marion Couldrey and Maurice Herson for being enthused about the topic and turning it into issue 55 of *Forced Migration Review*. In the wider Oxford community, I would like to thank Jocelyn Alexander, Ruben Andersson, Simukai Chigudu, John Gledhill, Dan Hodgkinson, and Myfanwy James for their friendship and encouragement and all my other colleagues at ODID for creating such a great place to work.

In terms of intellectual communities, I would particularly like to thank the participants at the Structures of Protection conference at St. Cross College in 2018: Marthe Achtnich, Roberta Altin, Hanna Baumann, Camillo Boano, Kamel Doraï, Diane Fellows, James Fenna, Maria Hagan, Cyrille Hanappe, Daniel Howden, Irit Katz, Faten Kikano, Cetta Mainwaring, Samar Maqusi, Craig Martin, Ashley Mehra, Petra Molnar, Renana Ne'eman, Polly Pallister-Wilkins, Toby Parsloe, Pauline Piraud-Fournet, Elisa Pascucci, Sarah Rosenberg-Jansen, Esther Schröder-Goh, Ioanna Theodorou, Robin Vandevoordt, Tom Western, Benjamin Thomas White, Catherine Witt, and Holly Young. Their excellent presentations all stimulated me to think more deeply about this topic. The conference was made possible through a grant from the Global Challenges Research Fund, administered by the University of Oxford. Staff at Berghahn Books helped turn the papers into an edited volume, and many speakers also came to present at an earlier seminar series on refugee shelter, which I organized in Oxford during the autumn of 2016. Thanks to Catherine Brun, Grainne Hassett, and Tom Newby for their contributions to this series, to Kirsten McConnachie for her inspiring academic work, and again to Irit Katz for blazing a trail in this area.

I would also like to thank the scholars who helped me think about the dynamics of humanitarian objects via three stimulating workshops held at the Universities of Edinburgh, Sussex, and Oxford between 2015 and 2017. Particular thanks to Uli Beisel, Jamie Cross, Catherine Dolan, Assi Doran, Mark Duffield, Maia Green, Alex Nading, Alice Street, Kristin Sandvik, Anke Schwittay, Tatiana Thieme, and Amy Moran Thomas for making me think harder about these issues. I am especially grateful for the kindness and friendship of Peter Redfield, whose insightful conversations have influenced a great deal of this book's wider framework. Over the past decade, Peter has been such an important source of stimulating ideas and unfailingly constructive feedback.

I would like to acknowledge all the students who have forced me to clarify positions and explain details and, above all, those who offered signposts to new research avenues. I'm particularly indebted to Aman Gupta for drawing my attention to the Mahmoud Darwish poem at the start of the book, to Jenny George for sharing her fascinating record of definitions in the shelter sector, to Irene Petraroli for teaching me so much about Lampedusa when it looked like it could become a key location for this study, and to Faith Cowling for all her brilliant work on Lebanon.

There is a long list of people who shared their time and insights during the research itself: Jalal Al Husseini, Mais Al Suradi, Sean Anderson, Lizzie Babister, Maryline Baumard, Antoine Bazin, Christiane Beckmann, Nikos Belavilas, Julien Beller, Francesco Bert, Dan Biswas, Tom Corsellis, Gemma Curtin, Tim de Haas, Ayham Dalal, Olivier Delarue, Sabine Dreher, Raphael Duetemeyer, Vincent Dupin, Haneen Faisal, Mona Fawaz, Clemens Foschi, Emmanuel Gignac, Harald Gruendl, Vinay Gupta, Martin Haller, Mona Harb, Nicholas Harcourt, Marie-Therese Harnoncourt-Fuchs, Barbara Holub, Daniel Howden, Elias Jourdi, Dennis Kanter, Johan Karlsson, Ahmad Kassem, Gunter Katherl, Sascha Kellermann, Daniel Kerber, Faten

Kikano, Maria Kipp, Kilian Kleinschmidt, Sascha Langenbach, Giovanni Lepri, Nasim Lomani, Caroline Maillary, Nazanin Mehraein, Stefan Mekiffer, Frank Merks, Kerstin Meyer, Matthieu Mirta, Jean-Louis Missika, Eliza Montgomery, Soman Moodley, Dimitra Mouteveli, Hans-Walter Müller, Saja Nashashibi, Tom Newby, Lefteris Papagiannakis, Mazen Riachi, Nicholas Rutherford, Jenny Rumohr, Jana Scholze, Rabih Shibli, Märta Terne, Sébastien Thiéry, Mathilde Vu, Don Weinreich, Uwe Wilhelms, Catherine Witt, and Michèle Zaoüi. Thanks to all of them for their kindness. I also had many conversations with refugees that informed this book, but who—for good reasons—spoke to me on condition of anonymity. Particular thanks are due to the residents of Azraq camp, Za'atari camp, Hotel City Plaza, Eleonas camp, Elliniko camp, Skaramangas camp, the International Congress Center shelter in Berlin, Karl-Marx-Strasse camp, Tempelhof Airport, Centre Ivry-sur-Seine, Centre Porte de la Chapelle, Haus Erdberg, the Kempelengasse office complex, and Haus Pfeiffergasse. I owe them a great deal.

Many other people helped with contacts and support for fieldwork, and I am particularly grateful to Stavros Alifragkis, Maha Al Ayyoubi, Ali Ali, Dawn Chatty, Cathryn Costello, Jeff Crisp, Ayham Dalal, Claudia Da Silva, Bashar Deeb, Alia Fakhry, Paul Fean, Andriana Fili, Lena Gold, Cannelle Gueguen-Teil, Dunya Habash, Zerene Haddad, Andrew Harper, Michelle Hoffman, Scott Key, Florian Kugel, Fotini Lazaridou-Hatzigoga, Valentina Napolitano, Ismail Mansouri, Bruno Morel, Christian Muhr, Ihab Muhtaseb, Rachel Mullin, Olga Nowak, Kate O'Reilly, Fotini Rantsiou, Katie Rickard, Cory Rodgers, Frédéric Roussel, Amelia Rule, Werner Schellenberg, Abeer Seikaly, and Florian Westphal.

Stanford University Press has been a great pleasure to work with, and I am particularly grateful to Kate Wahl for being enthusiastic about the manuscript in its early stages and to Dylan Kyung-lim White for shepherding it so supportively through the process and offering suggestions for the book title. I also want to thank Laura J. Vollmer for copyediting with such care and attention to detail.

A colleague once described the acknowledgments in my previous book as "terse." I hope fewer people will come to that conclusion this time around, and if I have forgotten anyone, I apologize wholeheartedly and will make it up by buying you a drink in Oxford.

Finally, I owe my greatest debt to my family, without whom none of this would be possible. Thanks to my parents and brother for all their love and advice and, above all, to my amazing, endlessly supportive partner, Morag—I'm only half a team without you. I have a book in progress that has your name on it, so this one is dedicated to our daughters, who have changed our lives in so many brilliant ways. They joined us on these field trips and always brought a fragment of home with them wherever they traveled. To Rosa and Thea, you are wonderful. This might not be the most riveting book you have looked at, but perhaps, one day, I will manage to write one better, inspired by you, about four clans and a dog.

FRAGMENTS OF HOME

INTRODUCTION

> Houses are killed just like their inhabitants. And the memory of
> objects is killed: stone, wood, glass, iron, cement are scattered
> in broken fragments like living beings. . . . Photographs,
> toothbrushes, combs, cosmetics, shoes, underwear, sheets,
> towels fly in every direction like family secrets broadcast aloud in
> the devastation.
>
> —*Mahmoud Darwish, A River Dies of Thirst*

THE JUNGLE STOOD ON A large patch of sandy wasteland
at the edge of Calais, bounded to the east by a country lane and to the west
by a highway that led to the port. To the north lay a vast, open beach where
one could look out over the waters of the English Channel to the cliffs of
Britain—a place that many of its residents aspired to live. Along the beach
stood the turrets of factories and a wide arc of warehouse roofs jutting up
from an industrial park. In the other direction, the urban skyscape dissolved into a coastal nature reserve and a shoreline punctuated by decaying
artillery batteries from World War II. These enormous concrete structures
had crumbled slowly over many years, revealing rusted iron skeletons and
cavernous, rain-stained interiors.

The Jungle was created here in early 2015 when refugees started to sleep
in the area while trying to get to England. They erected small tents under
scraggly bushes and threw plastic sheeting over the branches of small trees.
During the day, they slept among patches of woodland, and in the long

nights, they tried to board lorries heading to the ferry port. Such camps had long been a feature of Calais, and the name "jungle" was often used to describe them. It is a term thought to derive from the Pashto *dzhangal*, meaning "forest," indicating life in wooded areas, hidden from sight of the police.[1] These settlements had been dotted around the city since at least the 1980s, but the Jungle of 2015 was different in both scale and visibility. It was created after the local police began forcibly clearing the many smaller camps in Calais, tolerating their presence only in the tufty land at the east of the city. A new jungle emerged here over the next few months, which became larger than all the other settlements put together.[2]

At first, there were just a few hundred people living in tents spread over the sand and grass, but soon the camp grew and attracted more people. As the migrations of 2015–2016 gathered pace, the first few makeshift homes were given solid foundations: pallets lain on the muddy ground and wooden frames built around them. These were then wrapped in taut tarpaulin with tires thrown on top to weigh down the roofs. By 2016, there were thousands of people living in such houses, mostly constructed from wood and plastic sheeting. Some migrants opened shops from the front of their shelters, selling basic food and supplies. Others built places of worship, such as a large Orthodox church that was topped by a wooden cross.[3] There were schools and libraries covered in huge sheets of white canvas. Restaurants were also built next to ponds, providing food on carpeted decks wedged by the water's edge.

When I began visiting the Jungle in the middle of 2016, it was already clear that this informal settlement had become an important place of shelter. It was materially fragile and often squalid, but people nevertheless managed to find many forms of assistance in its temporary streets.[4] Its flimsy buildings were bathed in mud throughout the winter, and by spring, they were saturated with moisture, yet the settlement offered something crucial to its inhabitants: networks of social support. You could sit on the battered sofas of refugee-owned cafes and meet legal activists helping with asylum claims. You could reminisce about long journeys and learn about onward routes. You could drink tea with local artists and borrow books from the camp library. It was not all self-help either; there were many forms of humanitarianism on display. Volunteers traveled from Britain with donated clothing. French citizens helped to nail planks of timber into framework

FIGURE O.1. Temporary shelters in the Camp de la Lande. Calais, France. © University of Oxford / Mark E. Breeze, 2016.

houses. An international medical charity set up clinics in a mobile caravan. Theater groups came to provide entertainment. Teachers worked in a temporary school.[5]

The most striking humanitarian project, however, was a formal section of the camp that had been made from converted shipping containers.[6] This was constructed adjacent to the original jungle, surrounded by a fence and placed on level ground. Unlike other initiatives, it was a professional intervention with government backing: the containers were fixed in a grid and stacked on top of each another. In order to enter the compound, you had to register and pass through a turnstile, which checked handprints against a database. The main part of the Jungle was open and unplanned, but the container camp was closed and controlled. The rest of the Jungle was vibrant, but the container camp appeared in a series of washed-out colors. Whereas the Jungle was free and chaotic, the container camp was restricted and calm. Whereas the Jungle featured winding alleys over undulating ground, the container camp was built on soil that had been flattened and squared. This "camp within a camp" had been designed to house 1,500 people in clean and sanitary conditions. The contrast between spaces was remarkable.

To live in the container camp, you had to sign up to a long list of rules and restrictions that concerned visiting hours, curfews, and cooking. These were meant to address the perceived disorder of the Jungle, but the result was a settlement without any community. To avoid the cumbersome process of entry and exit, it was common for residents to climb over the perimeter fence to get into the rest of the Jungle, where they could buy food in the shops, meet friends for coffee, and worship in the mosques.[7] Once over the barrier, they could even walk over to an old walled summer camp nearby, where a French organization offered free meals in cardboard trays.[8]

The two parts of the Jungle contained different ideas of what shelter involved. One was order and hygiene, while the other was spontaneous community. Together, they turned the Jungle into an important stop-off point for migrants—a place where people could rest, regroup, and find assistance.

As the settlement continued to grow, its residents soon found themselves in conflict with the police. This took place most spectacularly along the highway to the west of the camp, where migrants spent the nights trying to smuggle themselves onto lorries bound for the ferry port. The best way to

FIGURE 0.2. Shipping containers in the Centre d'Accueil Provisoire. Calais, France. © University of Oxford / Mark E. Breeze, 2016.

do this was to create what they called a *dougar*, a blockage or "mess," which forced trucks to slow down. The police tried to prevent people from breaking into lorries by fortifying the road and surrounding the camp, clearing a buffer zone along the road, and firing rubber bullets to drive people back. Yet the residents of the jungle kept finding ingenious methods to get around police lines. The operations intensified, and by the spring of 2016, the authorities had decided to clear the entire southern section of the camp, leaving smoke-filled skies and crackling wood. The network of fences between camp and city was extended, and migrants were forced into an ever-smaller patch of land in the north.

By the autumn of 2016, the government had decided to destroy what was left of the camp. The dismantling began at the crack of dawn in late October. Long lines of people waited with their coats and suitcases to board buses that would take them to new Reception and Orientation Centers (Centres d'accueil et d'orientation) around France.[9] Others resisted the clearance, starting fires that ripped through the tents and trailers, which worsened over the next few days as gas canisters exploded and flames licked the evening sky. By the third day, lines of armed police were pushing through the camp to clear any remaining people, and workmen followed in their wake, tearing each shelter down and stripping timber from wooden frames, pulling nails from plastic sheeting, and shredding canvas into pieces. Smoke started staining the clouds, and an eerie orange glow settled over the ruins of the Jungle. Soon, nothing was left except fragments in the sand.[10]

I visited the Jungle for the last time a few weeks after these fires had been extinguished, and by then, the shelters were lying in pieces. The dunes still rolled down to the ocean, and the industrial edges of Calais still crumbled into the countryside around, but the land around me was devastated. Scraps of discarded plastic blew past in a breeze. Bulldozers churned up the last of the shelters to bury what was left. Linoleum and wood lay where homes once stood, and toothbrushes and knives lay wedged in the sand around them. The items on the ground testified to hurried departures, sprinkled with the light frost of an early winter's day. It was difficult not to be moved by these fragments of former homes, their decay and disposability a reminder of the people who had once lived there. They evoked Mahmoud Darwish's poem about how buildings can be killed, their contents buried like secrets amid the devastation.[11]

FOUNDATIONS

I first became interested in humanitarian shelter when working on a related project about nutrition. It was the middle of 2012, and I had been studying how humanitarians provide for basic needs in new emergencies. One day, I was watching a group of camp planners from the United Nations sketch out a new settlement in the Jordanian desert, which later became known as Za'atari.[12] It was a blisteringly hot day, and I introduced myself while they were taking shade under a hastily erected tarpaulin. As we talked, one of the planners crouched down and began to unfurl a map on the ground, explaining how the camp was projected to grow over the next three years. Hundreds of refugees kept arriving every hour, disembarking from the back of buses onto a sandy patch of land, and I was told how they would be allocated a small plot for shelter, initially filled with a tent but later with more semipermanent structures. I was shown the design for these structures. It looked like a shipping container but with small windows and laminate floors, set out in lines and craned into neighborhoods.

Over the next few days, I shadowed the team as they marked out paths, plots, and water points. I watched as they worked with a bewildering array of standards, which shaped every element of the camp. Each dwelling met a minimum floor area per person. Standpipes were provided to a certain quality and flow. Streets had to be laid out to fixed proportions, and there were metrics that determined everything from the material in the walls to the equipment in the schools. It was an approach that suggested human needs could be standardized and controlled, an idea that reduced the issue of shelter to an engineering challenge to be solved with wires, walls, and steel. It would be several years before I had the chance to study the topic in more detail, but I knew there was more to shelter than this. Nevertheless, that day, I started collecting different examples of refugee shelter while reflecting on what worked and what didn't. I became particularly interested in the tension between universal human needs and specific cultural particularities.

When the "long summer of migration" arrived in 2015, I started to examine shelter in more depth.[13] The story began that year on April 18, 2015, when over six hundred migrants drowned in the Mediterranean Sea.[14] This was a horrific event that awoke many policymakers to the scale of global displacement and launched a long-running media story that shifted attention as the months went by. After beginning in the central Mediterranean, news reports soon focused on the "Balkan route," where thousands of dinghies began to land on the shores of Greek islands. At the start of September, the body of toddler Alan Kurdi washed up on a Turkish beach, and his photograph flashed around the world. Informal settlements like the Jungle began to grow, and soon Angela Merkel was leading a short-lived "welcome culture" in Germany. Shelter became an imperative for many states.[15]

I launched this project when media narratives remained exhaustingly negative, but there was still something positive beneath the surface—a story of remarkable people seeking a better life and others trying to assist them. It had become clear that refugees were staying in a troubling variety of places: some lived for months in ruined buildings, others slept on the floors of friends and relatives, and many had to rest under trees at the side of the road. Camps emerged over that summer in a disorienting variety of forms, and refugees also ended up sleeping in reception centers or detained against their will. The 2015 summer of migration above all showed how shelter could mean different things to different people. For some, it meant protection in a functioning nation-state. For others, it meant protection from the elements in its most basic form. In many cases, it meant securing one's own private apartment, ideally supported by aid agencies. Within each location, there were a wide variety of shelters, and even in that small area of Calais, one could find both a vibrant informal settlement and the linear modernism of a container camp nearby.

This all contributed to the remarkable uptick of interest among architects and designers as the year went on. By December, the design press had started to fill up with new proposals for refugee shelters. Many of these took the form of supposedly universal dwellings, which aspired to be compact, simple, and cheap. I was initially skeptical about these innovative ideas as they seemed driven more by novelty than by wisdom.[16] They included pop-up shelters that could be dropped from an aircraft, tents that transformed into clothing, and homes that could be packed down onto a flatbed truck.[17] As I looked more into the issue of shelter, however, I began to reassess my view. It seemed inappropriate to be too dismissive of new ideas when so many people needed a roof over their heads in such a short time. Before long, I developed a series of research questions that reflected my interest in the tensions of emergency shelter and the difficulties of definition. First, there was a descriptive question: How *were* refugees being accommodated in different countries after 2015? Second, there was an evaluative question: What was working, what was failing, and why? Third, there was a practical question: What was the role for architecture and design? I also developed a fourth, and more philosophical, question: What *is* shelter in the end? How can we define this basic human need?

CORNERSTONES

I began fieldwork in the spring of 2016, when the urgency of the summer of migration had faded away but examples of emergency shelter remained thick on the ground. The media were still focusing on the spectacular chaos of informal settlements like the Calais Jungle, so I first traveled to France, where I found many forms of humanitarian relief: professional and amateur, formal and informal, planned and unplanned. I traveled next to Germany, where I began to follow the fate of more unusual renovations of sites that were rich in history. This included Tempelhof Airport in Berlin—a huge Nazi-era building that had been repurposed as a massive shelter. I soon settled on seven examples to demonstrate the variety of approaches to this basic human need. My final list of cases to study included two mega refugee camps in Jordan, an archipelago of rented accommodation in Lebanon, a vibrant squatting movement in Greece, and some expansive and symbolic interventions in France.

From the start, I was motivated by the notion that there is not one approach to shelter but a whole spectrum of ideas, so I set out to speak to the people who designed and built different structures in order to understand what motivated them and how they defined the problem. It was already clear that many people became involved in providing shelter to refugees over the course of that summer. Sometimes, it was an act of self-help, as when refugees walking through the Balkans erected tents in the bushes. Sometimes, it was an act of pragmatic adaptation, as when engineers converted empty warehouses and department stores in Berlin. Sometimes, it was a fundamentally political act, as when activists worked alongside refugees to occupy buildings in Athens. At other moments, it involved architects constructing buildings from scratch or industrial designers coming up with mass-produced universal dwellings.

These efforts involved the work of many people: architects, engineers, civil servants, solidarity activists, professional shelter specialists, and, of course, refugees themselves. This book touches on many of them, but it approaches the topic through the prism of humanitarianism. I use this word in the broadest sense to describe the work of people trying to meet the basic human needs of others in emergency conditions. My approach takes its lead from recent ethnographies of the relief industry—such as Liisa Malkki's study of Finnish Red Cross workers and Peter Redfield's study of Médecins Sans Frontières—which uncover what humanitarianism means to different people.[18] In this book, I recount seven detailed examples of emergency shelter, which collectively represent something of the diversity in humanitarian responses that emerged in this period. As I conducted the research, I always posed three basic questions to my interlocutors. First, how did they conceive of "shelter"? Second, what shelters did they think were particularly successful? And third, what might these examples teach us about the nature of basic human needs?

These questions gave a new twist to an old topic. Shelter has long been a staple of anthropological inquiry, an element of human life that is striking in its diversity but rooted in a common experience. For many decades, anthropologists examined how shelter is shaped by social contexts, how it illuminates values and norms, how it can be a vernacular adaptation to local conditions.[19] In a humanitarian context, too, some new tensions emerge. In trying to universalize the issue, aid workers usually want to define a bottom line; they attempt to create common standards for shelter. They look to produce cheap designs that can be used in a variety of conditions, and they try to act quickly. Such tensions—between the specific and the universal, the short and the long term, the balance of quality and cost—help to shed light on the dynamics of the aid world as well as the nature of human shelter.

My methods in this research were qualitative and ethnographic but always driven by the idea that ethnography is best built on diverse foundations.[20] Long-term participant observation was infeasible given problems of access and the number of projects involved, so I relied on in-depth interviews, photography, and film. Although "being there" was certainly crucial to my research—not least because one can never really understand a space of shelter without experiencing its sounds, smells, and sightlines—my access was often limited by visiting hours and concerns about privacy.[21] Participant observation could only be undertaken in limited, guided, and carefully managed conditions, so the backbone of this book was consequently built on detailed conversations with aid workers, architects, designers, donors, and others involved in providing shelter to refugees. These humanitarians, loosely defined, constituted the community I was trying to understand. My interest was in following how these people framed the world around them, the way they understood the need for shelter and acted to provide it in constrained conditions. Such conversations were supplemented by extended site visits and detailed documentation of shelters through photographs and architectural plans, which I collected over a three-year period from 2016 to 2019.[22]

BRICKWORK

As we can see from the brief description of the Jungle that opened this chapter, shelter has many elements. It can be a social practice as well as a material practice. It has a soft side as well as a hard side. It exists in buildings but also in human relationships. How, therefore, can we define basic shelter? This was one of the central questions that motivated my research from the start.

The essence of shelter seems, at first glance, to be rather obvious. Shelter is widely recognized as one of our most fundamental human needs, placed at the base of Abraham Maslow's famous hierarchy.[23] It has something to do with protection, defense against the elements through a roof or covering, yet it easily bursts from these confines while pushing outward toward greater complexity of form. To illustrate this, consider the silver-and-gold space blanket, which was a common sight in media reports during the 2015 summer of migration. Crinkling gently in microphones and glinting powerfully in the sun, these blankets were often distributed during maritime rescue missions to wrap around wet, shivering bodies and provide a thin layer of immediate protection. They are perhaps the most elementary form of shelter but are only ever useful for a few hours.[24]

When we try to define "shelter" at the most basic level like this, it immediately wriggles and jumps from our hands. It is clear that basic shelter has to involve something more than a blanket, but where does it start and end? Consider next a simple structure that provides a roof or covering. This might come in the form of canvas, a sheet of corrugated metal, or the protecting branch of a tree. Many migrants in Europe found this kind of shelter while walking on foot along the "Balkan route" from Greece to Germany, especially when hiding from the authorities. Some humanitarians assisted these journeys by providing migrants with tents or tarpaulin, by renting abandoned warehouses, or by converting empty buildings into dormitories. The conditions in such shelters were rudimentary and often insanitary. In many cases, people were crammed into small spaces, living under bare roofs in damp conditions. Again, we face a problem if we see this as the essence of basic shelter. Such structures can provide some respite from the rain, and they might prevent death from exposure, but the protection they offer is minimal and hardly sufficient.

Let us turn next to more complete prefabricated structures. Shelters in this category include the converted shipping containers in camps like Za'atari or mass-produced flat-pack shelters, such as those funded by the IKEA Foundation (considered in the next chapter). Such designs certainly improve on a warehouse or tent. They offer a private space, a lockable door, and a degree of privacy. They adhere to the widespread humanitarian standard that stipulates a covered floor area of at least 3.5 square meters per person—a metric that has been accepted for many years and is meant to prevent people from sleeping in overcrowded spaces like caged animals.[25] It is the closest thing we can find to a common definition of "basic shelter," but for most people, it is still too limiting. A shelter might meet the minimum floor area, but it could still lack insulation, a space to cook, properly sealed rooms, airflow, and other aspects that we consider essential for a decent standard of living.

The idea of "health" is often introduced at this point to define a minimum requirement for shelter. Indeed, a well-known definition sees "shelter" as "a habitable living space providing a secure, *healthy living environment with privacy and dignity.*"[26] This draws our attention to another layer of shelter—specifically, the way that shelter should offer far more than four walls and a roof if it is to prevent human suffering. At the very least, a shelter needs to protect against extremes of temperature. It needs to provide enough comfort for proper rest. It needs to include a separate place to sleep and cook. It needs to provide sanitation and a place to wash. Another requirement for shelter may be access to energy and running water. Each of these features can be grounded in health, which leads to other elements that could demand inclusion too. Perhaps a basic shelter needs to include a chimney or flue to remove toxic smoke. Perhaps it needs glass in the windows to keep in warmth. Perhaps it needs properly sealed doors to block rodents from entering or access to washing facilities to prevent gastrointestinal illness. These may all be crucial to stay healthy, and they lead us to define basic shelter in a more expansive manner—pointing to something bigger, more solidly built, with a number of rooms and spaces.

Is this still basic? Does it extend *beyond* the requirements of an emergency? For some humanitarians, the emphasis on health is still not enough because it fails to fulfill our need for social life. After all, basic shelter surely has to do *more* than just promote good physical health if it is to prevent human suffering. What use is excellent health if you're trapped in a remote area in the middle of the desert with no one else around? One document from the United Nations clarifies that basic shelter should provide more than just "protection from the elements" and "access to clean water" but also "secure tenure," "personal safety," and "proximity to places of employment and educational and health care facilities."[27] This takes us into a new realm with an emphasis on economic and social life, which is particularly important in contexts of forced migration. The result is an idea of shelter that fills new horizons. It is not just about a roof, privacy, and health but also about connecting people to "livelihood opportunities" and "essential community services." It means thinking about shelter in terms of education, employment, and transport.[28]

Where does shelter go next? After pushing beyond health and physical needs to embrace social and economic requirements, shelter must finally reckon with our cultural and creative lives. A good illustration of the failure in this regard can be seen in those soulless refugee camps that offer long lines of identical shelters but very little life. Such places might offer physical protection (and even access to good quality services), but they can do nothing for human flourishing. Resembling rabbit hutches, they fail to recognize the importance of art, culture, and aesthetics to human life. They may, at first glance, appear to lie beyond the realm of the "basic," but there is growing evidence that protracted exile in monotonous refugee camps has an appalling effect on mental health.[29]

Some humanitarians have addressed this by insisting that refugees should get involved in building their own shelter, while others have reached for the well-known adage that shelter is "a process not a product."[30] This draws our attention to the question of *how* shelter is provided, not simply *what* is provided. It underlines the idea that the inhabitants of a shelter need to be actively involved in defining what matters to them—a theme that will recur often in this book. In the extensive literature about architecture and humanism, many writers have also suggested that shelters should help fulfill one's ideals of a better life. Gaston Bachelard, for example, describes the house as a place to nurture the imagination, a place that "shelters day-dreaming" as well as the body.[31] Marina Warner writes of how shelters need to contain a range of imaginative equipment, becoming places "where fantasy and invention, memories and improvisation can happen."[32] It may seem like a long journey from the crinkling of a space blanket to the most expansive of human aspirations, but the various strands of shelter are embroidered into a complex fabric, which are hard to disentangle in practice.

SEVEN FRAGMENTS OF SHELTER

In this book, I look ethnographically at how humanitarians respond to such complexity, how they define the need for shelter, and take urgent action. In what follows, I build an account of what shelter does and how it is thought about in seven detailed examples. The study shows that shelter has many elements. It involves dignity, control, aesthetics, social connections, politics, solidarity, and harm. Humanitarian practitioners may not want their work to be about all these things when they engage in the provision of shelter, but every one of them is important. The chapters each consider a project that focuses on a particular aspect, defining the central task of shelter in a way that is summarized via a single word in the chapter title. These projects show how any attempt to pin down the meaning of "basic shelter" will end up in fragments. Humanitarians may try their best to define the central issue, to boil things down to their essence, to design something with the perfect balance, but the results are profoundly disjointed. The alternative, I suggest in the conclusion, is to prioritize the principle of autonomy, which can allow refugees to define what matters themselves.

In chapter 1, I begin with a design from Sweden that arrived in two boxes. This was funded by the IKEA Foundation, and it claimed to capture the essence of shelter in a single structure, which could be dismantled into hundreds of parts, flat packed, and then reconstructed in the wake of disaster. This gets to the heart of shelter as a humanitarian problem. How did these designers define the essential elements of shelter? What did they exclude and include? And what was the result? The chapter shows how the idea of a universal flat-pack shelter tried to boil things down to the basics, to break shelter down into little parts that could be reassembled where needed, but the result became contentious. Some people accused the shelter of being too luxurious; others criticized it for being too mean. Many aid workers claimed that the shelter was overdesigned and unsustainable since it involved sending packets of prefabricated plastic overseas rather than using local materials. Some architects, in contrast, said that the problem was a *lack* of good design, comparing the shelter to a portable toilet. These disputes introduce the central problem of precision, which followed the shelter as it was deployed around the world. Some countries blocked the shelter on the grounds that it offered conditions that were better than those of citizens. Others condemned it for being culturally inappropriate and a fire risk. The example shows how shelter is always contextual, and, as well as illustrating the difficulties of defining basic shelter, it highlights the tendency of aid workers to impose culturally specific ideas onto people from very different backgrounds.

The second chapter turns to Jordan, where two enormous refugee camps were created in the desert. Here, the planners tried to provide everything refugees might need, from supermarkets to schools, piped water to paved roads. It was a model that went beyond the minimum four walls and a roof to provide all the services of a small town, which raised various questions about the proper scope of this sector. Should humanitarians work with a comprehensive checklist of everything required from a shelter? Might such detailed metrics miss something important? In these camps, the huts stretched out in monotonous gray uniformity. Each house was identical to the next, and there was no variation or color. Refugees were not permitted to alter their shelters, and they could not create a place that felt like home—they were even forbidden from planting vegetation to improve the surrounding environment. The chapter shows how even the broadest definitions of "shelter" can miss something crucial about the nature of human needs. It demonstrates how the value of shelter can be found not in a list of metrics to be counted and met but in what shelter allows one to do.

Chapter 3 examines a radical alternative to the refugee camp, which was founded in downtown Athens. Here, a group of activists occupied a hotel that had been empty since the 2008 financial crash, creating a self-governing community for refugees. It is an example that raises important questions about the relationship between shelter and politics. Is shelter always implicated in structures of power and control? Can refugee shelters ever be apolitical? Or might people, conversely, be bound to realize political objectives through shelter? The activists in Athens criticized other approaches that claimed to stand outside politics while remaining controlling and hierarchical. As an alternative, they developed a form of housing underpinned by the values of equality and community. They asked that all residents participated in the daily running of the hotel, taking on chores from cooking to cleaning, and they ran general assemblies to make all the important decisions. It was an inspiring idea, but it still had critics. Some argued that squatted buildings could never provide shelter at scale. Others suggested that the approach simply reproduced hierarchies rather than doing away with them. Many people condemned the squat for its close connection to radical anarchist movements. The activists saw this as a good thing—as an attempt to deal with the root causes of refugee needs—but critics wondered whether people should have to sign up for the destruction of nation-states in order to get a bed for the night. Through following the fate of this scheme, the chapter explores the distinction between a communal vision of shelter and one that facilitates people's individual, longer-term aims.

Chapter 4 turns to Lebanon, which hosted more refugees per capita than anywhere else in the world. This generated a context in which many citizens feared permanent settlement, and the result was a limited range of options. Camps were forbidden, and forced migrants ended up living in an assortment of inadequate and improvised buildings scattered across the country, which raised crucial questions about the relationship between protection and policy. What happens when governments prohibit the creation of emergency shelters? How can humanitarians adapt in the face of such restrictions? Many refugees were left living in terrible conditions: in old factories, chicken farms, warehouses, and empty shopping malls. They were forced to squeeze into the gaps, finding a place to sleep where they could, while aid workers found their hands tied. Unable to construct new shelters, they set about providing piecemeal improvements to the inadequate accommodation refugees had found. The result was a situation whereby humanitarians followed the decisions of refugees but without being able to transform their circumstances. The chapter describes this as an instance of shelter by tactics and concludes that humanitarian shelter must be led by a clear strategic vision; otherwise, it will end up subservient to the interests of more powerful actors.

Chapter 5 turns to Germany, where the idea of transforming old buildings into refugee shelters became central to the strategies of government.

Many iconic buildings in Germany were requisitioned for this purpose, including the former Stasi headquarters in Lichtenberg, the buildings of Dachau concentration camp, and the enormous Tempelhof Airport in Berlin. Focusing particularly on the empty airport, this chapter raises crucial questions about adaptation and renewal in the search for basic shelter. Does basic shelter have to involve constructing something new? Or is it better to adapt what we have, giving buildings new life? At Tempelhof, thousands of asylum seekers found shelter in a building that was originally designed by Nazi architects in the 1930s. Vast, empty aircraft hangars were repurposed, shower blocks installed, and refugees slept in bunk beds separated by thin dividing walls. The use of such buildings was symbolically risky, but it represented a pragmatic approach to shelter that was driven not by ideal conditions but by the need to avoid refugees living on the street. It was a system that provided basic shelter but in a way that restricted inhabitants through a voluminous list of rules and regulations. Drawing on this example, the chapter shows how paternalism emerges in shelter, imposing serious costs on inhabitants.

Chapter 6 considers a creative approach to mass shelter that emerged in Vienna. The city was dealing with a large number of refugee arrivals, and the local authorities, desperate for space, adapted empty office blocks to provide emergency housing. Such buildings were deeply unsuitable, but they were modified with an eye to the emotional quality of internal space. This generated important questions about the relationship between shelter and the senses. Are emotions important in the provision of shelter? Should humanitarians consider how places make people feel? Rather than concentrating on ambitious structural alterations, the architects in this project focused on modest changes to allocated buildings with small objects and items of furniture. They used blankets to absorb sound, cushions to add comfort, and nylon curtains to provide privacy and controllable lighting. Drawing on the work of Bachelard, the designers argued that basic shelter could involve a "poetics of space"—an awareness of how buildings make people feel. Critics argued that this was hopelessly idealistic, but the architects suggested, in response, that the experience of a building is crucial to its function. The chapter concludes that the cumulative effect of small hardships can be easy to ignore in shelter but that this can be addressed through design that promotes autonomy in small but significant ways.

The final chapter examines a striking refugee shelter in Paris, which took the form of a taut, inflatable bubble of bright-yellow plastic. This was erected in a decaying railway yard in the northern fringes of the city and was visible for miles around, rising over the tarmac of the abandoned industrial site and extending over eight hundred square meters. It was a fascinating and creative example of shelter that raised some fundamental questions about the relationship between humanitarianism and aesthetics. Does beauty have a role in basic shelter? If so, what part should good design play in humanitarian emergencies? In the case of the so-called Yellow Bubble, the mayor wanted a shelter that could become "a signpost of humanity," an emblem of compassionate intent, but the architecture was symbolic rather than practical, and it contributed little to the experience of refugees inside. Most importantly, the optimistic symbolism of the bubble took on a different hue when the shelter became part of a project to sort migrants for deportation. It began to look like the striking design was used to make a place of misery look more attractive. The chapter concludes that aesthetics is important to emergency shelter, but it can easily become entangled with the pursuit of political objectives.

FROM FRAGMENTATION TO AUTONOMY

This book could have included many other instances of refugee shelter, but the seven chapters have been designed to provide an overview of some striking ways that humanitarians and designers have approached the problem. As should be clear from the summaries above, the key lesson from all these chapters is that emergency shelters consider just one fragment of a much bigger picture. The first chapter shows how shelter can be reduced to its basics. The second describes the idea that shelter can be constructed through metrics. The third suggests that shelter can be a form of politics. The fourth then examines what happens when shelter becomes a matter of tactics, working *around* political constraints and finding opportunities for advantage. The fifth chapter describes shelter as pragmatics, and the sixth chapter turns to a more Bachelardian approach, in which shelter is seen as poetics. The final chapter looks at how shelter can become dominated by concerns of beauty, symbolism, and aesthetics.

Taken together, these chapters show how shelter is provided in a way that tends to be partial and fragmented. With little time to act, humanitarians paternalistically impose their own ideas of shelter, rarely asking refugees what they consider most important about this basic human need. At the end of the book, I make a suggestion for how to address this—a design proposal of sorts. Refugee shelter, I argue, can either reproduce or resist the paternalistic restrictions faced by refugees in wider society. Shelter is too often saturated by grand ideas—symbolic architecture, expansive metrics of human life, ambitious political stands—but its most significant effects play out on the microscale: shaping where people wake, how they eat, and the conditions in which they sleep. The best examples of shelter, I conclude, seek to provide greater autonomy for people living in circumstances that are deliberately designed to deny it. The most important element to consider—which is so often neglected—is the ability to *control* simple things, from when the lights come on to what gets served for dinner. Such elements of life may seem trivial, but when people lose their homes, there is a sense in which their whole world falls apart. Places, people, and routines crack up around them. Without a home, everything becomes fragmented, as John Berger writes, but prioritizing the principle of autonomy might allow refugees to pick up the pieces and rebuild on firmer ground.[33]

1 | SHELTER AS BASICS
The Flat-Packed Home from Sweden

IN NOVEMBER OF EACH YEAR, a humanitarian trade fair arrives in Brussels, occupying an enormous hall in one of the city's outer suburbs. It is an area famous for the Atomium building, which was constructed in the 1950s from nine silver spheres to create the magnified shape of an iron crystal. This striking, futuristic building gives the whole neighborhood a sense of optimistic modernism. The sun reflects off the spheres in patches, illuminating the concrete walkways with soft, flickering light. A complex of art-deco buildings stand nearby with soaring facades carved in golden stone. The trade fair lies behind this and exudes a similar sense of confident modernism—a feeling certainly helped by the hundreds of humanitarian designers who gather inside this building each year, eager to display their products.

When you enter the trade fair, you will first come to a huge hall punctuated by small colorful kiosks and a multitude of humanitarian designs. You can find calorie-dense rations in one stall, lightweight latrines on another. There are jeeps and radios, tents and tanks, and a range of other products that can be flown into a disaster zone at a moment's notice. Among the booths, you can also find a bewildering array of shelter designs, which take many different forms. Some stack together like Styrofoam cups. Others collapse and expand like accordions. There are shelters built around demountable domes, hexagonal frames, and wooden arcs of great strength.[1]

Their designers are all trying to make a product that is small and strong but economical to produce and quick to transport. The idea is to reduce shelter to its fundamental components and produce it at scale for a fast-moving humanitarian marketplace. This may seem a simple proposition, but if you spend any time walking among the stalls, you will soon learn of the challenges. The designers will tell you how difficult it is to convince aid workers to move away from the tent. They will explain how it is tricky to produce a shelter that is cheap enough to be competitive. It is particularly hard, the designers will add, to find a way to break into a market that is dominated by a few big buyers and their favored suppliers. At this point, the designers may incline their heads toward a shelter that has dominated proceedings for a decade. It often stood at the center of the exhibition floor, illuminated by spotlights and surrounded by a brightly colored banner: the IKEA Better Shelter.[2]

The "IKEA shelter"—as it is known—looks modest at first glance, but it casts a long shadow over the industry. It has been the most successful of all recent shelters and is often featured at events like this. In terms of design, it has straight sides, a pitched roof, and four small windows; it is small, white, and squat, with a simple rectangular base. It is simple in form—its designer even describes it as like a "house a European five-year-old might draw"—but it can be dismantled into pieces and transported in fragments.[3] Despite the simplicity—even banality—of this design, however, the IKEA shelter has been declared a game changer. It has received millions of dollars of investment from the IKEA Foundation and the backing of the United Nations Refugee Agency. It has been lauded in the media and featured in numerous exhibitions. It even won the Beazley Design of the Year, awarded by the London Design Museum in 2016.[4]

When I visited the humanitarian trade fair, it looked as though the IKEA shelter had triumphed. It stood proudly in the middle of the exhibition hall, surrounded by glossy brochures. Yet the critics had already descended. The shelter was accused by some people for being too expansive and by others for being too restrictive. Some countries blocked the shelter on the grounds that it was luxurious compared to local conditions, whereas others condemned it for being culturally inappropriate and seriously insecure. The main designer had wanted his product to balance "the needs of millions of people living in different cultures, climates and regions" through "rational production . . . a single solution."[5] But was this even possible? Could designers reduce the problem of shelter to fundamental components? And was it reasonable to expect this to be brought together in a single product that might be shipped off anywhere in the world?

THE GOLDEN TICKET

I began my inquiry by traveling to Stockholm on a bright spring morning in 2017. A cold Nordic light streamed over the streets of the Swedish capital as I made my way south to the organization's headquarters, which lay in an old Ericsson telecom building near a busy railway line toward the south of the city. The managing director met me at the door and immediately started explaining what they were trying to achieve. "Here we are working with emergencies," he said. "The end users are by definition unknown." The whole project, he continued, involved finding the simplest way to meet the human need for shelter while responding to some central questions. "What is the common denominator for all people on this planet in terms of shelter? How can we produce this in a rational way? . . . How, in other words, can we put it in a box?"[6]

The director gave me a tour of his offices and then took me down to the workshop, where the latest iteration of the shelter had been erected in a corner. He showed me how the shelter could be broken down into pieces and fitted into two boxes, ready to be assembled in a refugee camp. I looked at the racks of different materials, the components that had been scattered around with spare parts all labeled and lined up on a shelf. Steel brackets, bolts, hinges, tension cables, and hundreds of other parts, from tiny screws to large plastic panels, all organized into categories. These were later sent for packing in a huge warehouse over the Baltic Sea in Gdansk, where workers carefully fitted panels, poles, and other pieces into cartons alongside an instruction manual. I later watched a film of the process, seeing forklifts beep and whine their way around towers of brown cardboard boxes. The containers were finally stacked, wrapped in plastic, and then labeled by a machine.[7]

When I sat down to talk to the director in more detail, I learned that the shelter had been conceived in a more modest environment. It started, he said, as a small and simple project to improve upon the tent. Tents, of course, do not offer refugees a very comfortable way to live. It is hard to stand up in tents and difficult to secure them from thieves. Lights can cast shadows on the canvas, making everything visible from the outside. Tents

FIGURE 1.1. IKEA-funded Better Shelters boxed and ready for dispatch. Gdansk, Poland. © University of Oxford / Mark E. Breeze, 2018.

let in dust, they are poorly insulated, and they quickly disintegrate.[8] The original intention of the IKEA shelter was to develop something similarly practical but more solid and longer lasting, something with vertical walls and a decent lifespan. As the designers explained, the idea was to produce a shelter in which people could stand, a shelter where people could enter without ducking, a shelter where people could lock the door and feel more securely enveloped by walls that were firmer than canvas.

By the time I saw the IKEA shelter at the humanitarian trade fair in Brussels, it was being manufactured on a huge scale and it had all these features. It had straight sides with enough headroom to stand; it had a proper entrance that was wide enough to walk through; it had a secure door and materials that were more durable than a tent. It also came with a few nifty technological additions, such as a photovoltaic panel, a lamp, and a cell-phone charger. Other designers were struggling, but this shelter seemed to have prevailed. So what was the key to its success?

When I asked this question in Stockholm, the team admitted that they had got lucky. We were speaking in the workshop, surrounded by old plastic panels and hundreds of hollow poles resting on a nearby shelf, their dark interiors lit with a circumference of glinting chrome. The main designer told me that, in the end, they had received a "golden ticket." Compared with other attempts to produce a universal shelter, they had been boosted by a funder with a great deal of "financial stamina." Their ideas had been taken up and tested in refugee camps, then guided through the complicated United Nations procurement systems. "It can be quite an obstacle getting a new product into the aid sector," my interviewee explained.[9] This is especially true when the competition is so tough and aid managers are so flooded with new designs. But their shelter was lucky enough to receive an advantage in the form of a prominent sponsor, IKEA, and a partnership with the new innovation unit at the United Nations High Commissioner for Refugees (UNHCR). I looked around the workshop, and it offered material proof of such support. There were detailed iterations of different designs printed in full color and tacked to a whiteboard. The sunlight streamed in through the window and illuminated the rising banks of steel components.

IKEA had certainly given this design a great deal of time, space, and money. But my interviewee told me that things had not always been this way. The founder and now director of the Better Shelter, Johan Karlsson, had little experience of the aid world when he started this project. Indeed, his involvement had been something of a coincidence. After graduating from industrial design school, Karlsson had joined a now-bankrupt foundation called Formens Hus, which had been collaborating with the Swedish Rescue Services Agency—a government body that was responsible for emergency response. Formens Hus then launched a project to improve on a particular design of an emergency tent, which had been distributed for the 2008 Pakistan earthquake. The founder's original involvement had been the result of a chance encounter. "They called my professor and asked, Do you have anyone in industrial design who could work on this project? We don't have a lot of money, but we need someone good with textiles." Karlsson fitted the profile, so he joined the team at Formens Hus, but he soon discovered how little he knew. "Not knowing the industry, not knowing the complexity around humanitarian operations," he told me, "I just asked, Why do we even send people tents? . . . Why don't we send them more durable, semipermanent shelters?"[10]

It was a reasonable question. Tents did not last, and they needed regular replacement. They were also clearly insufficient, and Karlsson wondered why they were still being used when refugees were in exile for many years. The problem was that emergency funding was being earmarked on an annual basis, making longer-term structures hard to finance. Tents were cheap, compact, easy to store, and they got around legal restrictions on more permanent shelters. This made it hard to think beyond them. Karlsson started to instead consider the idea of a simple lightweight hut that might be constructed with similar advantages. He tested shapes and started looking into materials. His aim was not so much to improve on the tent as to replace it.

Karlsson soon turned to an organization called Shelter Centre for advice and support. Led by an architect called Tom Corsellis, it had been trying to get aid agencies to agree to some specifications for a "fly-in transitional shelter." This notion of a transitional shelter, or T-shelter, involved distributing a high-quality frame that could later be expanded. The idea was to start with something simple and politically palatable but enable it to transition into a longer-lasting home. The material covering the frame might be slowly upgraded. The foundations might be strengthened. More sections of the shelter might be added bit by bit in order to increase the floor area. This would allow a better-quality shelter to emerge, but one that still started as something light, cheap, and seemingly temporary. It allowed for a more limited design in the first instance, but one that could change and develop when required.[11]

The idea of a transitional shelter promised to solve some of the political issues, but there were financial ones as well—soon tackled by the IKEA Foundation, which Karlsson contacted around this time. The relationship began when a board member of Formens Hus, who was also a well-known IKEA designer, suggested that Karlsson approach the Swedish multinational. The answer, initially, was that they did not fund this sort of thing—as one staff recalled, their reply was that "we make what is in the house, not the house itself." But by 2010, the IKEA Foundation was starting to expand its humanitarian work, and a series of meetings took place between Karlsson and the new director of the IKEA Foundation, along with a member of staff at the UN Refugee Agency. One member of the group described this as "a meeting of the minds," bringing together people who shared the "frustration of not being able to innovate" and were committed to creating some kind of alternative to the tent.[12]

Inspired by the idea of transitional shelter and with support from the IKEA Foundation, Karlsson began working on a rectangular frame made from strong steel tubes and held together with sturdy brackets. He found some suppliers who were "crazy enough to believe in the idea" and who were able to manufacture at a decent price. The next step was to convince the shelter specialists at UNHCR, many of whom were skeptical of this Swedish industrial designer. As Karlsson admitted, he had never been in a refugee camp before, and many people at UNHCR were not persuaded by the idea of a transitional shelter, which they saw as too complicated and time consuming. There were also concerns about what a transitional shelter would transition *into* if there could be no long-term security of residence for refugees.[13] UNHCR remained committed to assisting host governments, many of whom had an interest in keeping refugees living in temporary conditions. Politics, inevitably, hung over the design.

Karlsson, meanwhile, continued to develop the basic frame. As he told it, a key moment came when one of the veteran shelter specialists at UNHCR approached his prototype at an exhibition. Karlsson was displaying the latest iteration of the frame, and the shelter specialist began peering at the model. "The poles looked skinny," Karlsson explained, "and so this guy started to shake the frame." After some minutes of peering at the corners, he decided to test its strength, "like when you buy secondhand cars, you kick the tires." He grabbed the center of the crossbar and pulled his whole weight upward, expecting it to fail, but it held. "Of course, there's no connection between making a pull up and good shelter design," Karlsson clarified, but in retrospect, he saw this as the moment that convinced many in UNHCR that a freestanding frame might be the basis of a new kind of refugee shelter.[14]

With the frame finished, the key challenge was how to seal it. Initially the idea was to deliver it bare, allowing the frame to be covered with local materials, such as leaves, grass, straw, wood, corrugated iron, or whatever else was available. But UNHCR wanted the shelter to come in a complete package—an industrial solution with outer panels that could be stacked in warehouses and deployed immediately when required. The design team began to test materials to produce this outer envelope, experimenting with everything from nonwoven textiles to light foams. They tested these materials against high winds, which involved putting a fully built shelter in a wind tunnel to see how it behaved. They tested them against strong sunlight, which involved seeing how the panels were affected by ultraviolet rays. They examined how air flowed through the building and how it behaved in fire. The team even tested the shelter to see how much snow it could take, piling sand and other materials on the roof.

FIGURE 1.2.   Poles and panels stacked in the Better Shelter workshop. Stockholm, Sweden. © University of Oxford / Mark E. Breeze, 2017.

Unfortunately, however, the team was given no detailed brief during this process. UNHCR had now become a formal partner, but they had not provided a detailed list of specifications. Karlsson described the guidance as frustratingly limited. "It was basically: see if you can make a self-standing tent or a tent with a frame that can carry itself. . . . Take the tent and make it so that you can stand upright inside, a bit like a house. . . . That was it."[15] Perhaps this should have given the team some pause. One of the biggest humanitarian agencies in the world, the cluster lead for shelter, an organization whose logo shows two hands forming a protective roof over the figure of a refugee, was reluctant to provide a set of guidelines for a high profile, well-funded attempt to design a universal basic shelter. Was this an indication that the idea was flawed from the start? Was there, in fact, no such thing as a design that could meet so many requirements?

THE "KNOCKINESS" REQUIREMENT

It is certainly easy to understand UNHCR's reluctance to boil down the need for shelter into a single brief. Shelter is always contextual, rooted in a time and a place, and the difference between a shelter made from bricks and one made from straw, between a shelter covered in slate and one covered in iron, is not simply down to finance or skill. The form of these shelters has already been determined by culture, environment, and local conditions.[16] Shelter responds to climate and the availability of certain materials. It is also shaped by traditions and social structure.[17] Any design that is shipped around the world, therefore, will soon have to confront the fact that housing looks extremely different depending on where one is. And wherever it is sent, a shelter can be easily criticized as inappropriate.

The head of communications for Better Shelter acknowledged this when I met her soon after my arrival in Stockholm. As she put it, the Better Shelter "is, in every way, a very western looking house." "In that sense," she conceded, "it might be difficult to adapt it to certain local cultures." Some people "might not feel at home in the shelter because it doesn't look how their homes usually look."[18] An external critic agreed, pointing out that the design was not just Western but also specifically Swedish. It resembled, he said, a Swedish summerhouse with a gable roof. "Everyone builds what they know," this critic argued. IKEA is "very good at designing for mass manufacture; the Swedes have a decent understanding of the outdoors, and here, they have made a model of what they think shelter should look like." In reality, he suggested, it was a design that was mostly unsuitable, a design infused with Swedish assumptions about how people live.[19]

This is not specific to IKEA. Any attempt to build a universal basic shelter will see its design imprinted by context—a phenomenon that can be traced through the centuries. We might even say that this relationship has its roots in the very foundation of architectural theory. In 1753, a famous essay was published by Marc-Antoine Laugier on the idea of the "primitive hut."[20] This text can be seen as an early example of how cultural assumptions drive supposedly universal principles of shelter design. In his essay, Laugier begins with an imagined state of nature, a man living perfectly alone like Crusoe on his deserted island, whose first task is to create shelter from the natural world. As Laugier describes it, this man starts by turning to the resources he has around him. "Some branches, broken down in the forest are the proper materials for his design. He chooses four of the strongest, which he raises perpendicularly and which he disposes into a square. Above he puts four others across, and upon these he raises some that incline from both sides. This kind of roof is covered with leaves put together so that neither the sun nor the rain can penetrate therein; and now the man is lodged."[21]

Laugier argues that this "primitive hut" led to the most elementary principles of architecture. "The little rustic cabin that I have just described," Laugier writes, "is the model upon which all the magnificences of architecture have been imagined."[22] The thick branches, fixed into the ground, became columns. The horizontal wood, lain on top, became entablatures. Laugier argues that humans have always looked to the natural world to find their ideals of beauty and the primitive hut formed the origins of classical architecture with its columns, entablatures, and pediments. This grounding in the natural world, the argument goes, was why the buildings of ancient Greece and Rome were so revered for their simplicity and balance.

The problem, of course, is that Laugier is describing a very cultural idea of beauty, building on a very skewed state of nature. He is claiming to identify the universal principles of architecture but simply reflects the norms of society at the time. His argument is typical of Enlightenment thought experiments, reflecting on individuals in a state of nature without any attachments. These men (and they were usually men) were imagined without culture, kinship, or belief, able to construct a rational world from scratch. Laugier's primitive man, for example, is concerned only with the most general meteorological issues—such as the rain, the wind, and the heat of the sun. He protects himself with the materials around him, which happened to be the wood of a European forest. The idea was to generate universal principles, but he instead produced a remarkably narrow model of architecture, which also, incidentally, seems strikingly similar to the straight sides and pitched roof of the IKEA Better Shelter.

The notion that the primitive hut can be a universal model for architecture is as absurd as the idea that the IKEA shelter can be a universal model for refugee shelter—a solution that responds to "different cultures, climates and regions" in a form that just happens to resemble a Swedish summer house. Like the primitive hut, the IKEA shelter makes a claim to universality, but it is also firmly rooted in context. It mimics a Nordic cabin. It reflects a long tradition of Swedish modernist simplicity.[23] It can even be compared to the one-size-fits-all approach of Scandinavian social welfare more broadly—a model that can hardly apply everywhere and, like so many others, contains assumptions about the problem and how it can be solved. Even on a practical level, it would be impossible to design a shelter that is truly universal because environmental conditions around the world are so different. As one engineer put it to me, "it's very unlikely that you're going to find a single shelter design that will work everywhere because it's hot, it's cold, it's rainy, it's filled with ants, and so on."[24] Each place has its own challenges, and a single product simply cannot respond to them all.

The IKEA shelter was, therefore, partly a cultural product, but it was also determined by the concerns of the aid world. Its form was driven by dominant ideas circulating in the late 2000s, and most notably, it was based on the replicable rectangle of a "transitional shelter." It was then influenced by the desire of donor governments to offer something temporary and the limitations of purchasers reliant on annual funds. In the end, the metrics of success for the project came down to three simple things: price, weight, and volume. Karlsson understood that the major aid agencies wanted "something that is like the tent or better, which costs the same or less, and is cheaper and lighter and has less volume."[25] The new shelter, therefore, had to be longer lasting, it had to feel more solid, and it had to stay as close as possible to the price and weight of a tent.[26]

In this process, the concern of refugees was more or less excluded. To the extent that there *had been* some consideration of their needs, the design team ended up focusing more effort on privacy and security. This was stipulated by the UN Refugee Agency as a common concern and articulated through the notion of "knockiness." The material of the shelter, the United Nations advised, should be "knocky." Once the frame was sealed and wrapped, the shelter ought to be "somewhere you can knock, and someone on the inside has to

FIGURE 1.3.   Better Shelter units lined up for inhabitation. Milan, Italy. © University of Oxford / Mark E. Breeze, 2017.

give permission for you to enter."[27] This gave refugees the sense that they had their own domain. One of the design team admitted that this was a "fluffy definition," but it nevertheless captured a challenge they all understood. The key thing was that the material had to "convey the feeling of structural house and home."[28] In short, it had to be a place that felt secure.

The notion of "knockiness," however, also illustrates something important about the political constraints of emergency shelter. Residents wanted something more solid than the tilted canvas sides of a tent, but governments were still demanding that the shelter be clearly temporary. Karlsson explained that the benefit of a knocky material was that it can "give a surprisingly strong impression of being more permanent than it actually is." The wording here is crucial. It gave an *impression* of permanence without the *fact* of permanence. All the same, Karlsson continued, the design team "often made a joke" about this concept, asking each other, "How knocky is this? Does this material meet the knockiness requirement?"[29] They ended up with a material they named "rhulite," which was a polymer developed specifically for the shelter. It had the spongy texture of swimming floats and was light but vibrant when tapped. It was easy to pack into boxes and opaque enough to cast no shadows at night.

By 2013, the shelter had been designed and assembled into a finished product. It had been constructed around a balance of price, permanence, and politics. Now it was ready for its first "real-world" test overseas.

THE LAGOM SHELTER

The first proper outing for the IKEA refugee shelter was in Dollo Ado—an arid region in the south of Ethiopia with five large camps for Somali refugees. It is a landscape of red earth and thorn trees, burning sunlight and dusty ground. The sleek white sides of the IKEA shelter stood out starkly against this contrasting backdrop, and aware of such conditions, the design team fitted the shelter with sensors that could collect data on radiation, air movement, air temperature, and humidity. They employed researchers to talk with refugees about their experience of living inside, a process that eventually led to amendments, but the fundamentals had, at this point, already been fixed. The dimensions of the frame were locked in, and the outer panels had been created. All that was left to tinker with were the smaller details, such as brackets, bolts, and placement of the windows.

The head of communications acknowledged that it was difficult for refugees to be frank about any shortcomings at this point—not least because the researchers were asking questions while accompanied by armed guards.[30] But the test was significant for a different reason—because it marked the beginning of an intensive period of media interest in the shelter. The press release issued by the IKEA Foundation around this time had striking photos and a compelling storyline. Many newspapers could not resist the connection between refugee housing and the huge furniture multinational. The *Guardian* described how IKEA had brought its "flatpack, no frills efficiency to the problem of refugee housing."[31] NPR described it as a "new kind of IKEA hack."[32] The connection proved to be an easy hook because Western consumers were familiar with constructing this kind of economical furniture. There was something intuitively attractive about the idea of a basic shelter arriving in two boxes with a text-free cartoon manual like other products from IKEA. As the Better Shelter head of communications explained, many people have "an emotional attachment to IKEA. . . . We've all been there, and we've all bought our flat-packed furniture."[33] This meant that a global audience could draw connections between refugee housing and their bookcases and coffee tables at home.

From the perspective of the design team, however, there was a downside. The IKEA connection may have brought publicity and opened doors, but soon everyone was calling this the "IKEA shelter," which they deemed incorrect. When I first visited the team's headquarters in Sweden, I was told that the proper term was Better Shelter and that the product was not made or owned by IKEA at all.[34] Indeed, the shelter was actually produced by a social enterprise, also called Better Shelter, which had very few formal connections to IKEA except through funding. This social enterprise was owned by a philanthropic organization called Housing for All, of which the IKEA Foundation was just one investor. The IKEA Foundation, in turn, was institutionally distinct from the furniture manufacturer. By explaining this complex arrangement, the designers were anxious to distance themselves from the idea of an "IKEA shelter" because it implied that the giant multinational had manufactured the product to profit from human misery. At the very least, it implied that the shelter was an act of corporate social responsibility rather than a project with independent origins that had been led from the start by Karlsson and his team.

In some ways, however, even the formal name Better Shelter created another problem, closing down precisely the issues that needed to be opened up. After all, the new name was explicitly the result of a publicity exercise concerned with blurring the institutional connections between IKEA and the shelter, which were byzantine but nevertheless strong. In reality, the IKEA Foundation had a controlling stake in Better Shelter as well as owning the multinational company in a complicated corporate structure whose complexity, the *Economist* argues, seemed to be a way to avoid taxes.[35] It is not exactly far-fetched, therefore, to see IKEA's involvement in refugee shelter as a rather cynical form of corporate publicity. Photos and articles about the shelter appeared in not just newspapers but also IKEA catalogs around the world. Exhibits of the shelter stood prominently in IKEA stores, and IKEA also influenced the design by offering advice on logistics, flat-pack technology, and text-free manuals. It seems that the term Better Shelter was an attempt to play down these connections while uncritically positioning the product as "better." Yet the questions remained: Was the shelter genuinely better? And if so, how?

These questions were soon answered because the narrative of a "better shelter" provoked a backlash. Before long, criticisms started to emerge from two opposing directions. Some critics suggested the shelter did too little, arguing that it was a mean little space, which looked like a garden shed or, owing to its plastic panels, a portable chemical toilet. It was easy to see their point. From the moment I saw the shelter, it struck me as distinctly underwhelming. It was a small, bare, simple hut. It had just a few tiny openings by way of windows and a low, flimsy door. Its crude, hand-tightened fittings were fully visible from the inside, and there was no floor to speak of, with just a piece of tarpaulin covering the earth. The designers admitted that the external appearance of the shelter was somewhat "brutalist" but suggested that this did not matter as their motivation for this shelter was practical, not aesthetic.[36] The aim was to make something that was viable for aid agencies to purchase in cash-strapped circumstances, not something that would win awards for beauty. Yet architectural critics still pointed to numerous failings in the design, from the lack of foundations to the absence of insulation, from the "windows," which were just vented openings, to the fragile clips and meager metal pegs, which were inadequate to hold the shelter together in high winds.

All this made the shelter seem a flimsy, uninviting place to live. As one critic put it, architecture should respond to the site and the needs of the inhabitants. Yet the Better Shelter was a mass-produced design with no adaptability or control. It might work for a few nights but could not be recommended beyond that. Good architecture, another critic suggested to me, should create sensitive and carefully planned responses to specific problems, not ignore basic elements, such as insulation, flooring, and natural light. Architecture should be pleasing to the eye. It should be based on the Vitruvian triad of architectural virtues: *firmitas* (strength), *utilitas* (functionality), and *venustas* (delight or beauty). The IKEA shelter had somehow managed to fail on all counts. It was flimsy. It was flawed. It was ugly.[37]

These criticisms of the shelter were balanced by a rather different set of problems, which were raised by humanitarian workers. Those in the aid industry argued not that the shelter did too little but that it did too much. The Better Shelter, they argued, was too expensive, too complicated, and too fussy. It provided a fully integrated, flat-packed solution when this was not appropriate. Many aid workers pointed out that tents are perfectly suitable in emergencies, and they remain the best solution when money is short and time is scarce. The IKEA shelter was too complex, and it took too long to build. One experienced humanitarian complained that it had an "unimaginably enormous component count" and that its various fragments always got lost. A UNHCR employee described the difficulty and time it took to build the shelter, involving a confusing set of instructions and tricky procedures. Another humanitarian showed me a scar on his thumb from installing the poles into the sharp metal brackets during a long and frustrating day.

From this perspective, the key problem with the shelter was its overly complex form. It involved flying in a prepackaged solution rather than working from the bottom up. The designers of the shelter appreciated some of these concerns, and one of them acknowledged that "bringing a big pile of plastic and steel to Africa, produced with Western money in a Western country and then shipped there by Western companies" was not an ideal model of sustainability. Perhaps that kind of money could be used differently, to really build an economy where it's needed, but Karlsson clarified that this product was "for situations where local materials are not an option." It was designed for circumstances where there is "a very high influx of refugees and you need respond to in a very short time."[38] Some humanitarian critics accepted this defense, but many others maintained that the whole initiative broke the cardinal rule that shelter should be a "process, not a product."[39] This well-known aphorism in the shelter sector captures how most people are perfectly capable of finding or building their own shelters, even in emergencies, so humanitarians should be focusing on the process of supporting them with cash or materials rather than flying in their own prefabricated packets of steel and plastic.

The IKEA shelter was caught between these two broad criticisms from the moment it was formally launched in the middle of 2013. It was clearly more a product than a process, so it was "too much" for humanitarians, who concluded that it was overwrought, top-down, and too complex. At the same time, it aspired to be cheap and portable, so it was considered flimsy, light, and "too little" for architects with more expansive ideas about what design can achieve. When I told the team at Better Shelter my interpretation of these criticisms, they responded by reaching for the Swedish word *lagom*. This is tricky to translate, but it means something like "the right amount," "neither too little nor too much." It is a distinctly Swedish, and rather hackneyed, celebration of balance. The way they explained it, the whole project had tried to find a delicate equilibrium from the beginning. It was not just a balance between price, permanence, and politics; it was a balance between two potential criticisms. The shelter was poised on a knife-edge between the risk that it would do too much and the risk that it would offer too little.[40]

THE FIRE TESTS

In 2015, when the migration crisis hit Europe, the Better Shelter was already in production, and it began to be distributed to a range of new locations. Around the continent, one could see it placed under olive trees on Greek islands, on the concrete ground of Italian reception facilities, and in contexts as diverse as Iraq and Sweden to house people who were suddenly on the move. In each place, the balance of sufficiency shifted, and two events, in particular, illustrated how universality could be strained in both directions. The first event took place in Switzerland. The second took place in Lebanon.

The Swiss event was by far the more spectacular. It began when the city of Zurich began testing the Better Shelter and found the design to be wanting. Like other municipalities, Zurich was looking for simple accommodation—shelters that could be erected on sports fields, in empty warehouses, and on the tarmac of vacant lots—to house asylum seekers in a rush. Part of their assessment involved fire tests, which the Better Shelter failed dramatically. Videos appeared online showing a small interior fire, illuminating the translucent sides of the shelter and then quickly engulfing the entire structure in flames. The failure became a big media story. Clients became concerned and orders ended up canceled. The architectural critics argued that the Swiss fire tests proved their point, demonstrating that the shelter offered "too little" and that it was unsafe, insufficient, and limited. At the very least, it showed that the shelter did not live up to the standards that had been established in Switzerland.

The second event, which took place in Lebanon, demonstrated the opposite criticism: not that the shelter offered too little but that it did too much. Lebanon had a huge number of refugees on its borders and had long been governed through a precarious system that relied on confessional representation.[41] The prospect of integrating over a million Syrian refugees, mostly Sunni Muslim, was highly sensitive. After UNHCR accepted a small shipment of IKEA units for rural areas, they transported some to Akkar, in the north of Lebanon, for a test. The official in charge told me how his team was halfway through construction, putting the frames together, when a group of locals approached, armed and angry. They waved their guns and demanded that the shelters be removed, indicating the Syrian refugees were unwelcome in their neighborhood. My interlocutor tried to talk to them but quickly realized that the IKEA shelter was politically unpalatable. Its knockiness suggested that the refugees would be staying permanently. Many of its features appeared too luxurious, with bright white exteriors and frames of glinting steel. In the end, construction had to be abandoned. In the highly fractured political environment of Lebanon, the shelters were considered "too much."[42]

The events in Switzerland and Lebanon demonstrated the problem with universal shelter when it confronted real-world conditions. By using the word *lagom*, the designers expressed their desire to find a middle ground between comfort and cost. They had planned for their shelter to be deployed within careful parameters, but events had overtaken them. I discussed this with Johan Karlsson, asking why the shelter had been received so differently in Switzerland and Lebanon and suggesting that it placed the *lagom* shelter in doubt. After a pause, he agreed that it raised thorny questions before explaining that they had embarked on the scheme with a very particular vision of how the shelters might be used. The idea, he said, was to imagine a "refugee camp somewhere far away in Africa," where "it is not explicitly said, but there is some conception that [an IKEA shelter] is better than anything [and] that they should be glad for the shelters they are provided."[43] In other words, he had started with an image of a specific community—the remote African refugee camp—and then defined the boundaries of the project from there.

Such boundaries turned out to be flexible. The edges had been defined by the notion that the shelter would end up in places like Dollo Ado, where the first tests took place. The migration crisis of 2015, however, changed the terms of engagement. It saw the shelter thrust into a range of new locations, each with different cultures, levels of wealth, and politics. When it was transported to Switzerland, the IKEA shelter was perceived as unsafe, poorly insulated, and dangerous in fires. When it was transported to Lebanon, the same shelter was seen as too solid and luxurious. The shelter had tried to be universal, but events had shown standards to be very different around the world.

The designers responded to these events with a rethink. Hostility to the shelter in Lebanon did not come as a surprise because the possibility of government restrictions had been baked in from the start. The response in Switzerland, however, was more worrying. The team felt that the shelter was being held to exacting standards in Zurich, which was troubling because, as Karlsson explained, "if we could always put refugees in places meeting Swiss building norms, then we wouldn't have the refugee problem as it is today." His central frustration was that *any* emergency shelter would have failed the Swiss fire tests. "A wooden shelter, a tent, a container: you fill it with furniture, and of course it will burn down aggressively."[44] To make matters worse, how to respond to the fire tests was hardly straightforward. There was still no written brief from UNHCR, and the design team remained unclear about what they needed to do to restore confidence in the shelter. The team began working on a new material that responded slightly better to fire, but they were left in the curious situation of experimenting with new panels and sending them for fire tests without knowing what the standard should be.

Throughout this period, the same, central issue kept rearing its head. What was insufficient? What was "good enough"? And what might constitute something "better"? The team felt pressured by excessive standards, but they could hardly point this out publicly because they had staked so much on the idea that their shelter was *already* better. Most significantly, they could not defend themselves against the Swiss fire tests by saying that the municipality had made an unfair comparison with a permanent residential building because this would involve acknowledging that their shelters were designed for a different category of person: a refugee who should not expect to live in such high-quality accommodation. One of the designers lamented how the whole redesign had become "a guessing game." "Tent standards don't apply, and housing standards don't apply," he concluded.[45] The only solution, they decided, was to try and fudge something in between.

DON'T TOUCH

There have been many proposals for a universal basic shelter over the years, each reflecting different ideals, standards, and contexts. The International Style modernism of the 1920s saw the arrival of Le Corbusier's "domino system": a simple structure made from concrete slabs and reinforced columns with modernist flat roofs that could be replicated in identical units.[46] After World War II, there was Alvar Aalto's more organic modernist proposal, which involved emergency shelter "cells" that could grow and expand to produce more personalized individual dwellings.[47] In recent years, Alejandro Aravena's "half house"—a project that involves constructing half a house, with the other half to be completed by its occupants—has pursued similar aims in a different register.[48] The architect Shigeru Ban has also promoted emergency architecture based around lightweight cardboard tubes, drawing on the idea that if people love a building, then it will find some kind of permanence through their care.[49]

The IKEA-funded Better Shelter is just the latest in this long line of proposals, but more than any other, it demonstrates the difficulties of pinning down the essence of basic shelter. Some accused the IKEA-funded shelter of being too complicated and expansive, bursting the limits of basic assistance and reaching too high into exalted ideals. Others argued that it was too restrictive and mean, failing even to meet the "moral minimum" required of shelter. The designers, meanwhile, tried to find a balance of their own, seeking the middle ground between comfort and cost. These attempts, in the end, simply showed how hard it is to design a "universal" shelter because things change from place to place. Cultures have such different expectations that even the moral minimum will change with context.

It was against this background that I ended my exploration of the Better

Shelter by traveling to London and New York to find out why the IKEA refugee shelter had been so lauded in the design community. By then, it had been displayed not just in the London Design Museum but also in Stockholm, Berlin, Edinburgh, and the Museum of Modern Art in New York. I had already met the jurors in London, who had told me that its attraction came from compact accessibility. The shelter seemed like "a scaled-up version of your drawers at home," one juror told me. It was mass-produced and viable. "Sometimes, with design, you have a great idea," this juror explained, "but unless the infrastructure is there for it to be manufactured well, for it to be user friendly, for it to be transported effectively, then the design will come to nothing."[50] In this case, the juror believed, the practicalities had been solved: the shelter could be delivered in compact boxes, set up with no training, and even the instruction manuals with cartoon IKEA figures indicated a product that had considered all the details.

I sat in the Design Museum after this interview, surrounded by sleek gray furniture and feeling the bulk of its enormous concrete walls, while thinking about how the award reflected the peculiarities of our age. From precariousness to commodification, from humanitarianism to ephemeral architecture, the shelter just seemed to click into our most contemporary concerns. A statement from the museum said that the IKEA shelter tackled "one of the defining issues of the moment" while demonstrating "the power of design to respond to the conditions we are in and transform them."[51] It seemed an exaggeration, but I then remembered that the jurors had never seen this shelter in the field. They had never tried to build it. They had not spoken to anyone who lived in it. The shelter had been presented at the museum in an incomplete form, with just the gable ends mounted on a wall. The jurors had engaged with it as an idea, not a fully rounded shelter that people might inhabit. In such a context, it was perfectly possible to maintain that the right balance had been found.

This partial presentation—in a prominent exhibition, accompanied by laudatory description—was a common way to encounter the shelter. Soon after my meeting in London, I took a trip to New York to see how it featured in the Museum of Modern Art. Here, the IKEA shelter had been erected in full, placed in the very center of a space called Insecurities. It had been aestheticized and extracted from a real-world context, provided with a spotlight and a gallery attendant. Like the other exhibits, visitors were not allowed to get too close. Over the sound of an air-raid siren coming from a nearby audio installation, I kept hearing the attendant's refrain echoing around the exhibition hall: "Don't touch. Don't touch." It seemed that many of the visitors wanted to interact with the object, to feel it and get a sense of what it was like to inhabit it, yet the attendant was constantly reminding them to move away.

It later occurred to me that it was only here that the IKEA shelter could be truly *lagom*. In a museum or gallery, it did not need to negotiate with the difficult and compromised act of sheltering real human beings. It did not need to confront different cultures, climates, and regions. Here, it could retain its purity. Many critics felt that its notions of modesty and balance had prevented the shelter from doing anything more ambitious. They could not understand why its designers had failed to rethink emergency shelter from the bottom up, moving beyond the rectangular footprints and linear designs that were so common in refugee camps. They wondered why the IKEA shelter had mimicked the failed transitional module promoted by Shelter Centre, why its dimensions had been restricted by the size of tarpaulin distributed by the Red Cross. Some saw this as a missed opportunity, a failure of imagination. Why not make a shelter with a circular footprint? Or one that was hexagonal? Why not promote a design that was more flexible?

The fact is, whatever its form, a universal shelter will always be limited and bound by circumstance. The IKEA shelter was shaped by the cultural background of its Swedish designers, by the political context of governments looking for impermanence, and by the social context of a shelter sector that already had agreed on its parameters. The basic form was locked in by rectangular designs, limited budgets, and frames wrapped in replaceable envelopes. It seemed as though the gallery attendant knew that the shelter could not survive in the real world with so many pressures bearing down on it. She valiantly tried to repel any attempts to engage with it as a real place where people might live. I tried to thwart her, sneaking inside the shelter when she was distracted, but was discovered and reprimanded. I retreated guiltily into the corner of the gallery and watched as other people approached. They tried to tap, knock, and bring the IKEA shelter back to reality, but the attendant's refrain continued: "Don't touch. Don't touch. Don't touch."

2 | SHELTER AS METRICS

Refugee Camps in Jordan

FOR MANY YEARS, THERE WAS a testing ground for new shelters at the edge of Azraq refugee camp, a dry and empty field where temporary structures were driven into the gravelly ground and monitored as the elements battered them day after day. The sun beat down on their roofs, sand flew through their doorways, and temperatures regularly rose above forty degrees Celsius—conditions that became an ideal place to see how designs like the IKEA-funded shelter stood up to the rigors of life in a real-world refugee camp. I was introduced to the testing ground on an early summer day in 2017, soon after starting my study of the Jordanian camps. Each morning, I joined an aid convoy that drove out from Amman at seven o'clock, following a line of blue-bibbed aid workers as they streamed through the plate-glass UN headquarters to climb into jeeps and begin the ninety-minute journey to the camps. The road led out through the vast steel gates of the UN compound, past the suburbs and toward the north of the country.

Azraq was one of two gigantic camps that lay in the arid edges of Jordan. It had been planned in 2014 to house over 35,000 refugees and was surrounded by huge areas of desert and a razor-wire fence. I arrived at the testing ground on that first day just after nine o'clock in the morning, and the difficulties of designing an adequate shelter for such a harsh terrain became immediately clear. The prototype shelters, erected in a row, had buckling walls, sagging roofs, and slowly disintegrating exteriors. On the horizon lay the main camp, with its long lines of boxy shelters in the distance. The planners had decided on a structure with straight sides and a pitched roof, made from a metal frame clad in white corrugated steel. They were secured to the ground with deep anchors to ensure they couldn't fly away in the high desert winds. A single door entered directly into the living area, and an internal door led through to a much smaller kitchen. The heat inside was stifling.[1]

By noon in the summer, the shimmering heat haze barely softened the relentless view of so many small and stark metal homes. With few people outside, the streets felt abandoned. The population of the camp had ebbed and flowed over the previous two years, with some sections left empty as numbers declined and neighborhoods left to fragment. The steel panels of their vacant shelters had been wrenched away from the frames and left clanking in the wind. There was no vegetation, and the world appeared in a few washed-out colors: gray, brown, and cream. The grit thrown up from aid-agency jeeps enveloped the buildings as we passed, which glinted weakly through the sand-smudged air.

Azraq camp extended to fifteen square kilometers, and from a nearby hill, it was possible to appreciate the scale of the camp. At one side lay an enormous solar farm, which was spread out on the edge of the settlement, with lines of panels stretching into the distance. On the other side, there was a workshop to fix damaged shelters, with steel sheets and bags of concrete piled in a yard. Between these two landmarks were tall fences, wide roads, and an enormous supermarket, which lay at the center of the camp. Towering pyramids of tinned tomatoes stood alongside heaps of rice and flour at the market, where refugees could spend their allocated subsidence using an iris-scan system. At the checkout, they bent to put their eyes against a sensor so that the cost of their shopping could be deducted from a digital wallet. From the top of the surrounding hills, one could see them leaving the store, walking through the wasteland with bright-yellow shopping bags glowing like beacons through the haze.

Despite its grim and lifeless appearance, Azraq refugee camp had been built with an expansive vision of shelter. It was meant to be comprehensive and did not so much reduce shelter as scale it up. Rather than disassembling shelter into its separate components, as with the IKEA shelter, the planners had linked shelter to an extensive infrastructure. Rather than focusing on a single dwelling, the planners had knitted the houses together with shops and electricity, schools and health. There were markets, power stations, and welfare centers. The idea was to produce a checklist of everything required for human sheltering and capture them all in one place. From superstores to schools, piped water to paved roads, the designers of this camp had looked to provide all of life's necessities together.

Yet something was missing. People's physical needs were met, but the camp contained no space for beauty. Homes stretched out in gray uniformity with no variation in the plan. The whole camp was organized into smaller neighborhoods, each with access to a plumbed sanitation block, but movement through the settlement was closely regulated, and people were monitored as they crossed the perimeter fence. None of this affected the enthusiasm of the technical specialists, who showed me around that first morning with pride, pointing out the well-maintained gravel roads, the shelters that met minimum standards, and the services that came with quality benchmarks. In the view of the technical specialists, this was a camp that met all the core standards. It was clean. Trash was collected on time. Each dwelling had an electricity supply. The gaps between each shelter met the most stringent fire regulations. One of them even described it as a "model camp" because it had fulfilled all of the humanitarian metrics governing emergency settlements.[2]

What was going on? There seemed to be a profound disjuncture between

FIGURE 2.1.   Azraq camp, showing shelters and electricity lines. Zarqa Governorate, Jordan. © University of Oxford / Mark E. Breeze, 2018.

the fulsome humanitarian description and the meager material reality. The camp was meant to be a model, but it was clearly a horrible place to live. This raised a question: Is it really possible to come up with a comprehensive vision of shelter, as this camp was trying to do? Is it reasonable to think that one can set out everything needed from shelter in a book-length list of guidelines?

HUMANITARIAN METRICS

Elizabeth Cullen Dunn and Martin Demant Frederiksen argue that there is something ghostly about refugee camps, which try to simulate human communities but nevertheless fall short.[3] Camps *nearly* resemble a town or city. They *nearly* offer social life. They *nearly* provide for human requirements, but they end up feeling lifeless. This sense of near reality stimulates revulsion, as Azraq certainly did for me. It was an attempt to engineer a whole settlement from scratch, and the result was appalling. It was a remote place surrounded by desert, and there was little to do. It was a place that somehow resembled a community with everything people needed. Yet it appeared disconcertingly empty, like a half-finished, half-dead town.

The idea of the "uncanny" in this context can be traced back to early robotics. When robots begin to resemble humans, the argument goes, they are more likely to give us the creeps. We can cope with a robot that looks nothing like a human, but when they begin to closely approximate us, they begin to tap into subconscious fears that we are predictable and replaceable. Like camps, robots are trying to replace something more organic. They are an attempt to recreate human labor, just as camps are an attempt to recreate organic human communities, and the closer they come to succeeding, the more eerie they become.[4] Camps are similar in that they seem to reduce the essence of humanity and its manifold needs into a template, which stimulates an uncomfortable sense of the uncanny. Camps represent a far more comprehensive idea of shelter than just a flat-pack dwelling in a box, yet they still end up giving us this strange sense of an unfinished, dead space.[5]

After my first visit to Azraq, I returned to the UNHCR headquarters and spent the next few days talking to the camp planners to try to understand their aims and worldview. What notion of shelter were they following in the construction of this site? What were they trying to achieve? And what did they think of the results? I spoke first to the head of the technical unit, who had decades of experience constructing and managing refugee camps. It was late afternoon, and we were talking in a room darkened by venetian blinds—a welcome relief after the bright and arid camp. He set the scene by saying, very clearly, that camps are not an ideal response to the problem. Camps, he clarified, are a "last resort." They create a range of problems, from isolation to restriction on movement, but they may still be the only option on the table.[6]

There has been a lot of talk about abolishing camps in recent scholarly literature.[7] The aim is laudable, but we first need to understand why they persist. It is common to criticize camps without understanding that their existence is not solely due to the malicious acts of government but also due to the advocacy of humanitarians, who often have decent intentions and pragmatic knowledge about the available options. When I raised this with the senior UNHCR officials in Jordan, they were clear that there was indeed a political context that had to be understood when talking about camps. In the case of Azraq, you have to begin, they said, by going back to the middle of 2012, a year into the Syrian civil war.

At the time, Jordan was seeing several thousand refugees arrive from Syria every day—a huge number by any account—and these arrivals were set against a complicated political context. Jordan has a long history of hosting refugees with variable social impacts on the country as a whole. Since the 1940s, there has been a large population of Palestinians, in particular, living in camps that are now over seventy years old. Many Iraqi refugees arrived in the 1990s as well, along with tens of thousands of Syrians as seasonal laborers. When Syrians began to arrive in even larger numbers after 2011, the government initially allowed them to settle in towns and cities provided that they had connections. The key requirement was to have a Jordanian citizen as sponsor.[8]

The increase in numbers and the rise of daily arrivals, however, soon changed this situation. By the middle of 2012, words such as "stability" and "security" kept appearing in official communications, and it was decided to round up people crossing the border and take them to a newly created camp.[9] The first camp was called Za'atari, and I visited it just a week after it had opened, shadowing the site planner as he projected its growth to one hundred thousand people.[10] At that point, there were few solid features except a concrete arch, a perimeter fence, and some shipping containers serving as UN offices. Tents were set up in perpendicular rows, and their loose fabric flysheets flapped in the wind. Bladders and water points stood at corners, filled regularly from trucks. Communal shower blocks were constructed at the end of each line of tents, and kitchens for multiple households stood on the corner of makeshift streets.[11]

At this point in my interview, the technical coordinator rolled out the common formulation that explained UNHCR's role in the creation of this camp. The agency, he stressed, was there to "support and assist the government." Opening camps, he explained, is first and foremost a government decision, a political decision, and UNHCR was there to offer advice. This had already been clarified by officials at the UN Refugee Agency many years ago when they tried to draw attention to state sovereignty as the central building block of the international system. As one official put it back in 1995, "Host countries, not UNHCR, have the primary responsibility for refugees residing within their territories. . . . UNHCR does not control all the options."[12]

When I spoke to humanitarians about the arrival of camps in Jordan, many of them made the same basic point that, for all their faults, camps are the only option, and they can be useful for delivering relief. They may be described as a "last resort," but they remain an important part of the humanitarian toolkit for good reason. Even UNHCR's policy on alternatives to camps describes them as part of the arsenal, a way to "facilitate the rapid provision of protection and life-saving assistance in the event of a large-scale refugee influx."[13] In this respect, they have long been described as a "paradigmatic humanitarian space."[14] It is in camps, after all, that new procedures for emergency relief are formulated. It is in camps that aid workers cut their teeth. It is in camps that aid agencies trial new techniques and collect information to assess human needs. Monitoring and assisting a vulnerable population are much easier, in other words, when the people are all collected in one place.[15]

When Za'atari camp opened, therefore, the aid agencies saw it as an opportunity to establish good quality services. It had not been their decision to create the camp, but many of them sought to make the best of it—taking the opportunity to monitor the vulnerabilities of those that came in each day and carefully document what they needed. In this way, the camp provided decent amenities while also helping the government register, monitor, and—arguably—control the people arriving at the border. The process was straightforward. Refugees were brought to Za'atari and gathered together in large, covered waiting areas where they were fingerprinted, interviewed, and logged with the Jordanian security apparatus. The outer perimeter of the camp was guarded with sentry boxes and barriers. Once inside, the refugees were allocated accommodation and given food.

Why do governments establish camps? It is partly because they want to relieve pressure on local services, ensuring that traumatized refugees are not overwhelming schools and hospitals in the local community.[16] It is partly to keep refugees close to the border so that they can be more easily repatriated home. It is partly to ease communal tensions, maintaining a sense of refugees as separate from the rest of the population. It is partly to separate and contain noncitizens, avoiding thorny questions of long-term political membership.[17] All these factors—which are sometimes framed as moral issues and sometimes framed as an act of realpolitik—can play a role. But most often, camps are justified on grounds of security. Governments use them to monitor and screen people moving around unstable borderlands, and although security issues are often exaggerated, they are sometimes acute.[18]

Many of these factors were at play in the decision to open Za'atari camp in 2012. The Jordanian government was fearful of Da'esh fighters posing as civilian refugees. Officials were concerned about urban services being overwhelmed. They were reluctant to incorporate Syrians into the citizenry and wanted to ensure that refugees were kept near the northern border to make repatriation easier. Yet the humanitarians also benefitted from the decision to establish this camp as it made their job far easier. Keeping refugees all in one place certainly helped forms of surveillance, but it also helped provide people with what they needed to survive. The camp fed the government's desire for containment and control, while it also benefitted aid agencies by attracting donors and international attention.

FROM TENTS TO CARAVANS

I mentioned all this in the offices of UNHCR that afternoon, where there was evidently not much enthusiasm for a discussion of the political dynamics of the camp. When academics write about refugee camps, they tend to frame them with reference to some all-encompassing theory of power, which is not attractive to aid workers dealing with more complex negotiations on the ground. Some scholars compare camps to Erving Goffman's "total institutions," where people are cut off from the wider community and live an enclosed life administered by centralized authority.[19] Others reach for the work of Giorgio Agamben, stressing how camps can strip lives of political significance and reduce people to a form of "bare life."[20] Perhaps the most common approach is to draw on Michel Foucault, highlighting how discipline and biopower become central to the management of basic needs.[21] Yet mentioning these theories in a conversation with aid workers is likely to lead to a lot of eye rolling. Not *everything* about a camp, they are apt to say, is this totalizing and controlling.

My interlocutors at the UN Refugee Agency certainly held this view. They acknowledged that there were many restrictions on freedom in the camps, with control and surveillance from government authorities, but they stressed that the camp had a dual purpose. Camps are not just about control, they said, but also about care—a position that reflects the endpoint of a long-standing debate among humanitarians who were divided for many years between those that believed camps could only serve a political purpose and those who saw them as a useful humanitarian technology.[22] Most aid workers have since settled on a compromise position. Camps are both. They are never simply humanitarian spaces, but nor are they purely about repression and containment. The camps in Jordan were no exception. They were places of tents as well as fences, health centers as well as surveillance centers, water points as well as police posts. Through caring, these camps controlled, and through controlling, they could care. Indeed, it was precisely because they were so controlling that they could be so efficient for delivering aid.[23]

Much of this has already been integrated into academic theories of the camp, but the aid workers I spoke to were also keen to emphasize how totalizing models fail to capture the sheer diversity of refugee settlements around the world. It impossible to take a single approach to power in the camp, they say, because camps differ. Some are large; others are small. Some are urban; others are rural. Some are indistinguishable from the surrounding city, whereas others are clearly demarcated in remote border regions. Camps are different, too, in their architecture, landscape, history, governance, and culture.[24] Some camps are closely controlled, while others are effectively lawless. A single definition or universal theory, therefore, is simply inappropriate to make sense of what happens in a camp.

There is another way of looking at camps in the academic literature, however, which is to see them not as primarily places of care and control nor as places of politics and power, but rather as complex sites of cultural production.[25] Refugees are not simply governed in camps by powerful authorities, this literature reminds us; camps are not simply places where refugees wait passively to receive aid. Camps are also places where people create new identities, where they forge new ways of life and build social and cultural worlds.[26] Rather than just focusing on the dynamics of care and control, this literature reminds us that the bulk of camp life involves refugees taking action, subverting systems, and doing things for themselves.

Many people immediately seized on this point when I interviewed them, describing Za'atari, in particular, as an example of refugee political agency. This may have been a classic example of linear order in design, they said, but it was constantly being reworked and refashioned by refugees. I had seen this for myself when returning to Za'atari four years after it had opened. On my first visit, during the first week of its existence, tents dominated the landscape. Their grubby cream canvas constantly crackled in the high wind, and dust whipped up in vast clouds to cover the UNHCR logos in a fine film of yellow sand. These tents were fragile, insubstantial, and they began to disintegrate fast. At the end of a long day, I would often walk away from the main road to see how the landscape was changing at the edges, and I would find wide expanses of canvas straining and fluttering in the wind, their guy ropes held taut like kite strings in a gale. Further out, whole sections of the camp were uprooted, tarpaulin flattened, tents half buried in dust, their parts pinned against the wire diamonds of a perimeter fence.

This was how the camp began to change. The tents may have been useful as an emergency response—they are cheap to procure and quick to erect—but they became tricky to maintain when empty. Without anyone to weigh them down and keep them clean, the tents stood little chance against the elements.[27] Before the end of the first year in Za'atari, therefore, the tents began to be replaced by prefabricated mobile homes, which arrived on the ends of huge cranes, swung and lowered into place. The prefabs, known as "caravans," had similar dimensions to shipping containers but with two barred windows along each flank and a narrow door into the boxy interior. Their bottoms were made from plywood concealed by laminate flooring, and donor logos were stenciled onto their glaring white sides.[28]

By 2014, these caravans made up three-quarters of the shelters in Za'atari camp.[29] They may have been more solid than a tent, but they were still

FIGURE 2.2.   A caravan in Za'atari camp, showing window bars and initial adaptations. Mafraq Governorate, Jordan. © University of Oxford / Mark E. Breeze, 2018.

meant to communicate to Jordanian citizens that the camp was not permanent. As one planner put it to me, the hope was that the caravans "could be moved back to Syria after the crisis"—much like the refugees.[30] This was wishful thinking not least because the cost and energy required to relocate them would have made it unlikely. Yet the mobility of these dwellings nevertheless proved significant.

I saw why five years later when I returned to Za'atari in 2017 and found a completely different kind of camp. In the intervening years, the refugees had started to move their caravans into new locations and disrupt the linear plans of UNHCR. The head of the technical unit told me how refugees had done this by taking metal posts from the perimeter fence to create a chassis for the caravans, fixing wheels onto the posts with a welding machine and then pushing them about at night. "Thirty men were able to lift a caravan onto the chassis," he explained, and together, the refugees would "reshape the camp" according to their own desires.[31] Often, they positioned the caravans facing inward, with three or four together and a private courtyard at the center. Sometimes these compounds were constructed from just two caravans, placed in an L shape and surrounded by a corrugated iron fence. Other examples involved placing three caravans in a U shape, the fourth side then sealed from the street by a taut strip of fabric. The biggest compounds brought four caravans into a square and then concreted over the floor of their central courtyards, with lengths of tarpaulin stretched from each roof to offer shade from the sun.

As I walked around the backstreets of Za'atari, looking at these fascinating forms, I came across a team of shelter specialists, who were struggling to match their maps with the ever-evolving landscape. Each caravan had a number painted on its side, but the original caravans had been moved and hidden behind sprawling new compounds. The aid workers complained of disorder. They lamented that they had lost control, but there was no doubt that the results were peculiarly beautiful. Small patches of garden peeked around pale metal walls with irrigated vegetable crops climbing up partitions. Corrugated storerooms leaned against external fences with showers tucked around the back of caravans. The iron facades of new courtyards were often painted in a range of vibrant colors. Plots had been edged with stone and verges planted with greenery. Often, I found myself sitting inside a compound, talking to its creator and watching as sunlight filtered through stretches of canvas and illuminated delightful touches of personality. Refugees had transformed their characterless caravans into a smaller-scale version of vernacular Syrian architecture: a careful re-creation of home made from steel prefabs in the desert.[32]

The details were extraordinary. In some compounds, there were fountains fashioned from concrete or clay, water circulating in the middle of courtyards with a small electric pump. In others, the caravans had been adapted and divided, with one part for private sleeping and another for entertaining guests. The rigid urban plan had also been disrupted, with sterile plots gradually transformed into more vibrant social spaces. The market was perhaps the most well known, and by 2016, it had become a jumble of shops selling everything from bolts to bread, washing machines to wedding dresses. Guides would enthusiastically bustle through and demonstrate the range of products on offer. The main street—which was ironically named the Champs-Élysées—contained over three thousand shops that buzzed daily with donkey carts, bicycles, and deliveries.[33] This demonstrates how camps can quickly develop vibrant social and economic lives of their own, completely separated from the top-down intentions of the planners.

The aid workers always expressed great admiration for the creativity of refugees, but they nevertheless saw the lack of control as a problem. I followed as they knocked on doors and inspected compounds, noting down where caravans were disintegrating, walls were buckling, or floors were rotting from the daily sluicing that helped deal with the ubiquitous dust. The humanitarians saw themselves as responsible for the material condition of the camp, and they were simply trying to make lists of what needed to be fixed, as well as working out who owned the caravans so they could monitor people's vulnerabilities. This task, however, had become more difficult once the camp started changing. "Imagine the reaction of our team coming in each day," one senior UNHCR official explained, "when, across this huge surface area, the tents or caravans would just disappear."[34] The planners had arranged the camp according to a legible design that was reminiscent of a high-modernist settlement.[35] They wanted to know where people lived, and they disliked it when their plans were disrupted.

Despite all this, the shifting landscape and adapted caravans of Za'atari show how camps are not simply governed from the top down but can be altered and recreated by their inhabitants. It also shows how humanitarians perceive this as a problem, always keen to control difficult conditions.[36] The head of the UNHCR technical unit summarized the situation when he praised the vibrancy of refugee creations but nevertheless argued that Za'atari had become hard to manage. In his words, everything was back to front. "When you develop an urban plan," he explained, "you usually start with the large infrastructures: the network of water, the network of sewage. . . . You then build a road, you define your plots, and in each plot, you construct a house."[37] In Za'atari, however, this pattern was reversed. Rather than starting with the infrastructure, the aid agencies put down tents in a hurry. They then replaced them with longer-lasting caravans and eventually laid the infrastructure. This meant that refugees could move and shape their dwellings into new configurations, but it left the camp planners struggling to catch up. They were constantly trying to keep connections and track where dwellings had moved. Aid workers only imperfectly managed to attach each dwelling to services such as water and electricity. The result was a "spaghetti network": a complicated tangle of pipes and wires that was difficult to maintain.[38]

The camp planners responsible for Za'atari saw this as a failure. The facilities were not good enough, they said; the services were incomplete.[39] But soon, a new camp was being planned: Azraq. The camp planners saw it as an opportunity to draw out the "lessons" of Za'atari and to create an even more comprehensive settlement. As one put it, this was a chance "to repeat Za'atari, but in a more controlled and careful way."[40]

A TALE OF TWO CAMPS

Azraq was founded to the east of Amman in another dry military zone. It was meant to improve on Za'atari by offering better engineering and more control. The planners of Azraq tried to prevent shelters from being moved around by residents from the start; they wanted to provide better services and avoid the sense of chaos and insecurity that was a common lament in other camps around the world. This meant that they began by laying down the kind of infrastructure you would find usually in a modern city, including asphalt roads, a sewage system, and water networks. They built the camp on top of these networks by following up-to-date humanitarian guidelines. All this created a place that some in Jordan described as a "model" camp.[41]

These guidelines extended from the micro to the macro. They included minimum standards for individual dwellings, specifying at least 3.5 square meters of living space per person with an internal floor-to-ceiling height of at least two meters.[42] They included standards for the layout of the camp, which calculated the total area based on forty-five square meters per person and a one-to-two ratio between covered living space and plot size.[43] The guidelines determined everything from the positioning of distribution points to the distance between each structure. There was meant to be a maximum distance of five hundred meters from any household to each water point and no more than 250 people sharing each tap.[44]

Such metrics created a comprehensive vision of shelter. The aim was to maintain control over basic standards and prevent the plan being disrupted. The landscape was divided into zones, which were called "villages," with markets created in each. The handbooks specified the gradient of the overall site as between 2 and 4 percent. They recommended specific gaps between shelters and periodic firebreaks, which should be thirty meters wide for every three hundred meters in the plan. The metrics covered everything down to the size of classrooms in each school and the latrines in every market.[45] There was such trust in numbers that the camp planners even sought to control and measure the thermal performance of each shelter, tracking the air temperature and relative humidity inside.[46]

Refugee camps are often defined by this kind of detailed control; although, in practice, the implementation of such metrics is more ad hoc.[47] Azraq is simply an extreme case. Few camps are designed quite so intricately and with such generous budgets, and this made Azraq the apex of an ideal realized through metrics. Camps like Azraq, my interviewees stressed, are where "people can be fed, watered and schooled," places that contain "everything refugees need."[48] In this respect, they involve a broad vision of shelter but also a shallow vision since it reduces shelter to what could be checked and monitored. The idea is to set human needs down with precision. There is no space for variation, beauty, or surprise. Success is measured in units. Humans are put in boxes. As Dunn and Frederiksen put it, places like Azraq are built not for people but for "an abstraction of a person—a 'person-unit' that requires a given amount of space, just as it requires a given number of calories."[49]

The camp, therefore, was laid out with precision. Every street and shelter was mapped, and every unit in the marketplace was registered. Each of the "villages" was divided from the others by an open buffer zone so that any gathering of people could be quickly identified and dispersed. Visitors could not walk into the camp but had to enter along a long approach road that was watched over by checkpoints. The camp management was situated in an isolated area, making it hard to organize protests.[50] Every shelter had a clear identification number, which was matched with a register of residents and tied to open-source map software that became updated in real time.[51] Unlike Za'atari, there was no risk of the camp being reorganized or of camp planners losing track of people. Each refugee had to sign an agreement with UNHCR and the Jordanian government when they entered the camp, which made it clear that they were not permitted to move or maintain their dwelling, effectively denying them the ability to make a home.[52]

Critical commentators often describe the central problem with Azraq as one of control—precisely the thing that humanitarians found attractive about the place. But the flipside was that the refugees had no control at all. There was no freedom, no chance to move or change one's shelter. "Beyond relief and subsistence, it's a disaster," one critic told me. "It is just boredom. Nobody wants to go there."[53] Most refugees needed permission to enter or leave the camp, and even when this was granted, they found themselves a long way from any urban centers. Conversations with inhabitants always came back to a desire for freedom and the inability to move and live elsewhere. Many expressed gratitude at having safety and security in the camp, but they spoke of feeling trapped. "The most important thing for us right now is to be granted permission to leave," one told me. "Even if you are living in a palace, you will die and eventually be buried under the soil and covered by a piece of cloth. The same if you are living in a camp. . . . But we are always hoping for better things, and right now, we want our freedom."[54]

Conversations often lurched violently like this, from religious fatalism to a yearning for liberation, but the problem of control was not just a matter of free movement. It also concerned people's ability to make a mark on the world, to leave some kind of scratch on a soulless landscape and make it distinctively their own. When walking through the camp, it was possible to see the odd flash of life emerging between upright sections of corrugated steel. Children found places to play in small yards demarcated by discarded panels. Washing was hung colorfully, despite long-standing camp rules. Indoors, people let rip remarkable displays of creativity. If invited for tea, you could find rich-red tapestries hanging from the interior walls of a shelter and golden tassels tied around beds. It was common to see strips of insulation cut into intricate shapes, turned inside out to reveal their glinting silver interiors. Homemaking went on inside despite the restrictions and in ways that reflected a gendered division of labor.[55]

Personal expression may have been possible inside, but public spaces in the camp remained empty and untouched. Adaptation was forbidden and vegetation restricted because one camp manager reportedly insisted that he should have an uninterrupted view from one end of the camp to another.[56] Some refugees dug the earth around their homes to plant flowers

FIGURE 2.3.   Panorama of Azraq camp. Zarqa Governorate, Jordan. © University of Oxford / Mark E. Breeze, 2018.

and bushes, which was tolerated as long as foliage did not grow beyond a certain height, but trees were not permitted. This was justified on security grounds, with the government believing that tall vegetation could be used to provide cover for armed groups, but it seemed an unrealistic notion. How would masked gunmen be camouflaged by a few scraggly trees in an open desert?[57] The sense of a place governed by emptiness was even deeper in Village Five, an area within Azraq that operated as a camp within the camp. This was a fenced-off section where new refugees from certain areas of Syria were sent for security clearance, and it was surrounded by a high chain-link fence with only one entrance. The people inside could not leave without permission, and Village Five stood like a prison, visible from all sides and threatening ever further confinement.[58]

FROM CAMPS TO CITIES

The author Brian Keenan, who spent four and a half years as a hostage, wrote a beautiful book called *An Evil Cradling*, which describes not just the experience of captivity but also what it means to be reduced to a bundle of basic human needs. The book contains a particularly memorable moment when Keenan is given a bowl of fruit by his captors after living in solitary confinement for many months. He simply stares at it, reveling in its textures and smells, its shapes and its colors—the apricots, oranges, nuts, and cherries. He described how he wanted to absorb this sensory abundance, how he derived so much joy from looking at the bowl of fruit that he could not bring himself to eat it. Blue-green mold started furring the surface, and the colors became mesmerizing. This left him in "quiet rapture" as sights and smells spun through his head. Keenan's guards thought he was mad as he refused to eat the fruit, and he screamed in fury when they tried to take the rotting mess away, but Keenan was taking his nourishment from sensing the fruit, not eating it. "My soul found its own completeness in that bowl of color," he later wrote. "The forms of each fruit. The shape and curl and bend all so rich, so perfect."[59]

I often thought of this anecdote in Azraq because it seemed to articulate what the bare metrics of shelter can miss. We tend to think about survival in terms of the body rather than the soul, but this is a false division. For Keenan, the fuzzy feel of an apricot skin and the sight of a bright orange against the monochrome walls of his cell became just as important as the vitamins he might gain from eating it. His story shows how surviving in brutal conditions is not just a matter of meeting physical needs but also a matter of finding beauty and variation in the world. With shelter, too, we need not just roofs and walls but difference and delight.[60] When walking around Azraq, I frequently wondered if the feel of the place might change if the restrictions were eased, if etches and scars could accrue on the buildings and the passage of time could roughen those sharp steel lines into something more varied. It seemed ironic that the camp planners spoke of "villages" and "communities" when such organic forms of living were impossible to impose from the top down. Despite the detailed guidelines, this camp missed a great deal about what it means to be human. It contained no beauty, no cultural life, and no basic freedoms.

None of this was lost on aid workers, who often drew a different lesson from the tale of two camps. One was the former manager of Za'atari, a grizzled humanitarian called Kilian Kleinschmidt, who had left his job just as Azraq was opening its gates. Rather than endorsing the intensification of control in the new camp, he started arguing that camps should be transformed into bustling, entrepreneurial cities. His idea was simple: that aid agencies needed to shake off the idea of camps as temporary settlements, resisting the temptation to manage every element of life, and instead, they should try to harness the natural dynamism that was evident in a place like Za'atari in order to change the nature of a camp. Refugees were already creating markets, opening shops, and reshaping their environment to create thriving communities, he pointed out. So why insist on top-down control? Humanitarians need to learn from refugees, Kleinschmidt concluded. They need to encourage greater autonomy, thinking about camps as the "cities of tomorrow."[61]

Turning a camp into a city requires more than good infrastructure. Azraq had that infrastructure in spades, but it was nevertheless a sterile, eerily dead space: a creepy facsimile of a city. Perhaps it is best to imagine the infrastructure as a kind of groundwork: a necessary but insufficient condition for camps to evolve into more vibrant metropolitan centers. If the right networks are in place, the argument goes, then camps are ready to develop—but they still have to evolve organically. Indeed, camps seem to change most profoundly when centralized control begins to weaken, when commerce begins to develop, when tents turn into buildings, and when they slowly spread as neighboring conglomerations sprawl to meet them. This can take years, if not decades, but when these things happen, the effect can be transformative. Indeed, there are many examples of camps that have become urban centers and, as a result, have lost that sense of the uncanny.[62] Kleinschmidt argued that this could be achieved not just through building infrastructure but also by reducing controls and restrictions.

The story of cities over the past two hundred years has involved homes gradually becoming linked to a growing array of networks. First, there was piped clean water. Then, there was electricity and gas. More recently, we have seen communication networks, such as telephones and broadband. This ideal of the "networked house" has become the model for camps as well.[63] Each shelter has to be linked in a web of wires and pipes and roads, and the upshot is that camps need to be planned as though they were future cities—a notion that goes back to the earliest humanitarian shelter handbooks.[64] But the tendencies toward top-down planning still have to be overcome because camps are, by definition, populated by people with constraints. Refugees cannot come and go as they please. They cannot make long-term plans or create businesses or navigate bureaucracy as easily as citizens. Kilian Kleinschmidt favored a settlement that could be driven by the market rather than by humanitarian metrics, and his idea was to provide refugees with a framework of rights that would encourage entrepreneurialism and reduce aid dependency. The aim seemed to be to turbocharge a process of development: establishing infrastructure and then stimulating the entrepreneurial dynamism that might replace that drab uniformity with change from the bottom up.

This is certainly an attractive idea, but it remains flawed because there is no formula for a successful city. The modernists of the 1950s and 1960s found this to their detriment, trying to carve buildings and forge new human communities from the blank slate of the open countryside. This often led to ugly environments, fractured societies, and destruction. It failed because the architects assumed that places and people could be detached from their contexts and backgrounds and made amenable to rational plans.[65] Too many camps have been designed according to a similar blueprint, with their tight grid formations and their "trust in order and hygiene."[66] As many scholars point out, these are settlements that resemble other high-modernist schemes for human improvement, with a related failure to understand local contexts.[67] The recent call to foster "entrepreneur-ship, self-sufficiency, and new investment in jobs" may not be enough to overcome such problems.[68] Economist Paul Collier believes that camps can contribute to an "economy-in-exile," providing "the job havens that incubate the future economy."[69] This drive to transform camps, however, has a serious flaw. Camps will always remain camps as long as they are built for a single category of people at a single moment in time. Most definitions of a camp emphasize how they are clearly demarcated territories where exceptional arrangements of governance are exerted over noncitizens.[70] No amount of liberal optimism can contain these political pressures.

Consider the differences. Cities are vibrant spaces that become a melting pot of cultures. Camps, however, are designed for a specific class of noncitizens. Cities are "dense and permanent settlement[s] of socially heterogeneous individuals."[71] Camps, however, are rarely dense, rarely heterogeneous, and are not meant to be permanent. Cities are highly concentrated urban areas with a vibrant range of activities. Camps, however, tend to sprawl out in endless suburbia and contain large empty spaces to improve surveillance and visibility. One UNHCR staff member made these differences crystal clear when he told me that Azraq was a "dream" for monitoring and evaluation. Everything had been laid out so clearly, he said. Everything could be known and then quickly fixed if there were any problems.[72] Even the food that people eat in a place like Azraq could be monitored and logged through the iris-scanning system at the supermarket. Cities are never places with such intricate legibility and control. In contrast, they are places of relative anonymity, places where ideas can circulate, and places of openness and freedom, where people can hide and dissent.[73] Camps are designed to specifically *prevent* these characteristics from emerging. They are arranged in order to cut people off from precisely the diversity and openness that might help a true city arise instead.[74]

These issues cannot be wished away. If humanitarians want to break the top-down control within camps, then they need to find another approach. One suggestion is to give refugees more control over the governance of refugee camps.[75] There is a strong moral case for this, but on its own, it hardly represents a radical departure from the status quo. Another suggestion is to encourage the retrofitting of existing shelters by articulating a right to "appropriate" the places allocated.[76] This is an important and pragmatic way to improve the quality of shelter, but it does not eliminate the wider framework of control. Some scholars would like to abolish camps entirely.[77] This is a noble idea but may not be pragmatic given the state system we live within. We are, therefore, left with the push to turn camps into cities, which risks being little more than a rebranding exercise: a limited way to make the isolationism, the poverty, the poor design, and the absence of rights look like a temporary feature on the road to a brighter future.

3 | SHELTER AS POLITICS

Squats and Solidarity in Greece

I FIRST MET NASIM IN a smoky bar in Exarcheia, and he was very clear from the start: Hotel City Plaza was not just a building; it was a political idea. Situated in a drab concrete block on a busy road to the north of Athens, the hotel had stood empty for many years accumulating dust and shedding masonry—just one of the many dejected buildings signifying the effects of the 2008 financial crash. Nasim knew it was empty, and after witnessing the rising numbers of refugees sleeping rough during 2015, he decided to break in. Along with a group of other activists, he reconnected the water, rewired the electricity, and cleaned the rooms.[1] I entered the building a few months later, and City Plaza had already become a brightly lit community. The noise of conversation echoed down the marble stairs, and colorful photos lined the walls. There were posters announcing language lessons and music classes, with hundreds of refugees making their home in the rooms above.

Nasim and his colleagues were trying to do far more than just provide a bed for refugees when they started squatting in the hotel in 2016. They wanted to challenge the government's whole approach to shelter. As the refugee crisis had intensified over the previous year, the Greek government had built many new camps in neglected corners of the country. By 2016, the borders began to close, and tens of thousands of refugees were trapped, with those not in the overcrowded camps left sleeping on the streets. Nasim's occupation of this building was meant to raise big questions about the wastefulness of vacant urban spaces, the harmful policy of encampment, the priorities of politicians, and even the existence of nation-states. As one statement declared, "as long as they build camps and detention centers, and as long as there are borders, we will also be there to fight for a better world."[2]

Nasim said something similar when I met him in Athens. He told me that City Plaza was a political project that had been designed to empower refugees and allow them to stay in the heart of the city. It was partly aimed at preventing people from being forced to live sequestered in isolated camps, but it also aspired to build a political movement that encouraged refugees to take action. Refugees would not just receive aid in City Plaza but also be educated about their situation with the hope that they would be able to "think about their dreams, their ideas, and their aims in life."[3] The idea was to build a more egalitarian community where migrants and citizens would live together. The architecture may have been uninspiring—a squelch of laminate floors illuminated by overhead spotlights set in suspended ceiling tiles—but this was a place with a stirring political vision. One statement even described the hotel not as a shelter but as a "workshop of solidarity and resistance."[4]

The exterior of the squat had little to indicate what lay inside. Years of neglect scarred the bricks. Paint was peeling from the walls, and the entrance was hidden down a dingy alley littered with cigarette butts. Mucky letters spelled the hotel's name in vertical protrusions above the pavement. A large banner across the front of the building declared, "People are dying in the camps. . . . Open Borders! Open Buildings!" Awnings made from blankets were hung across the windows, and the whole facade looked like a patchwork of textiles, which hid the activity inside.[5] Behind this blockwork, four hundred people stayed in the building each night, sleeping in over ninety bedrooms set along long corridors. "It's like a street, you know," Nasim told me. "It's like each room is a house and everyone is a neighbor."[6] Stacks of leaflets in reception declared that refugees and activists were "living and struggling together." The idea was to create a bustling city in miniature.

Politics has been famously defined as the struggle to determine who gets what, when, and how.[7] The activists in City Plaza were certainly engaging in politics in this sense. They were trying to challenge the government's idea of what refugees should receive. They were pointing out that people in the camps had no power or resources—they just lived as refugees in isolated

FIGURE 3.1.   Hotel City Plaza from the street. Acharnon, Athens, Greece. © University of Oxford / Mark E. Breeze, 2017.

places waiting for news about their final status while living in terrible conditions. Those on the street were even more destitute, dependent on charities for their daily necessities. City Plaza wanted to break such "relations of dependency."[8] The building was managed through self-governing committees and assemblies in which everyone took part. Timetables stipulated who should do the cooking, cleaning, and security. Everyone took turns to keep the place running, an approach that was meant to create a flatter—that is, more horizontal, or nonhierarchical—structure while offering a challenge to humanitarians and governments.

There was another notion of politics going on here, too, which emerged from the work of Jacques Rancière. This was politics as a struggle, politics as the fight for inclusion on the part of disempowered people.[9] The aims of City Plaza were often articulated in this way: to ensure that refugees were fully recognized as equal participants in every aspect of life in the building. The experiment not only threw down a challenge to mainstream approaches to shelter but also raised deeper questions about the relationship between shelter and politics. Can refugee accommodation ever become genuinely egalitarian? Or is shelter inevitably implicated in structures of power and control? The activists wanted to remake the world, creating an alternative to hierarchical refugee camps that would break destructive relationships of dependency. But could their own shelter shake free from these ubiquitous networks of power?

TWO CONNECTED CRISES

When the old hotel was occupied in 2016, two closely connected crises were hovering behind the scenes. First and foremost, there was the refugee protection crisis, which had started the previous year with thousands of people crossing the Aegean Sea to arrive on the Greek islands each day. But the event also took place against the background of a second crisis—a government debt crisis—which had been bubbling along for six years. This was triggered by the global financial crash of 2008, and it led to years of crippling austerity, the sale of state assets, and the stripping back of welfare that led to rising poverty and the growth of self-support movements across Greece.[10]

In January 2015, a leftist political movement, Syriza, swept to victory in the general election. Their approach set the tone for the subsequent summer of migration. The previous center-right government had invested heavily in punitive detention centers and interdiction at sea, but Syriza adopted a more promigration stance, scaling back both incarceration and the interception of boats. This was partly motivated by a commitment to the universalist idea that "no migrant is illegal," but it was also driven by the sense that migration into Europe should not be Greece's problem. By refusing to act as border guards for the whole continent, the new government realized that migration could become a bargaining chip that might help them during negotiations with the European Union (EU) over debt and austerity.[11]

By the summer of 2015, however, the number of arrivals on the Greek islands had rocketed. At first, the new government responded by waving people through. The politicians understood that the majority of migrants had no interest in remaining in Greece but rather wanted to move through the Balkan corridor and onto the wealthier economies of northern Europe. By encouraging refugees to move on, the new Greek government achieved two objectives at once: they realized their ideological commitment to reducing punitive detention, and they shifted the pressure of migrant arrivals onto richer countries in the EU. As one border agent put it to a journalist that summer, their strategy involved taking fingerprints and then sending everyone onto Germany: "Finger, Copy, Merkel."[12] Most migrants did not spend very much time in Greece as a result. From the moment they arrived on the islands to the moment they crossed the Macedonian border, they generally kept moving, pausing only to rest, eat, make contact with smugglers, and negotiate the next part of their journey.

This policy of waving migrants through the country meant that shelter was not a priority—at least initially. Many migrants needed no more than a few days of accommodation, and they were always traveling north. Many people slept in ports, bus stations, or crucial stop-off points, such as the ferry terminal buildings in Piraeus. They also camped outdoors in public parks, such as the huge Pedion Areos in Athens.[13] Informal transit camps emerged at border posts, like Idomeni near the boundary with Macedonia, where nongovernmental organizations (NGOs) provided food, medical, and legal assistance. Yet none of these locations were really proper shelters; they were informal places to rest and gather information, places for pauses on a journey. Viktoria Square in Athens became a particularly important location in this regard, where people met and planned their next steps with the help of smugglers who congregated near the entrance.

At the start of 2016, however, the borders began to close. Restrictions first came into effect in the north when Macedonia started preventing certain nationalities from moving through the Balkans. Then, in the middle of March, the EU and Turkey reached a deal that closed the southern border as well, preventing the arrival of boats to the islands. This meant around sixty thousand people were stranded in Greece—migrants who had planned to move north through the Balkan corridor but were now unable to do so.[14] The informal camps and stop-off points soon became crowded as people were trying to move north but became stuck at their staging posts. At Piraeus Port, for example, thousands of people ended up sleeping on the floor of the terminal buildings for months on end.[15] In many other places, too, migrants were trapped with nothing but a blanket and no way to continue their journeys. At Idomeni in the north, a small, informal settlement began to grow and eventually over ten thousand people ended up living in tents and temporary shelters by the newly closed border.[16]

It was only at this point that the problem of refugee shelter became acute, and the Greek government responded by building an archipelago of camps with financial support from the EU.[17] These camps were often constructed by the army, who laid out settlements in the classical manner of grids on state-owned land. The migrants stuck in Piraeus, for example, were moved to a large new camp called Skaramangas in an old Navy dockyard in an isolated industrial area northwest of Athens. Here, four hundred white, rectangular container homes were stacked in lines on a concrete foreshore, surrounded by fences and butted up against the edge of the sea.[18] Other migrants were housed in poorly converted buildings, such as warehouses and factories. One notorious example was Softex, a ruined toilet paper factory that stood downwind of an oil refinery.[19] Residents complained of feeling trapped and cut off. They could come and go with few physical constraints, but the facilities were unpleasant and remote.

CAMP CONDITIONS

The poor conditions in many camps became painfully evident over the following year and a half. During the unusually harsh winter of 2016–2017, many refugees were still stuck in places that had been designed to last just a few months. Heavy snow fell on shelters that had not been properly prepared, and in some places, refugees were still living in tents and thin metal sheds as the temperatures plummeted.[20] When I visited Greece the following spring, many of these camps were still open, with asylum claims and relocation promises stuck in a massive backlog.[21]

I began by going to the Ministry of Migration in order to try to understand their version of events. The conversation began in an old building that overlooked a public space, and after showing my credentials, I took a cranky elevator up the building, which led to a weightily furnished boardroom with a large table, leather sofas, and padded doors.[22] A senior official got up from behind a dark wooden desk flanked with flags and called in a group of other civil servants who proceeded to make a promotional presentation. They explained how they had drawn up the best possible specifications for shelter and heroically mobilized resources to map out possible locations. The officials kept gesturing to a huge map on the opposite wall, with camps marked with pins of different colors: red for those due to be dissolved, green for those that would remain. A civil engineer unfurled a sheaf of plans on the tabletop, showing diagrams of sleek new container homes.

I took a visit to one of these camps a few days later, a place that had been laid out with all the pristine uniformity of Azraq. Rows of boxlike dwellings stood on the concrete ground, surrounded by lots of space. Local activists had complained about the soulless landscape, but this camp was at least clean and relatively close to the city center.[23] I was presented with all the successes—a story of speedy construction, of overcoming constrained conditions, of standards being met—yet this was one of the better camps in the country, and there were countless others that were unsuitable for an official tour. I saw the flipside a few days later when visiting the abandoned airport of Ellinikon. I had been hearing of a cluster of camps at the old airport for some time—camps that were unofficial, disorganized, and shockingly chaotic. Many government officials had been unwilling to discuss such camps on the record, and in the absence of official permission, there was no option but to go down there and try to get in.

Ellinikon was the main airfield for Athens until 2001, and it remained an enormous area surrounded by blocky suburbs. Tufts of grass spurted and swayed through cracks, bisecting the gray concrete runway in long, angular lines. Blue-and-white aircrafts lay rusted and unused on the vast expanse of tarmac. Parts of this area had been repurposed for the 2004 Summer Olympics, and the plan had been to transform the site into Europe's largest metropolitan park once the Olympics were over. The place still felt like a void in the cityscape over a decade later.[24] As the refugee crisis started to worsen toward the end of 2015, the Greek government decided to transform some parts of the airfield into emergency refugee accommodation. Teams of police had begun to clear some of the informal settlements in parks and ports around Greece, moving their inhabitants to stay in this crumbling airport terminal and the dusty stadiums alongside it.[25]

It was one of the ironies of 2015 that refugees so often ended up stuck in places that had been originally built to enable mobility: ports like Piraeus, Skaramangas, and the Ellinikon airport. Eighteen months after arriving, they were still there, and when I visited the camp on Greek Independence Day in 2017, it remained shockingly overcrowded and decrepit. The skies were a vibrant blue, but the ground sparkled with windows broken from neglect and vandalism. A deafening cluster of military planes passed overhead, with colored contrails sliced in formation, while traveling to Syntagma Square. Tall floodlights extended high above the empty airfield on posts of white and red. In the old terminal building, I picked my way past skewered metal shapes and rusting forms to get into the battered buildings beyond. Children played barefoot around overflowing rubbish bins. Wet clothes hung on rusting chain link fences and cars roared past on the main road nearby. The low building to the front of the terminal building was smashed and sprayed with graffiti, with shards of glass speckling the painted curbstones beneath.

This was, without doubt, one of the worst places I visited that could be called a refugee shelter. Ministry officials had been happy to organize trips to the most clean and organized camps, but they had wanted me to avoid places like Ellinikon. Its status was complicated: it was not an official camp, but nor was it condemned. NGOs offered support, with food served from visiting trucks, but their scraps were often left scattered on the concrete for the gulls and pigeons. Some of the residents were keen to illustrate their living conditions, which involved sleeping in tents on the floor of the large terminal building. Cords and guy ropes were strung from pillar to wall, with extra blankets creating partitions. Hundreds of people milled through the corridors, sitting under airport signs and walls scrawled with pen. On the ground floor, a bank of blue cubicles provided sanitation, but this was one of the few adaptations that had been made in a structure that had always been profoundly unsuitable for long-term accommodation.

The officials in the ministry informed me that Ellinikon was the unfortunate result of a "need to place an increased number of people somewhere," saying that it had been an emergency measure and was not a proper accommodation center, "just a place of temporary stay."[26] Yet by this point, over a year later, it was still occupied and still as bad as ever. Before being thrown out of the site, I sat on the pavement speaking to families eating prepared meals from metal trays. One father told me how his younger child had grown from a baby to a toddler while living in the camp. The child ran past us, chasing her brother around a line of disintegrating bus stands with a faded Christmas message overhead. An abandoned set of passenger stairs had been left to rust nearby with a strange, severed statue of a man mounting the first step, a line of bags behind him.

ALTERNATIVE ASSISTANCE

Official refugee shelter in Greece ranged from cold and clinical to squalid and chaotic, but there was another story of assistance that summer, which was led by ordinary citizens rather than the state. Hotel City Plaza was one prominent example, but it was just a small part of a much wider scene that included fishermen rescuing people from punctured boats, villagers offering a bed to passing travelers, and office workers coming into the camps to provide food and conversation. Many ordinary people were going out of their way to help refugees across Greece, a movement that grew rapidly throughout 2015 and into 2016.[27]

These initiatives ranged from the ad hoc to the well structured; Hotel City Plaza lay at the organized end of the scale. It had aims that were common among the solidarity groups emerging with particular strength after the debt crisis and subsequent austerity measures of 2010. During that period, thousands of people lost their jobs in Greece, and the social security system seriously struggled. Self-help networks began to fill the gap, with services like collective pharmacies and soup kitchens replacing the welfare state for many Greek citizens.[28] Lots of these groups conveyed an explicitly political message, demonstrating opposition to austerity and authoritarianism. Some were radically socialist or anarchist in orientation. Their spirit of resistance and solidarity extended quite naturally to include the problems faced by refugees once they began to move through the country in greater numbers during 2015.[29]

The Greek solidarity networks were profoundly different from the traditional humanitarian agencies that also began operating in the country in larger numbers from 2015. UNHCR had declared an emergency that summer, and many aid institutions had followed suit by establishing new projects, but these took a long time to mobilize, and—just as in the era of austerity—solidarity networks were quick to fill the gap. The activist groups positioned themselves in opposition to the large bureaucracies and faceless authorities that characterized both state welfare and international relief. They saw themselves as nimble rather than cumbersome. They responded to people rather than statistics. They worked for nothing rather than being paid high salaries. Perhaps most crucially, they presented their work as intrinsically political, opposing borders and standing in solidarity with migrants rather than claiming to be neutral or impartial.[30]

This fascinating combination of amateur assistance and political positioning was particularly prevalent in the aftermath of the 2015 summer of migration. It attracted volunteers from across the world. These young and inexperienced activists were filled with enthusiasm but had no humanitarian qualifications, and they became attracted by the extensive media coverage of the refugee crisis in Greece and the ease with which they could travel. As one journalist put it, "there was a sense that people of conscience from all over the world should rush to Greece to take part in a sort of test of humanity."[31] Once the trickle started, volunteers came in ever-greater numbers. The young activists mixed with experienced community organizers and became radicalized, leading to a melting pot of informal humanitarian assistance combined with effervescent ideological debate. A commentator described how "they all crashed into each other"; in the industrial zones outside cities, on the hillsides of Greek islands, outside the formal refugee camps and transit centers, there were young international volunteers channeling their outrage and working with experienced solidarity activists to develop new and creative forms of assistance.[32]

Professional humanitarians soon recognized the successes of such informal assistance. As one report put it in 2017, "Much of the water, food and healthcare provided during the critical months of July, August and September 2015 came from local independent and subsequently international volunteer groups. . . . It was not until October 2015 that the international response really began to catch up with the scale of need."[33] Yet despite such acknowledgment from the formal humanitarian sector, the relationship between traditional aid agencies and the new grassroots activists was not very cordial. The solidarity humanitarians resented how professional humanitarians came to dominate when they finally arrived. Many objected to their timid, apolitical stance. As one activist said to me, traditional aid agencies had a terrible sense of entitlement. They arrived late, with a lot of money and very little understanding of the local context. They rolled out inappropriately standardized systems and focused all their efforts on providing short-term relief. They "fought no long-term battles" and then "left for lengthy periods while feeling really good about themselves." All this, I was told with bitterness, constituted a form of "humanitarian colonialism." Employees of large aid agencies ended up "living in luxurious hotels, sitting around the swimming pool, drinking their martinis"—precisely the opposite of engaged, grassroots activists.[34]

Here, solidarity humanitarianism involved a contrast to the professional aid world. It involved activists living alongside migrants, cooking food together and discussing politics late into the night. They were more hands on, developing a level of compassionate intensity that professionals found difficult to muster. When the borders finally closed in March 2016, therefore, the solidarity response became a thriving concern. The activists had previously been doing small but important things—helping people to get around border restrictions, distributing food, and offering a bed for a night—but once the refugees were stuck in Greece, supporting them required a deeper and longer-term engagement. They no longer needed just information and basic care; they needed a place to stay for months on end. They no longer needed information about how to travel north; they needed help navigating the complex bureaucracies of state.

Meanwhile, refugees were being shepherded into camps by the authorities, many of which were located a long way from urban areas. Most activists saw these camps as an inhuman disaster, and most refugees preferred to live in the city. Opposition to bureaucracy and state power combined with the need to take durable action. The task of the solidarity activist began to require more ingenuity and commitment. It involved more than just giving out food and criticizing the government-run refugee camps. It involved creating an alternative model of shelter.

SQUATS AND CITIES

It was against this background that Nasim and his colleagues occupied Hotel City Plaza in the spring of 2016. The EU-Turkey deal had marked the end of the long summer of migration, and the activists realized its significance.[35] The deal shut the door on migrant journeys through Greece and effectively trapped people in the country. Now they needed a place to live that was safe and inclusive, somewhere that brought the refugees into social communities rather than pushing them to the edges. There was a sense among many activist groups that the borders were getting closer, that authoritarianism was expanding. In 2015, it had been possible for migrants to move relatively smoothly through Greece, but by early 2016, they were faced with a new fence in the north and pushbacks in the south. People were packaged off to distant camps and enclosed refugee shelters. The best way to resist this creeping curtailment of free movement, many activists thought, was to find spaces for refugees to live in the heart of the city.

The solution was found in squats, which have a long history in Athens. The neighborhood of Exarcheia, in particular, has a radical past, with a network of occupied buildings that sometimes made it feel like an independent republic. Its residents had long tried to keep the government at bay, but from time to time, they were subjected to massive concentrations of state power in the form of police raids. Many of these squats were not just about shelter; squatters staked out much bigger arguments about politics and social organization. Some squats had a hard anarchist ethos that was opposed to all forms of authority and hostile to outsiders. Others had a tight hierarchy and a clear leader, motivated by socialism or communism. Some squats were feminist, open only to women, and after the summer of 2015, there were also squats run by refugees. All these places had a different emphasis and feel, but they tended to be highly suspicious of governments and formal organizations—even researchers. Most opposed borders and the global system of nation-states.[36]

Hotel City Plaza stood in this diverse and complex landscape. It was occupied after a collapse in property prices that led to many vacant buildings; from bankrupt theaters to empty schools, there was no shortage of space for new squats like this. Yet unlike other projects to occupy buildings, City Plaza looked to gain exposure. Rather than pushing away outsiders and researchers, it welcomed them. Its aim was to offer an example, to generate publicity, to create a "crack" in the dominant public discourse, and to present an alternative to mainstream policy.[37] Its activists encompassed a broader spectrum of leftist political views than many squats, and they had a more accepting relationship with the ruling party. Rather than hiding away and seeking anonymity, they organized public events. Rather than being suspicious of visitors, they embraced them.

City Plaza had an active presence on social media and maintained a professional website with a prominent fundraising campaign.[38] The idea was to inspire others and to encourage the occupation of other empty buildings. Activists like Nasim had a particular notion of "the city" when they presented their case to the world. They saw cities as inclusive and multicultural, as locations of support and community. In this respect, the city was the opposite of the refugee camp: whereas refugee camps isolated people, cities put them in networks; whereas camps were organized from the top down, cities could be lived from the bottom up.[39] When City Plaza was occupied in the spring of 2016, the idea was to give refugees a place inside this idealized vision of the city. Cities were everything that camps could never become: open, cosmopolitan, and welcoming.[40] Cities were sites of resistance, standing in opposition to the fundamentally repressive nature of camps. Cities were places of sanctuary, a place for oppositional politics and an alternative locus of power.[41] Cities, in this narrative, were presented as a "utopic project," an attempt to remake the world.[42]

One activist later described the entry of refugees into this vision as a dramatic moment of political theater. Olga Lafazani was part of the collective that first opened the building, and she presented the action as a way of opening up hostile terrain. On the very first day, she explained, "it was chaos. Many neighbors, along with the owner of the building and her friends, had gathered outside and were swearing at us, threatening to call the police. . . . Members of the neo-Nazi party Golden Dawn [were] demanding that we leave immediately. At the next corner, there was a group of migrants who had previously stayed at the Camp of Hellinicon [Ellinikon]. . . . Because of the whole mess, they could not reach the door."[43] The activists broke into the building and formed a human chain to lead the migrants into the hotel. The shelter became a form of political activism from the very start.

The official name of the new squat expressed its ideals and aims. It was not just called City Plaza but Refugee Accommodation and Solidarity Space City Plaza. This emphasized both the political activism and the accommodation it provided. The leaflets explained how the project had two central objectives: first, "to house refugees in the centre of the city"; and second, "to create a centre of struggle against racism, borders, and social exclusion."[44] These aims were intimately connected, which became clear as soon as one rose up the staircase and entered the communal areas of the hotel. Inspirational statements adorned the walls, marked in block letters and inscribed on white paper alongside timetables and other announcements. "Fences can't stop giants," read one. "The crime is the borders, not the solidarity," read another. A large poster said simply, "Solidarity will win!"

INSIDE CITY PLAZA

By 2017, there were over four hundred people living in City Plaza from ten different countries, all housed in over a hundred rooms. They each had a door they could lock and a conformable bed, which made the facilities already feel better than many camps. The fittings were sometimes old and faded, but they offered privacy and community. Alongside the beige lampshades and pale-blue carpets, each room had its own bathroom, its own stash of soap, and three meals were served each day in the hotel's kitchen. All this was all funded by donations from across Europe, which also enabled an impressive array of activities and services, such as a library, a clinic, and a kindergarten.

In return for room and board, each resident at City Plaza was asked to work a minimum number of hours. This was designed to demonstrate their commitment to the community, and it was managed through various working groups. There was a committee running the kitchens, a group coordinating social activities, and a unit managing relations with the media. There were teams organizing the cleaning rotations, the storage of food, and the reception of new residents. This last task was one of the trickiest in the block. With only four hundred places and tens of thousands of eligible refugees, it was hard to decide whom to admit. As one activist explained, the task was to "balance the needs of migrants with those of the project."[45] The committee looked not just at vulnerability but also at the profile of residents, considering a range of factors. They wanted to prevent a single nationality from dominating, they wanted to maintain a gender balance, and they wanted to sustain the basic operations of the project—which meant prioritizing translators, cooks, carpenters, and others with specialist skills.

These principles of admission often created problems. There were three issues in particular that illustrated competing demands: a closed-door problem, a horizontal-structure problem, and a free-rider problem. The closed-door problem was primarily about who arrived in the squat, and it emerged from the limited capacity of the hotel and the need to lock external doors. Many of the activists were committed to openness, but they also had a duty to protect the inhabitants, who were often vulnerable. This meant regulating who came and went from the hotel—preventing strangers from coming in from the street and ensuring that the number of residents was capped so the hotel did not become overcrowded. Such actions sat badly with many of the activists because they concerned policing boundaries and restricting human movement, which was precisely what many of them had devoted their lives to prevent. Locking the external door also meant turning away the needy people that kept arriving. As one activist explained, refugees would often "knock on the door looking for a place to stay, begging to sleep in the dining room or the corridors." But the project had to refuse them in order to stay afloat.[46] This illustrated the closed-door tension in its clearest and most painful form.

The second tension was the horizontal-structure problem. Despite the desire to create a truly egalitarian community, many subtle hierarchies remained in place. Some people dominated discussions due to the force of their personalities. Others brought preexisting notions of authority from their home society, which were based on sex, class, or position. Some people had a disposition that was nervous or withdrawn, opting to stay quiet in assemblies even when given the opportunity to speak. To complicate matters further, many refugees looked for leaders as soon as they arrived. One activist explained how people from conservative backgrounds would seek the "person in charge," the director to whom they might address.[47] Despite the desire to create a flat structure through participatory assemblies, therefore, there were many obstacles in practice.

This generated a third tension: the free-rider problem. Rather than equal participation in the running of the building, some people did more work than others. In this nonauthoritarian space, there were still leaders and followers, and some residents contributed little or nothing to the community. Many people felt this was unfair, but it was difficult to enforce a rule that every adult should share the basic chores because many of the refugees were so vulnerable. Some residents were listless, despondent, perhaps traumatized. It was impossible to make them work. Yet many activists thought that equal participation should nevertheless be a prerequisite for residence—it was a matter of keeping the community functioning. There was simply so much work to do in order to keep this huge residential block,

FIGURE 3.2. Entrance sign, Hotel City Plaza. Acharnon, Athens, Greece. © University of Oxford / Mark E. Breeze, 2017.

with over a hundred rooms, running smoothly. Many activists also believed that equal participation was important to break the assumption of dependency, to ensure that refugees were treated as "members of a community with responsibilities."[48]

These three problems were internal—they were issues that activists and volunteers were thinking about as they did their daily work. Yet there were external tensions, too, which came from people who were critical of the squatting movement as a whole. Some objected to the political message, which they said was not in the interests of refugees. "No papers, no borders," one aid worker argued, is only ever the indulgent cry of people already living in a safe and functioning nation-state. Refugees *need* papers and usually *want* protection behind borders; they are rarely in favor of the complete abolition of the state system.[49] Others pointed out that the approach would never work at scale—a criticism that came primarily from employees of established humanitarian organizations. They acknowledged that City Plaza provided an important sense of community but argued that it could never house everyone in need. Finally, in a more general sense, some critics were troubled by the sense that refugees were being force-fed an agenda and had few options to refuse. As one journalist put it to me, Are a group of vulnerable people *really* in a position to say no to the political agenda that comes alongside an offer of shelter? Is it fair to place refugees in a position where they have to sign up for the destruction of nation-states in order to get a bed for the night?[50]

TYPES OF HUMANITARIANISM

These external critiques only intensified as the project moved into its second year. The politics of City Plaza stood in contrast to many mainstream humanitarian agencies, which adhered to a version of political neutrality instead. Their more "classical" approach to assistance suggested that aid should meet basic needs without being ideological.[51] This was a view that the activists opposed. Many of them felt aid was always ideological, and they hated NGOs for hiding their politics—or, worse, for having no values at all. My interlocutors often described mainstream agencies through the metaphor of a vampire. The large agencies had "no heart," one said. They were "sucking money from all around." They were concerned only with maintaining their own existence. Another suggested that the NGOs were "empty inside," taking action not from any kind of ethical commitment but simply from self-interest.[52]

Scholars have not really agreed on a label for this approach, but some have settled on the terms "subversive humanitarianism," "solidarity humanitarianism," or "grassroots humanitarianism."[53] It is important to remember that there has always been variation in the humanitarian movement, with some humanitarians opting for classical principles and others openly taking sides in a conflict and making high-profile statements of support for certain groups. Such a commitment to solidaristic principles always follows the same central thread: a concern for human life combined with an internationalist egalitarian belief that sees suffering as always worthy of assistance.[54] City Plaza can be seen as fitting into this longer radical story. Their dispute with mainstream NGOs was, in many ways, a battle of humanitarian ideas: one approach had been institutionalized and subscribed to an ideal of neutrality; the other was more radical, activist, and politicized.[55] The activists of City Plaza were following that foundational commitment to basic human equality right down to its roots. Instead of simply responding to the symptoms—the call for housing and the urgent need to get refugees off the streets—they had decided to campaign on what they saw as the fundamental cause: the system of borders and nation-states.

Arguments about the activist squats in Greece always came back to the role of politics. For some aid workers, the problem with places like City Plaza was that they were *too* ideological, *too* politicized. They forced a certain perspective of the world on needy people that crossed the building's threshold. There was no accountability for what went on inside their walls, and the conditions for vulnerable people were often not addressed in a professional way. Politics took precedence over protection.[56] Yet the counter argument was that these places facilitated more equal relationships and offered a sense of belonging. Rather than hiding behind a principle of neutrality and a minimalist set of obligations, the activists and organizers at City Plaza were actually living alongside the refugees. They tried to remove hierarchies from their work. They engaged forced migrants as friends and equals, getting them involved in every element of the community and campaigning with them on the injustice of border control. In other words, the activists had a deeper concern with the problem of shelter, and their beliefs were explicit and clear.

In addition to arguments about politics and relief, there were also disagreements about scale. The professional NGOs claimed that the squats could never meet the extent of need. They were too small, and they relied on an astonishing degree of commitment by the organizers, which could never be sustained. Living and working alongside refugee communities, they argued, meant work-life boundaries could never be maintained. It required an exhausting level of constant presence—day and night—with long community meetings and fractious assemblies. It was simply not an effective way to manage the tens of thousands of people needing somewhere to live.[57] In response, the activists claimed that they were working on a humane scale. They argued that the mainstream aid agencies treated refugees like animals in a zoo, putting them in camps and failing to see them as anything other than passive victims. As one activist put it, "at times, refugees are not properly recognized as human beings; they are just numbers in a report."[58] The squatters also pointed out that there were around four thousand empty buildings in Athens alone, which could be renovated by reallocating funds they saw as wasted in the official response.[59]

This then led to a final set of arguments, which concerned participation and autonomy. The activists were suspicious of regularized authority, of systems, procedures, and faceless bureaucracy. Most of them were anarchist in orientation, and they had an intense distrust of state power. They believed that NGOs acted in concert with the most authoritarian elements of the state, deliberately collaborating with violent border enforcement to provide a velvet glove of care that covered the fist of formal power. Even well-meaning aid workers, I was told, did little more than provide crumbs of assistance while failing to empower refugees or fight the root causes of their predicament. The mainstream humanitarians, perhaps predictably, had a very different view of the world. Their approach was Hobbesian rather than anarchist. They feared an absence of regulations and rights. They criticized the squats for being too chaotic, and above all, they were concerned about the ability of charismatic individuals to manipulate others and prey on the most vulnerable. They argued that true autonomy in the squats was prevented by the imposition of an inflexible leftist ideology: rather than being freed from control, they argued, refugees in these places were never really free to develop their own views or pursue their own aims.

CLOSING CITY PLAZA

The activists of City Plaza left the building on July 10, 2019, more than three years after the occupation began. They were responding, once again, to external events. The shelter had been founded just after the EU-Turkey deal, which had turned Greece from a corridor into a prison, and it was closed just after a new government declared its intention to evict all the squats. The activists saw the writing on the wall, and they acted quickly, but City Plaza had been struggling with questions about its future for many months. Indeed, the decision to wind up the occupation had been taken over a year previously, back in June 2018, when the community stopped taking new members and tried to find new places for its existing residents to live.

Their reasoning for closing the squat demonstrated the limitations of this model. It showed that the problem of sustainability was serious. The activists could not maintain the level of commitment required to keep running the shelter indefinitely, and they did not have a stable enough population of refugees to whom they could hand over the keys. The community's public statement was clear that this was not a squat that could "stay closed for a couple of days in August without any problems." It was a space that required "a daily commitment, responsibility, and presence." Self-organization was described as a "struggle," in which "enthusiasm, commitment, and participation dwindle[d] over time—especially when circumstances . . . [were] so demanding."[60]

There were two options for the future. The first involved "normalizing and legalizing the squat"—that is, turning it into an officially registered nongovernmental organization. The second was to close the squat completely and try "to keep the community it created alive in a different context." After much discussion, the assembly went for the latter path. As the final statement explained, the first option was "politically undesirable, as it clashes with City Plaza's character as a political alternative to NGOisation."[61] Yet the second option seemed to vindicate the criticism that such shelters could not be sustained forever. It was clear that this decision was taken by many activists with a heavy heart and only on the understanding that the struggle would be continued in other places.

In the twelve months after this decision, no new residents joined City Plaza, and people gradually left. Just days after the election of the right-leaning New Democracy Party, however, the assembly of City Plaza decided that it "should rightly close the way it began . . . as a political project." Its last moments, like its first, became an opportunity to take a stand, to remind everyone what grassroots activism could achieve. They declared that the squat had shown how activism could provide decent quality accommodation far cheaper than official NGOs, that solidarians could act fast, while cumbersome bureaucracies dithered, and that shelters could offer more than just a roof but also a true community. Rather than retreating to more comfortable circumstances at the end of each day, the activists had stayed in the building alongside refugees, worked with them in the kitchens, and campaigned on what they saw as the structural causes of violence and suffering. The closure statement declared that City Plaza had become "a political event far greater than the sum of its parts." "Without exaggeration," it continued, City Plaza was a "pan-European symbol, which concentrated resistance to the racist and repressive migration regime of the EU [and] . . . served as a strong counter-example at a time of pessimism and demobilisation for the left."[62]

Many of the other squats in Exarcheia were evicted soon after.[63] By September 2019, seven of the most prominent squats had closed, but they still endured as an idea: an alternative model and a reminder that politics is important. Rather than abstracting political issues, these shelters had barged into the heart of political debates. Even their challenges were an opportunity for political engagement. Their limited capacity was an opportunity to think about justice in admissions. Their horizontal structure was a chance to think about the dynamics of power. The free-rider problem was a provocation to think about how participation can work. In the early months of the occupation, during City Plaza's first flush of fame, Nasim articulated the case for the squats in a newspaper report by writing that City Plaza "is not the solution to the refugee crisis . . . but it is a good example of how to do it better."[64] When I met him in Exarcheia, he put it more colorfully: "We can't solve every problem, but it's a huge question that we asked. What the fuck is happening here?"[65]

Certainly, City Plaza and the other squats were good at posing such questions. They worked best as a "counterexample," standing out precisely because they embraced the politics of shelter rather than suppressing it. All the same, the squats tended to develop a narrow narrative. They offered a communal vision of shelter rather than one that allowed more personal goals to emerge. This was the big challenge that the organizers constantly faced: that refugees and other migrants would often avoid immersing themselves fully in the running of squats because they had their own aims in life and no opportunity to create a home. Above all, most of the refugees wanted to stand on their own feet and build their own lives—ideally in northern Europe—which meant that it was impossible for most of them to take control of the squat and make the idea sustainable.

What were the lessons? First, the squats remind us that method matters, showing how egalitarian ideals are not enough if one is not prepared to live them out. Second, they show that there is a human side to shelter, with a great need for community and close interpersonal connection that lies beyond the metrics. Third, and most importantly, they established that shelter is inevitably a political act. The designers at the IKEA-funded Better Shelter realized this when confronting the different responses in Lebanon and Switzerland. The humanitarian planners of Jordan came to a similar conclusion when they implemented the government's preference for camps. City Plaza reminded everyone that politics was always central to shelter. If shelter has to be political, they concluded, then it is important to think about what kind of politics to promote. As Nasim often said, camps are a choice, not a necessity, and reveal a lot about who we are.

4 | SHELTER AS TACTICS

Rental Accommodation in Lebanon

I FINALLY UNDERSTOOD THE CHALLENGE of shelter in Lebanon when I visited the offices of the UN Refugee Agency in a southern neighborhood of Beirut. I was standing at the top of a huge building with views over the suburbs of the city and a large map of refugee settlements pinned next to me on the wall. I looked closer at the map, which was marked with countless colored dots showing where refugees were living, and I saw how the specks were sprinkled over the entire inhabitable surface of the country, around each road and region, converging in darker clusters in some neighborhoods and spreading out into rural areas along wavering lines out of town. Lebanon had the highest number of refugees per capita in the world at the time, and apart from two streaks of blank paper—the parallel mountain ranges that stretched across Lebanon from north to south—the map indicated over a million refugees living in every district and municipality. The specks indicated a range of shelters that included everything from rented buildings to self-built homes.

I had already visited a number of refugee settlements by the time I went to the UNHCR headquarters. My trip had begun with a visit to the fertile Beqaa Valley, where I saw thousands of makeshift shelters constructed from canvas and timber on agricultural land. They stood in large clusters: unofficial shacks and tents surrounded by flat fields and partitioned by rubbish-strewn heaps, with the bulk of the mountains behind. I later traveled north to the area around Tripoli, where refugees lived in converted buildings behind thin dividing walls. Some of these were situated in empty warehouses, some in rented storefronts, and in one particularly bleak site, I saw a vast, vacant shopping mall with hundreds of people living in graffiti-covered concrete lodgings. Next, I visited the Beirut suburbs, where refugees lived in expensive rented accommodation. These were often unfinished buildings with breezeblock walls, bare wires, and huge holes in the walls. They were close to jobs and social networks but were terribly basic and cost a great deal to rent.

The diversity of shelter in Lebanon was not, therefore, what surprised me about this map. Rather, it was the sheer number of different settlements. The shelters were dispersed around the country in every possible location, which stood as a stark reminder of how hard it was to find decent shelter in Lebanon. At the time, there was one Syrian refugee for every four Lebanese citizens in the country, and the religious profile of the refugees meant that many Lebanese feared that their presence would disrupt the negotiated peace that had ended the country's fifteen-year civil war.[1] The official response to the influx was therefore cautious and neglectful. Rather than creating new homes for the million-plus refugees, the government disengaged. They refused to facilitate camps or allow the construction of official shelters. There was, in effect, a "no-camp policy" in place, which meant refugees had to squeeze into the gaps, living in all sorts of unsuitable spaces that were hastily converted and often exploitatively expensive.

The map I found in the UNHCR headquarters was a perfect illustration of the challenge. Forbidden from building official refugee camps, the aid agencies were left trying to help hundreds of thousands of people scattered around the country. They offered a bit of cash here, a delivery of materials there, and other small interventions, such as helping with the cost of small refurbishments, providing subsidies for private rent, and supplying insulation to improve the warmth of self-built homes. Their efforts seemed piecemeal, but they were limited by the political context and the restrictions imposed by the government. The conditions were so bad that some humanitarians were even arguing that large refugee camps should be reintroduced to the country—an approach that the UN itself had described as a last resort.

Lebanon's no-camp policy thereby raised a range of important questions about the consequences of government action. How can humanitarians adapt to restrictions on what can be built? What happens if states disengage from the issue of shelter? Since the government was refusing to build camps or provide centralized forms of accommodation, shelter became a matter of tactics. Refugees had to find what they could in an unregulated and splintered landscape. Landlords were taking advantage of lax planning laws to make more money. Aid agencies, in turn, were filling gaps without being able to transform anything. The whole terrain of shelter in Lebanon became short-term and "tactical" in Michel De Certeau's sense, involving daily practices of street-level negotiation and use of local knowledge.

FRACTURED LANDSCAPES

Lebanon has long been a country with a fractured political landscape. It has eighteen officially recognized religious confessions with none constituting an absolute majority of the population. This is partly the result of migration itself, with religious and ethnic minorities from across the Middle East finding refuge in and beyond the country's hills and mountains.[2] Such demographics have led to complex power-sharing arrangements, with seats in parliament divided between Christians and Muslims and key positions split between the main sects. The main constitutional roles are divided between the largest confessions, with the prime minister being a Sunni Muslim, the president being a Maronite Christian, and the speaker of parliament, a Shi'i Muslim. This division of power has meant that any change in demographics is controversial. With over a million refugees arriving from Syria, the country experienced serious opposition from across the political spectrum. If the refugees were naturalized or incorporated into the political fabric, the argument went, their presence could profoundly change the balance of power. This means that the naturalization of noncitizens in Lebanon has long been controversial. The issue is so sensitive that there has not been a national census since 1932, and the revised 1990 constitution clearly states that there should be "no settlement of non-Lebanese in Lebanon."[3]

The main group affected by these circumstances has been the Palestinians. They arrived as refugees in 1948 and settled in refugee camps, which eventually became crowded and precarious, inhabited by multigenerational households with no prospect of citizenship. These camps grew into permanent settlements layered with concrete on the edge of towns and cities, netted above with tangled power lines thrown out from the grid, yet the long-term presence of Palestinians generated concerns that permanent integration would follow, creating a far larger Sunni Muslim citizenry. The issue was complicated by the growth of Palestinian political autonomy in the 1970s, when many camps became militarized enclaves largely outside Lebanese government control. Many citizens attributed the start of the fifteen-year civil war to growing Palestinian power and independence, resulting in a deep opposition to disruption of the political settlement by the naturalization of other groups.[4] This fear of local integration—known as *tawteen*—has since become "embedded in the Lebanese political psyche."[5]

This background affected the reception of Syrian refugees, who began to arrive in large numbers at the end of 2012. Like the Palestinians, these refugees were also mostly Muslim, and by 2015, their numbers in Lebanon had grown to over a million in a population of only five million people.[6] Fears of permanent settlement and naturalization reemerged, and the government created a no-camp policy in response.[7] The idea was to discourage permanent settlement and to prevent the emergence of militarized ghettos, but this was always a "policy without a policy"—an approach that united many Lebanese political groups through an absence of action, which was never formally articulated.[8] It also indicated a path not taken rather than one that was carefully formulated. Ironically, the end result of this political paralysis was a large number of settlements that were camps in all but name. Formal encampment may have been banned, and international aid agencies may have been blocked from constructing new shelters for refugees, but the outcome was a wide range of informal ghettos that looked, from the outside, like poorly organized camps.

This situation contrasted starkly with other places in the Middle East, most notably Jordan. Rather than having large camps and clusters of planned settlements, refugees in Lebanon maneuvered into the gaps. Shelter became a matter of tactics as refugees used their limited resources and social networks to find a place to stay, however imperfect.[9] For those working as agricultural laborers, this meant constructing basic shelters with wood and tarpaulin on fields with the consent of the landowner. The result looked a bit like camps but messier and more unplanned, with few services or official authorization. For other refugees, it meant renting an apartment in cities, becoming subjected to extortionate rents. Many wealthier refugees took this option, and landlords and realtors used the rise in demand to reconfigure buildings into smaller units and push up prices. It was not just apartments either. Many refugees rented deeply unsuitable spaces through the shadow economy, living in pump rooms, peri-urban warehouses, and even chicken farms. This was all the result of a fractured landscape with no real planning and no effective strategy. Refugees were relying on their own tactical abilities. Informality in the planning sector and deep reserves of refugee self-reliance combined to produce the only options available.[10]

The humanitarian response, too, was limited and largely tactical. After being forbidden from any large-scale production of new shelters, aid agencies tried to adjust and improve the imperfect shelters people found. This involved small interventions, such as offering a layer of plaster, a bag of insulation, perhaps an injection of cash, or an agreement with landlords to improve apartments in return for payment. The world of international aid has always been shaped by the external political environment, but the no-camp policy in Lebanon meant that the whole approach to shelter shifted from the large-scale, top-down, and strategic provision of shelter to the smaller-scale, tactical support of refugee decisions. Shelter became a matter of doing what was possible within government constraints—for refugees and for humanitarians alike.

THREE TYPES OF SHELTERS

Humanitarians in Lebanon divided the world of shelter into three main types. First, there were "collective shelters": large buildings or structures, not originally intended for habitation, which had been subdivided into smaller units to house refugees. Second, there were "informal tented settlements": clusters of self-built shacks, which had been built on agricultural land from wood and tarpaulin. Third, there were "private rentals," where families rented apartments in various stages of repair, usually in urban areas.[11] These three categories disguised many smaller varieties, but they all were driven by urgency. None were designed by humanitarians as the categories were created by aid workers describing events after the fact.[12]

Consider, first, the collective shelters. This type took many forms, with refugees inhabiting garages, farms, shop fronts, engine rooms, and construction sites. Many were carved out of old warehouses, divided inside with slabs of thin plywood and fabric doors. I visited one with hundreds of people living in the dark interior of a high-roofed warehouse. Rivulets of wastewater and sewage bisected the earthen ground, and whole families were crammed into small rooms with no ceilings. The noise of everyday life bounced off the corrugated metal roof above, and a winding central corridor linked each small boxed-off area from its neighbors. A further set of iron shelters leaned against the external walls.[13] Other collective shelters were created in abandoned shops. I visited one that was created from a whole mall buried into the edge of a hillside on Mount Lebanon. The interior of each shop had a single set of windows looking out and a dark core, where mattresses were lined up in the gloom. Outside, the noises of enforced communal living echoed up the stories, with clothes strung from windows and children running past piles of trash. Cars passed by with a hard, rumbling sound that reverberated around the courtyard.[14]

Similar shelters had been created in other places by subdividing large buildings, from barns to unfinished schools. In each case, a landlord might charge a small fee for residence and would allow for rickety conversions. In one warehouse, I found crumbling, filthy dividers that had created compartments for large families. The roof, high above, was leaking, dripping rain into the living areas of the partitioned spaces below. Aid agencies worked to improve the building as best as they could, contributing some sanitation facilities and a makeshift toilet block situated outside the warehouse, but the earth was still sodden and marked by pools of stagnant brown liquid. I got the sense that the landlord was renting an inappropriate building in the

FIGURE 4.1. Nazih Karami Warehouse, showing flimsy shelter divisions. Miriata, Lebanon. © University of Oxford / Mark E. Breeze, 2018.

most awful conditions with impunity, treating refugees like the commodities that had previously occupied the space.

Next, consider the informal tented settlements. Many of these shelters emerged from longstanding relationships between employers and laborers on agricultural land. Before the civil war began in 2011, there were already a large number of Syrians employed in Lebanon, mostly men working in construction or as seasonal laborers in the fertile fields of the Beqaa Valley.[15] They would frequently live on site, in temporary accommodation, and when the war started in Syria, they used their existing networks to turn these short-term residences into longer-term shelters. For around half the year, they had been working in the fields before returning to Syria for the winter, but when the war escalated, these settlements became an opportunity for refuge. The landowners gave permission for longer periods of stay while collecting more rent, which became "a major new opportunity for quick revenue."[16] Laborers brought children, spouses, and other relations into Lebanon, following well-established migration patterns. The addition of these families quickly led to over a million refugees. As one commentator put it, "When the war started in 2011, you already had 250,000 workers right here. Each one of these workers had at least four or five people in their immediate family, and when they brought them, we quickly got to one million plus."[17]

To accommodate all these new people, fields were turned from crops to housing. Landowners set about preparing the land, compacting the soil, and even concreting the ground to create more stable foundations for informal shelters. The refugees then built bigger shacks from materials purchased in the local market. The quality of services in the informal settlements differed wildly. Some had firm, leveled ground and networks of water and sanitation. Others had just a few taps and no groundwork, leaving refugees to build foundations. The whole arrangement was unauthorized, although the settlements were tolerated to different degrees by the local municipality. Some mayors allowed them to grow, whereas others prevented them entirely.[18] Officially, the no-camp policy should have prohibited such settlements, but some municipalities turned a blind eye as long as the structures remained temporary and the local residents remained happy. Often, Lebanese citizens were benefiting a great deal from the refugee industry, and landowners in particular collected thousands of dollars in ground rent. Traders also made a killing by selling plastic sheeting at inflated prices.

The conditions in informal settlements often depended on the density of settlement and the degree of support and cooperation from the landlord. They did, however, all share certain features. The homes were initially made from tarpaulin and wood but often became sturdier and more complex as money and materials allowed. One example can illustrate this: a family in central Beqaa whose home was situated on flat land near farms and fields.[19] They lived in a shelter of simple origin, clustered with many others around messy lanes and heaps of refuse. It had begun with a wooden frame wrapped in tarpaulin, and like many other homes in this area, this plastic sheeting came from disused advertising hoardings: huge sheets of waterproof material that had previously been strung up by the nearby highway and were sold to refugees on the cheap. These sheets were still emblazoned with images of cars, designer clothes, or contented faces—incongruous images that once beamed down from enormous billboards but were now used to seal the frames of refugee houses. The tarpaulins were held in place by cable ties and weighted down by the thick black doughnuts of discarded tires.

This particular family had been living in their shelter for five years, making improvements each year. They had begun with a basic frame, fixed together with nails on bare earth. The concrete floor came later and was the first big investment, which was only possible once the older men in the family had earned some money as laborers. The family later received some

FIGURE 4.2. Informal tented settlement, showing reuse of advertising tarpaulin. Beqaa Valley, Lebanon. © University of Oxford / Mark E. Breeze, 2018.

blankets from UNHCR and eventually some extra tarpaulin, so they grad-ually sealed the outside and made the shelter watertight. In dribs and drabs, they created "something out of nothing," as they put it, but the shelter re-quired constant maintenance.[20] The tarpaulins wore out, deteriorating in the rain and sun each year. It was tricky to heat the shelter in winter and ventilate it properly in summer. Aid agencies provided "weatherproofing kits" containing insulation and "fire kits" containing extinguishers, but they could never change anything significant. The rule was clear: no aid agency was allowed to create a lasting shelter, which meant they could only "repeat activities again and again," carrying out small improvements each year with no longer-term strategy.[21]

The annual renewal of these shelters was an inefficient use of resources, but it was the only way to allow improvements without breaking the rules. The settlements could end up lasting for years as long as they appeared to be temporary, but there was no security of tenure. Landowners had a huge amount of power. Some offered residence on the land in exchange for labor on the fields, but this only underlined how much refugees relied on em-ployers or their intermediaries.[22] Such a precarious situation was further exacerbated after 2014 when the government introduced new restrictions— including a new $200 fee for residency permits, required by all Syrian ref-ugees over the age of fourteen. This proved extremely expensive for most refugee families, as well as making them even more dependent on employ-ers. Regular renewal of residence permits could be done in two ways: by registering with UNHCR or having the sponsorship of an employer. Regis-tering with UNHCR had the disadvantage of prohibiting paid work in the country, which meant that the only way to gain income and legal residence was through an employer. However, taking the sponsorship of an employer involved submitting to a position of weakness as, within the *kafala* system, being fired could also deprive a refugee of their residency permit and thus their protection.[23]

PRIVATE RENTALS

The gold standard of shelter, therefore, was the third main category: the private rentals. This actually constituted the most widespread type of shel-ter in Lebanon, though it took many forms. Around 70–75 percent of refu-gees lived in rented apartments or rooms in residential buildings, but these tended to be overcrowded spaces that contained extended family units or several households. They were often rudimentary, with bare cinderblock walls, uncovered floors, and the twisted pigtails of steel reinforcement cable emerging from unplastered concrete pillars. Unfinished buildings like this were common throughout Lebanon. They were the result of a loophole that meant taxes could be avoided if new buildings remained incomplete. This had long been useful for large families, who could leave reinforced columns protruding from a flat roof so that an additional floor might be added at a later date, perhaps when funds were more plentiful, perhaps when a son or daughter needed an apartment of their own. The upshot was a large number of incomplete buildings strewn across the landscape of Lebanon.

The rent in such buildings, when finished, was not particularly cheap, even when the conditions were poor. Compared with informal settlements in the Beqaa Valley, renting an apartment in one of the large cities was a hundred times the price.[24] This was primarily because it brought all the benefits of living in a city—like employment, social networks, and cultural life—but such advantages were outweighed by the fact that rented apartments were cramped, often with multiple families living in rooms made with hastily erected internal walls. They were not necessarily furnished either. I visited a number of apartments in a shocking state, with rough and uneven floors and piles of debris in the corner. Some aid workers seemed surprised that so many people failed to move away from the informal tented settlements, but circumstances in the cities were rarely better.

The humanitarian approach to helping refugees in rented buildings was, again, mainly tactical. Aid agencies offered subsidies, materials, and cash but no meaningful alternative to the status quo. One innovative approach involved paying landlords to improve buildings in exchange for a rent-free period for refugees. Aid, in other words, was given directly to landlords to fund infrastructure with the agreement that the apartments would be made available to refugees for a limited period of time. This was meant to be a win-win situation. It gave landlords some money to improve their unfinished apartments, and it provided refugees with some accommodation that met a minimum threshold of safety and comfort. The attraction for aid agencies in this fraught political landscape was clear: Who could object to such a scheme, in which Lebanese citizens would receive funding to finish their empty apartments? Landlords would receive a benefit and refugees would receive a home—being allowed to live in the apartment for a specified time, usually a year, without paying rent. The scheme was known as "occupancy free of charge."[25]

The agency that pioneered this approach, the Norwegian Refugee Council (NRC), formulated the scheme in order to reduce social tensions and navigate political constraints. The idea was that Lebanese citizens received benefits in the form of investments in their properties, which could be rented in the future as a complete building. Refugees received benefits in the form of housing with secure tenure, which they received free of charge for a fixed period. The government, meanwhile, could maintain their position of not sponsoring camps while seeing some benefits to society at large. One of the specialists involved in the scheme emphasized that the funded improvements were all "fairly basic."[26] The aim was not to create luxury apartments, he said, but simply to work with the landlord to bring each home up to a set of minimum standards: somewhere dry with safe water and electricity. Sometimes the aid agencies paid for external rendering, but the improvements primarily involved changing bare, unwired buildings into something more immediately habitable.

The process worked as follows. First, the aid agency would scope out an unfinished building and discuss improvements with the landlord, agreeing what kind of work was needed. Then, they would determine how to bring the apartment up to minimum standards and calculate the cost. From here,

FIGURE 4.3.   Residential block in Lebanon. Waha Complex, near Tripoli, Lebanon. © University of Oxford / Mark E. Breeze, 2018.

a negotiation led to a funding agreement and a set period of free rent. As an NRC specialist explained, "a Bill of Quantity is signed, a Cooperation Agreement is entered into, and then the landlord is left to get on with the works."[27] Apart from monitoring whether the work had been completed, the aid agency had no direct role in construction, which made the project easier to manage. As the renovations went on, aid funds could be used to boost the local economy and provide work for local laborers as well as improving the housing stock. They would also offer an incentive to expand the availability of shelter for refugees, creating greater willingness to rent to people who might otherwise be blocked from the rental market due to discrimination or lack of availability.

Compared to the short-term and incremental improvement of tented settlements, this approach was meant to be more strategic—although there were still many challenges. The whole arrangement required trust in both directions. The aid agencies had to trust that the landlord would not renege on their agreement to offer free occupancy to refugees. The landlords, in turn, had to trust that the aid agency would pay for the renovations once they were completed. Both parties then had to trust that refugees would adhere to the terms of the rental agreement and that the contractors would complete the work at a decent standard for the price that had been agreed upon. The refugees, finally, had to trust that they could enjoy a rent-free period of accommodation in a finished apartment without disruption. A lot of paperwork was completed in order to provide a framework for these relationships, but aid workers admitted that there was actually little capacity to enforce these agreements through legal means if the trust broke down. More seriously, the key disadvantage for refugees was that they ended up with shelter for only twelve months, and little stability beyond this period. The *idea* might have seemed more long-term and strategic, in other words, but from a refugee perspective, there was very little in the way of lasting benefits.[28]

What happened once the rent-free period was finished? I asked this question of the shelter specialist at NRC, and he said that the twelve-month period was long enough to build "resilience." While living in apartments for free, the theory went, refugees would gradually build "social capital and social networks, which would give them some sort of social insurance at the end of that twelve months."[29] This optimistic approach drew on a long-standing ideal of refugee self-reliance, combined with a fear of dependency that has underpinned many interventions since.[30] It shaped which properties were prioritized for investment and occupancy, which had to be near jobs, schools, markets, and health facilities—anything that would help refugees build lasting networks. "We're looking to put people into an enabling environment," the shelter specialist explained, "so that refugees can access livelihoods and create social capital."[31] The aim, in other words, was for humanitarian support to end once investment in the property was complete.

The scheme seemed ingenious, injecting some long-term thinking into a political circumstance that seemed deliberately designed to disallow it. Yet the model of occupancy free of charge was, in many respects, an impersonal transaction in which money for material goods was exchanged for a time-limited tenure for refugees. The landlords received concrete benefits in the form of plaster and tiles, sinks and worktops, wires and pipes, and in the end, they ended up with an asset that they could use: a newly renovated apartment to rent or reside in. The refugees, however, ended up with nothing of lasting value—just a negotiated period of rent-free accommodation followed by more insecurity, which was all paid for by aid agencies. The final effect was simply to transfer wealth from humanitarians to landlords for property renovation. On the face of it, this hardly seems like a good use of funds, and it hardly seems strategic from a humanitarian point of view. The landlord retained most of the benefits and the refugee was left with no security of tenure beyond a year or so.

TACTICAL RESULTS

The three categories of shelter in Lebanon were therefore all short-term, piecemeal, and fragmented. In many respects, they offered most for those who needed help the least—that is, income for landlords, who already had a strong economic advantage. The effect of these schemes, moreover, was the production of precisely the kind of ghettoes they were designed to prevent.[32] They emerged from a prohibition on camps, but they ended up resembling camps. "Collective shelters" were whole buildings with a high concentration of refugees living in cramped conditions and with clearly demarcated boundaries. "Informal tented settlements" were a cluster of tarpaulin-wrapped temporary structures in remote rural areas. Renovated apartments were concentrated in poor neighborhoods, resembling camps within a city. In each case, refugees were living in closed, clearly bounded areas, with their movement further restricted by permits, checkpoints, and detention.[33]

Michael Walzer once wrote that a world without national borders would only produce "a thousand petty fortresses."[34] In Lebanon, it seemed that a country without camps was producing a thousand petty camps. There was a deeper irony, too, because many aid agencies had no-camp policies of their own.[35] As the UNHCR deputy representative in Lebanon explained, "the Lebanese authorities had decided on something that, *according to our own policy*, is the preferred option."[36] Yet the result was so messy and inadequate that many humanitarians were calling for camps as the only way to produce good-quality shelter at scale. If camps were done properly, the argument went, then "you can build a dedicated infrastructure, with health services, schools and so on."[37] In contrast, the government's no-camp policy had led to ghettos without careful monitoring, well-organized services, or shelters built from lasting materials—precisely the features that one might expect to find in a well-planned camp. Shelter in Lebanon, therefore, ended up being shaped by short-term, tactical interventions, and it suffered as a result.

What is the difference between strategy and tactics? The traditional idea is to see tactics as the art of arrangement, the skill of getting things lined up to reach a short-term goal. In this respect, humanitarianism tends toward the tactical. Aid agencies have traditionally focused on immediate suffering, saving lives in emergency conditions, and many argue it is not their job to think beyond this limited goal.[38] This may be contrasted with a more strategic approach, which involves thinking about how to strengthen and rebuild those systems and structures. Often this comes as a call to link up relief and development, engaging in bigger-picture thinking and longer-term aims. Being strategic, some believe, should involve considering the structural effects of an intervention, thinking about systems as a whole, and trying to address root causes.[39]

The challenge of being truly strategic is perhaps most clearly illustrated by the push toward camps. Even if aid agencies try to be strategic in a camp setting, they will end up constrained by political dynamics. They need to respect the limits of their authority and must retain their permission to operate in a country if they are going to do any work at all. Refugee camps are a typically tactical intervention because they tend to be opened in a hurry and they are designed to cope with a rapid number of refugee arrivals. There is rarely a plan for their closure, and limits on development are set by restrictive funding and political constraints. Designing them to be truly long-term is difficult because it is likely to violate rules or political norms against permanent settlement. As one humanitarian policymaker put it, "Camps are very practical in the early stages of a crisis. But then what? How do you manage a growing population without jobs or livelihoods? What do you do about temporary buildings when a crisis drags on? What is the plan for people in camps who cannot or will not return to their original homes?"[40] Without the ability to think and act on these issues, the same problems are likely to drag on, including restriction, inertia, and dependency.

The no-camp policy in Lebanon was therefore oriented around short-term tactics, but camps were not strategic either. In fact, the humanitarians who wanted formal camps were falling back on default solutions and demonstrating a serious lack of creativity. While camps might have offered some people a better quality of shelter—in a purely material sense—many humanitarians still failed to recognize the long-standing problems with the model. As a professor at the American University of Beirut, Mona Fawaz, put it to me in exasperation, "Why camps? Why create that state of exception? Why put people in this vulnerable situation where they will have to depend on you?"[41] Opponents of the no-camp policy were simply turning to what they already knew. They were bringing the idea of camps back to the table because it was simple, standardized, and easy to adopt.[42]

Fawaz had a different view. She believed that refugees know what they need. They make decisions all the time, she pointed out; one simply has to follow the refugees and see how they want to benefit their lives. This should be the starting point for aid policy, which tends to jump in too fast with a set of preestablished solutions from old humanitarian handbooks. Too often, aid workers try to *imagine* what people need and then construct it from scratch, when a far better approach is to wait, to watch what refugees are doing, and to intervene when that becomes clear. Fawaz described how the majority of refugees in Lebanon wanted to live in cities like Beirut, gravitating to areas with existing social networks and employment. The very idea of opening camps—where sociality and employment were rare—flies in the face of these desires and indicates a startling lack of imagination.

The movement of refugees, Fawaz observed, has proved that people can find places to live without camps. The next step, she continued, should be to find bigger-picture ideas that can transform the urban environment and improve cities for everyone. To put this another way, the aid agencies had, at this point, offered only piecemeal support. They had funded small improvements in individual dwellings, subsidized monthly rents, or offered small quantities of insulation. What they had to do next, she argued, was to intervene in the city. They had to think big and consider longer-term issues, looking at the problem "like an urbanist." This means improving the infrastructure of cities. It means "creating public space, improving the streets, improving the sewer networks, getting the neighborhood to work." "The market has already produced the private units," Fawaz explained. "What hasn't happened is the upgrading of the infrastructure to carry three times more population."[43]

Such interventions, Fawaz argued, could improve cities more generally, preventing ghettos and "anchoring the local population" in place. One problem contributing to the refugee protection crisis was that many Lebanese people were leaving areas of the city just as large numbers of refugees arrived. There was an exodus from certain areas driven by mutual suspicion and a sense of competition for space and resources. This led to "de facto camps" within the city: more of those petty camps that dotted Lebanon as a whole. Fawaz stressed that the aim of good policy should not be to create ghettos but rather to build a humane, "mixed city" and to change the rhetoric around refugees. To help build this policy, Fawaz has described refugees as "city makers," who create the vibrant urban spaces we know today.[44] "Beirut, historically, is a city that grew from refugees," she told me. The idea of seeing refugees as "city makers" draws attention to the benefits they bring to urban environments, the jobs they do, and the businesses they create. It shows how the long history of Lebanon has always involved generations of forced migrants contributing to the country, and this has tended to work alongside investment in city infrastructures to improve life for refugees and locals alike.

TACTICAL REVOLUTIONS

Not everyone thinks about strategy in positive terms, and even Fawaz did not actually use this word to describe her vision for humanitarian response. The notions of "tactics" and "strategy," in fact, have had a more specific meaning in architecture and urban studies that emerged from the work of De Certeau. Rather than seeing tactics and strategy in the vernacular sense—as distinguished by a short-term and longer-term focus, respectively—De Certeau suggested that they are fundamentally different. Tactics, he said, are the domain of the weak. They draw on local knowledge and involve adapting intuitively to one's environment—a bit like being "street smart." In contrast, strategy is the domain of the powerful. It implies an aerial or panoptic view of the world, drawing on abstract models and plans to make people legible and controllable. According to this view, strategy is employed by people in power who have the ability to act over a wider time and space, whereas tactics are employed by those in a subordinate social position who have few options but to subvert the dominant order. Tactics are everyday actions, dynamic, and bottom-up. They take place in the space *created* by strategy. Whereas strategies are planned, tactics are opportunistic. Whereas strategies involve controlling people, tactics involve resistance to that control.[45]

Tactics, in this view, are a way for people without power to identify gaps and opportunities, which they may seize for limited periods of time.

It is tempting to see the actions of refugees in Lebanon as tactical in this sense because they often found gaps in the urban fabric and sought a place in the face of hostility. They adapted to the repressive environment created by the government and often turned to their personal connections to find unusual places to stay. Such a view, however, is both romantic and simplistic. It is romantic because it seems to suggest refugees in Lebanon were finding a form of resistance through shelter, when in fact they were limited and restrained by circumstance. It is simplistic because it suggests a level of organization in the government's response that is not entirely warranted. Lebanese political leaders were not really acting strategically in De Certeau's sense as the policy response was so uncoordinated. It was fragmented by the decentralized nature of power in Lebanon and always framed by state absence. After all, the "policy without a policy" in opposition to camps emerged, in large part, due to the *inaction* of political leaders.[46]

Aid agencies, in turn, might be said to be acting tactically *or* strategically in De Certeau's sense. They certainly engaged tactically in some ways—by lining things up to meet short-term objectives—but this was a response to their environment rather than an explicit act of resistance. We might argue that aid agencies always act strategically in that they tend to impose order through models and plans, controlling people in concert with power, but this is also misleading because aid agencies can undermine the government's plans, and when they wield governmental power, they do so ineffectively and with a limited scope of influence.[47] De Certeau's model tends to divide actions into either strategy or tactics. It simplistically suggests that people *either* wield power and authority *or* they opportunistically subvert that authority. In reality, however, this binary breaks down.

Aid workers may wield some power, but they also have to act within constraints set by the government.[48] They might also subvert government policy, but they usually remain complicit. To confuse things further, De Certeau's work seems to imply a moral binary, in which tactics appear as morally good—something pure, oppositional, and disruptive—while strategies seem morally suspect.[49] This does not make sense for humanitarians, who rarely idealize the short-term act and, in many ways, *must* be strategic to have any lasting impact. In the shelter sector, more than any other, there has to be a bridge between the simple roof to keep off the rain and the requirements of longer-term residence with warmth, comfort, and good sanitation. If humanitarians only look at the short-term issues, they can do no more than put "band aids on malignant tumors," as the saying goes.

Debates between "classical" and "alchemical" approaches have divided aid workers along these lines, and my interlocutors at the UNHCR headquarters rehearsed many of these arguments when I spoke to them in Beirut.[50] Ultimately, though, ambitious action was tricky, and it was already a massive challenge to get assistance to the hundreds of thousands of refugees represented by the pointillist map on the wall. The humanitarians in Lebanon knew that they were frittering away precious resources by returning each year and offering ephemeral upgrades to substandard shelters, yet their hands were tied. Like many aid agencies, they were forbidden from providing longer-term accommodation that might imply refugees could stay, and they were blocked from taking steps to facilitate better integration when it conflicted with immigration policy. They were unable to do anything that might be considered political, so all that remained were these small-scale, tactical interventions—the rental improvements, the materials for better insulation, the limited attempts to relieve suffering in the short term. This made it look—to many people at least—like humanitarians were just subservient to power.

5 | SHELTER AS PRAGMATICS
Abandoned Buildings in Berlin

WHEN FLYING INTO BERLIN on a clear day, you can see a vast hole in the urban fabric, clearly visible from the air—an imperfect circle of empty green space surrounded by straight streets and densely packed apartment blocks. This is the site of Tempelhof Airport, now closed, where an empty airfield lies fragmented by a web of crumbling gray paths bisecting the grass from east to west. In one corner of the airfield lies an enormous terminal building following the gentle arc of a quarter circle, over a kilometer in length, which hugs the airfield boundary nearest to the city center. This contains seven empty hangars, which have been built to resemble the wings of an eagle when viewed from planes above. At the middle of this building lies a terminal hall, the body of the eagle, jutting toward a road junction that points straight to the heart of Berlin.

Tempelhof Airport was built in the mid-1930s as the monumental entrance to the Nazi's imagined world capital, Germania. Once completed, it was one of the largest structures on earth. By 2015, however, it stood empty, its huge hangars used to house temporary events until the refugee crisis that year led to it being turned into an enormous dormitory for refugees. After tens of thousands of refugees arrived in the city that summer, the German chancellor Angela Merkel led her country into an open-door policy by suspending existing asylum regulations and indicating that the country was open to Syrian refugees. "Wir schaffen das," she famously said. "We can do this!"[1] By September, the number of arrivals were still growing, and Berlin was receiving over a thousand people every day. The authorities were immediately overwhelmed, and the scale of the challenge became clear when families with young children were left sleeping on the street opposite the state registration office as they waited for their presence to be acknowledged. A huge building like Tempelhof seemed like a good option to give them a place to stay.

At the time, the municipality was scrambling around for accommodation, with a deficit of over ten thousand beds across the city.[2] Some kind of emergency response was required, and so the government began requisitioning buildings around Berlin. At first, this meant school gymnasiums, which were confiscated and filled with beds lined up on the floor in a process that was seemingly simple. "They just knocked on the door of the district mayor and said, 'You've got these three school gyms next door? Well, they now belong to us. . . . We'll give you one hour to organize the keys.'"[3] Over the course of September and October, more refugees arrived, and more school gyms were requisitioned. The whole process involved a constant negotiation for space. As the manager of the scheme explained, they were "always fighting with everyone. . . . No mayor would give up the sports halls voluntarily. They just pointed to each other and said, 'Well, we've created five thousand places, but you've got only three thousand. . . . So now it's your turn."[4]

Back at the state administration, there were still hundreds of refugees sleeping on the street and in the nearby park. Frontline workers explained their embarrassment at the lack of any effective planning, and the numbers sleeping rough were still high as winter approached.[5] By the autumn of 2015, the use of school gymnasiums was beginning to reveal their disadvantages. Despite the government-led idea of a *Willkommenskultur*, or welcome culture, many parents had begun complaining of disruption at schools.[6] The capacity of gyms was also limited, with only a hundred or so able to sleep in each, which meant that refugees were spread around the city, making it hard to monitor their progress through the asylum system and causing frustration for social services required to travel between sites. By winter, it looked like a more efficient housing system was needed.

It was at this point that buildings such as Tempelhof were considered. Rather than a hundred people here and a hundred there, the idea was to find buildings big enough to house thousands of refugees at a time. This would produce greater economies of scale, the argument went, and Berlin had many empty buildings that could work. It was always a city marked by remnants of the past. Scratch behind the battered walls in one location and you could reveal fragments of another era—casualties of war or ideology that had left acres of internal space. There was the vast intelligence wing of the former Ministry of State Security for East Germany, a 1960s bureaucratic monolith that had been empty for decades, where the Stasi monitored and interrogated the citizens of the German Democratic Republic.[7] There was the colossal International Congress Center (ICC), a white elephant of a building in West Germany, constructed in the 1970s to demonstrate economic might and hold huge spectacular events and trade fairs.[8] There was the abandoned C&A department store on Karl-Marx-Strasse in Neukölln, emptied of commodities and installed with dividing walls and bunk beds between its escalators and retail displays.[9] All these buildings stood as testimony to faded political dreams, and all became housing for refugees.

In many cases, these large buildings had become a headache for the municipality. They were protected by law for reasons of heritage but required some kind of upkeep. They were suitable for accommodation insofar as they were large, but many had troubling historical resonances and were sites of state repression as well. Further afield, refugees were housed in former concentration camps, such as Dachau in Bavaria, and Tempelhof itself had been a forced labor camp.[10] The decision to use these buildings could, therefore, be portrayed either as an instance of blatant insensitivity or a purifying act of urban transformation. Some argued that they were indelibly marked by their despotic histories, while others suggested they could be altered and put to the service of good. So how effective were these buildings in practice? Were they simply inappropriate as refugee shelters? Or could they become decent, effective, and pragmatic responses to a real emergency?

CHECKERED PASTS

Tempelhof was the largest emergency shelter in Berlin, and it had the highest profile mainly because of its symbolism and history, which traced the twists and turns of the nation's past. It was first used as an airfield in 1923, and a decade later, it became part of Albert Speer's futuristic plan for Adolf Hitler's new capital. Speer's vision was that the airport's enormous size and imposing symmetry would envelop visitors, depositing them with an awe-inspiring sense of scale at the foot of one of the gigantic boulevards that was slated to lead to the heart of the Reich. In the middle of the city, a huge, new parliament building was planned for construction, able to house over a hundred thousand people under a dome that would have been large enough to produce its own microclimate. Germania, of course, was never built, but its gateway, Tempelhof, was nevertheless completed to the designs of Ernst Sagebiel. Construction began in 1936 under the direction of Hermann Göring, and the enormous hangars were completed within a few years.[11]

When approaching the building today, its heritage is obvious, with remnants in the imposing limestone facade that can be seen through tall vertical windows, including Nazi mosaics, sculptures, and reliefs. There are halls of marble, spread eagles clutching rings, and the shadows of other detailing, such as a swastika that has since been destroyed. The whole complex has a monumental character, designed to overwhelm visitors with a sense of power. As well as receiving planes, the field was meant to become the site for huge rallies, airshows, and demonstrations of supremacy. The hangar roofs, which extend around the edge of this great airfield, were built with the gentlest of inclines in order to seat hundreds of thousands of people. Spectators could be led up the wide stairways from the street below to take in a capacious view of military parades. The hangars were also used for arms production during the war and then became a space for constructing aircrafts.

World War II was just the beginning of this building's fascinating story. After a brief Soviet occupation, the Americans took control of the airport in 1945, when the city was divided into sectors by the victorious powers. By 1948, the airport had become the center of the Berlin airlift, with American planes landing every couple of minutes to bring millions of tons of food and fuel into the isolated western part of the German capital. So-called "raisin bombers" dropped treats for children on parachutes, and the symbolism of the airport began to shift. It had once indicated the global ambitions of a totalitarian power, but it soon became a symbol of Western liberalism. Tempelhof was, by then, West Berlin's connection to the wider world. As one activist put it, the airport was a representation of freedom. It stood for the need to stick together, for survival against the odds, a lifeline for people who were surrounded by Soviet power.[12]

By the 1960s, Tempelhof changed again. Air travel became more common, and the airport became a regular stopping point for celebrities and movie stars. This made it into an important cultural emblem for the city.

The building served as a backdrop for many famous media appearances, with Billy Wilder, Gary Cooper, Marlene Dietrich, and Marilyn Monroe all photographed against its stone. The airport was still a representation of freedom for many people, but it also became a famous point of arrival for world travelers and a symbol of optimistic modernism. Its proximity to the city had always been one of Tempelhof's great attractions, situated only fifteen minutes via bicycle ride from the Tiergarten. This made Berliners very familiar with the airfield and its connection to capitalist culture.

In the 1970s, Tempelhof went into a long process of decline. Air traffic had increased, and jets were getting bigger, but this required runways that were longer than those Tempelhof could provide. The airport's location in the middle of the city was also a problem as there was no room to expand. A new airport for West Berlin was built at Tegel, and, after this opened in 1975, more and more carriers moved their base out of the city. Business gradually moved away from Tempelhof, and by the 1980s, the airport was in its death throes. The airfield remained a US military base for a few years, but even this role ended when the last American troops left in 1993. By the middle of the 1990s, only a few small commercial flights were coming into the airport, primarily for businesspeople attracted by its proximity to the financial district. By 2008, all operations had ceased.

At this point, arguments about the future of this site began in earnest. It was a huge area of prime real estate with a powerful symbolic past. The airport was handed over to the German government, and the complex of buildings were fenced off and separated from the old airfield. Its hangars were used for temporary events, such as fashion shows, music festivals, and business fairs, while the field opened as a public park in the spring of 2010. Developers began circling, and Tempelhof became highly valued by local citizens. It was a democratic and accessible green space right in the heart of the city, with abandoned runways that became a popular spot for people with roller skates. On warm days, the grass was filled with kite fliers and sunbathers. Local residents were protective of this new amenity, and they began to mobilize when, in 2013, the park seemed under threat. That year, a development plan suggested that apartments and commercial buildings be built around the airfield edge, and this led to a prominent campaign advocating that the whole area be left untouched.[13]

In 2015, when large numbers of refugees began arriving in Germany, these debates about the airport were still ongoing. As an article in the *At-*

FIGURE 5.1.   Tempelhof Airport terminal building, showing the huge sweep of hangars. Berlin, Germany. © University of Oxford / Mark E. Breeze, 2017.

lantic put it, the airport had been inverted from a place of transit to "a destination in itself."[14] All that grandiose architecture, all that scale and detail, all those journeys through the terminal building had now given way to a space that was being used and occupied in a thousand different ways. The airfield had evolved into "a playground of the human spirit": a place of leisure and enjoyment.[15] Inside the hangars, it had also become a space for asylum seekers to wait nervously for their claims to be processed. Many Berliners were suspicious about this development, keen to keep the area free from permanent settlement and concerned that accommodation in the hangars would pave the way for the construction of apartment buildings on the site. But with thousands of refugees living on the street in September 2015, they also recognized that the municipality had little choice but to do something bold. The city authorities insisted that this was just a temporary measure and that it would not set a precedent for the residential use of the site, but opposition continued to rumble on. The stage was set for a great experiment: a chance to provide thousands of forced migrants with urgent shelter by adapting an older building.

ADAPTED BUILDINGS

One of Tempelhof's big advantages was location. It was close to several multicultural districts with good infrastructure and social networks. This offered a refreshing contrast from life in many other refugee camps, where people ended up being pushed to the edge of cities. They problem, however, was that Tempelhof felt too imposing, and few people could forget their first impression of entering the hangars—these cavernous, echoing spaces stretching upward to steel girder roofs. Many refugees described a feeling of overwhelming remoteness on arrival, despite being in the middle of the city, and the airport was further cut off from nearby streets by miles of fencing and tarmac. Reaching the hangars involved ducking through a dingy tunnel beneath an old railway line and sinking down into the shadow of the perfunctory rear facade. Security guards constituted a final obstacle, checking papers and monitoring the coming and going within. This network of barriers was a legacy of its previous use as a munitions factory and American military base. It made an unwelcoming prospect for any new arrival.

I spoke to one of the people involved in running the shelter, who described how they felt when they came to the building for the first time: "I remember when I entered this hangar through this massive metal door and . . . well, it's just huge . . . big enough for airplanes. . . . A massive industrial hall with very bad light. . . . My first thought was that it would be very difficult to create a comfortable and inviting atmosphere."[16] These initial impressions proved correct. Over a long weekend in late October, the hangars were rapidly converted into accommodation by the German army, who used standard-issue white tents erected in rows on the old, tiled floor. It was a remarkable feat of speed and efficiency, but it did little for comfort and hospitality. Each tent was lined with twelve bunk beds, and over six hundred people lived in each hangar. When one hangar was full, another was opened. By the time four hangars had opened, with thousands of people living on site, local wholesalers were running out of beds.[17]

The biggest issue for Tempelhof in the early days was a lack of toilet and bathroom facilities. The building was protected by conservation laws, which made it very hard to adapt the existing structure. Drilling a single hole in the fabric of the building was forbidden, and all alterations had to be reversible. Unplumbed chemical toilets were initially lined up outside, but visiting these in the Berlin winter was a horrible experience. There was also trouble with the showers as the only way to get clean in the first few months was to take a prearranged bus to a local public swimming pool, where refugees were given a fixed time slot to use the showers once or twice a week. Life in the shelter, therefore, became more and more regimented, and soon there would be growing control over food, lighting, and other aspects of daily routine.

By the end of October, there were around three thousand people in Tempelhof, and there were plans to double the capacity to six thousand in the coming months.[18] Additional hangars were converted, and firmer cubicles were installed instead of tents—their white dividing walls made initially from exhibition screens, and their small openings covered by flimsy fabric that served as a door. Unlike the tents, these cubicles had no roof. They were partitioned from the sides but open at the top, so noise bounced off the brick hangar edges and the huge metal wall. Pendant lights shone down from above, relentlessly illuminating everyone inside until all lights were cut at the end of the night. Pigeons flew in and perched on the roof trusses, defecating on people from fifty-two feet above. Soon, there was graffiti and dirt covering these partitions too, messages and pictures scrawled by angry hands as the asylum process dragged on.

Refugees tried to counter the lack of privacy by constructing personal pergolas from fabric strung up around their beds. They began seeking smaller and more intimate spaces to shelter from the vastness of the surroundings. They also tried to get out of the hangars as often as possible, navigating along paths and around fences to get to the city or the park, but this was made more difficult by the layout of the site. Through the tall windows, refugees could look beyond the chain-link fence to see the joggers and sunbathers outside, but to join them, they had to travel the long way around by walking through the rear doors, under the old railway tracks, around a modern car park, and then passing out to the road before entering the field through a gate further down the street. This separation between the land of leisure and the land of needs created an uncomfortable juxtaposition. Visiting the park could relieve the oppressive sense of isolation in the hangars, but it was not easy. When I finally got out onto the airfield on my first day at Tempelhof, I watched as the cloudscape cast great shadows across the grass. The rain, when it came, swept and speckled the strips of tarmac in beautiful waves. The huge arc of the terminal building remained visible behind the fence, encrusted with layers of history.

FIGURE 5.2.   Tempelhof Airport from the airfield. Berlin, Germany. © University of Oxford / Mark E. Breeze, 2017.

LASTING PROBLEMS

The teething problems might have been solved with some more careful planning. There could have been beds and better showers from the start, as well as easier access to the field. The head of public relations admitted that things could have been more organized: "If you tell people that in a country like Germany, it wasn't possible to set up some mobile showers within two months it's, well . . . I still can't believe it."[19] Soon, however, some more structural failings began to emerge. As the emergency faded and the arrivals leveled off, those inside the refugee shelters found that their routines had become calcified and controlling. It seemed that the only way to gain a pragmatic advantage from organizing accommodation at this kind of scale was to structure everyone's life in a similar, routinized way.

The first issue was food. To ensure that thousands of people were fed each day, there were meals provided by external catering firms, who offered little choice and served only at fixed times. The quality of the food caused many complaints because it was culturally incongruous—initially based around sausages and bread—and mass-produced from cheap ingredients. Many Tempelhof residents described it as disgusting: "Just macaroni with watery sauce," one said.[20] It was heated up with microwaves on site, and refugees could not bring in their own alternative meals due to fear of rats,

rodents, and rotting food. They were not given access to any kitchen facilities, and this became the most troubling part of staying in Tempelhof
for residents who ended up living there for months and then years on end.
More than the quality of the food, the central issue here was a lack of control. "You have to be there in time for breakfast. You have to be there in time
for lunch and supper. You have to eat what is provided or you die," said one
refugee.[21] This lack of autonomy over food began to symbolize the complete
disempowerment of people within a system that managed so much.[22]

The problems with food were closely followed by noise. This was a constant complaint in the shelter: the background clamor, the murmurs and
shouts, the squeak of sneakers on tile. Bodies bumping against plasterboard
dividers created a recurring sound, and it was impossible to cut this cease-
less din out of one's life. Cubicles were shared with up to twelve people,
and since these had no proper ceiling or sound insulation, this meant that
everyone was effectively sharing a living space with up to eight hundred
others in the whole hangar. Each night, there might be fifty people cough-
ing, ten children crying, and thirty young people walking around, and in
such circumstances, it was very difficult to sleep.[23] It might be possible to
put up with this for a few weeks when the alternative was living on the
street, but after months and then years, it took its toll. As one refugee put
it, the most fundamental desire for those in Tempelhof was simply to have
a door—an object that could close and cut off the world outside with all its
commotion and complexity.[24]

Next, there was lighting. When it comes to basic needs, this may seem
trivial, but the ability to control lighting became serious for many people's
mental health. Lighting determines the character of the environment and
shapes so much about wellbeing. From when we rise in the morning to how
we finally fall asleep, controlling light is crucial to our routine. In Tempelhof, however, residents were not able to regulate the light. Pendants hung
high from the hangar roofs, which came on in the morning and were cut
off at the end of the evening. All day, the light shone down—unforgiving,
harsh, fixed. Combined with a curfew in the shelter, this meant that refugees had no real control over how their days unfolded. The pattern of their
personal life had to defer to the running of an institutional shelter, and the
result was an absence of autonomy over the most basic acts. The resulting
disempowerment had a slow but profound effect on mental health.[25] As one
member of the staff at Tempelhof put it, "We're talking about people who

FIGURE 5.3.   Inside a Tempelhof Airport hangar, showing bedroom divisions. Berlin, Germany. © University of Oxford / Mark E. Breeze, 2017.

didn't switch on a light for two years."[26] The most crucial element of shelter became the ability to control one's immediate space.

Bad food, interrupted sleep, constant noise, and uncontrollable lighting—these might seem like small irritations, but they became more serious over time. Some refugees began to develop tactics to ameliorate their conditions, such as smuggling in kettles or hotplates to make simple meals. They stashed bread under their pillows and hung blankets from the bedframes to create a refuge from the light and noise. They spread mats on the floor to receive friends, trying to create a facsimile of home with boundaries they could control. Yet these tiny acts of hospitality always flew in the face of a tightly controlled atmosphere. Security guards checked everyone and prevented residents from bringing in food. Gatherings of friends and family were blocked off at the gate. Contractors in high-visibility jackets sat stony-faced at each internal door, checking movements from one hangar to the next. One interviewee explained the horrible feeling that "security is everywhere," saying how it made him feel guilty and listless. "Every time security asks questions: Where are you going? What are you doing? But we just want to be free. So I sleep."[27]

PRAGMATICS AND CONTROL

The idea of "pragmatics" has many meanings—philosophical, linguistic, and vernacular—but all definitions have a similar core. It is a word that directs attention to the conditions that exist rather than obeying our ideals. It is a word that concerns the ability to solve problems in the present, considering what works. The word has a root in the Greek *pragmatikos*, "relating to fact": a thing done, a thing fit for action. The pragmatic approach to shelter in Germany, therefore, involved coming to terms with constraints, finding something fit for purpose given the facts of the case. It meant ensuring that refugees did not have to live on the street in the context of rapid arrivals, and it meant using a surfeit of empty buildings in order to keep people safe.

This last element—safety—was the core justification for tight controls within each shelter. Humanitarians kept pointing to the importance of maintaining order. There were so many people in the shelter, they said, so it was important to have rules. If everyone brought guests, then the numbers would spiral very quickly. With so many vulnerable people inside the shelters, there was also a risk of drug dealing, trafficking, and prostitution.[28] The managers had concerns, too, about far-right activists who might find their way into the shelter. They pointed out that providing refuge involves shutting some people out so that others can be protected.

This makes intuitive sense as control over the external frontiers of the shelter was surely a pragmatic decision given the tense political debates around migration. Refugee shelter in Berlin was always likely to be infused by restrictions over entrance and exit, even though the extent of these controls was frustrating for those on the inside. One journalist, who spent a lot of time in these shelters, told me that they were "shocked to see the extent of these rules. People had to show ID going in, they had to sign in and out, they couldn't bring visitors to their room, they had belongings scanned."[29] Many such controls were as much about governing *internal* space as they were about policing external boundaries. They were consistent with theories of hospitality, which show how acts of welcome involve rules about acceptable conduct.[30] It is often said that hospitality is a way to deal with potentially hostile strangers by controlling interactions that surround them.[31] Many aid workers in Berlin ran the shelters in this way, speaking of how the atmosphere in a shelter could easily bubble over into disagreements. As one put it, "You need to have rules and security because if something kicks off, it is all really very quick. Suddenly you can find yourself in the middle of fifty fighting men."[32]

Over sixty years ago, when surveying the ruins of postwar Germany, Martin Heidegger wrote an influential paper on what it means to truly live in a place. In it, he makes a distinction between the act of taking shelter and the more profound sense of *dwelling* in a building.[33] To dwell is not just to be inside a building. It is to *belong* there. It is to see the building as a place one can feel at home, a place one can be at peace with the world. It happens when a building becomes familiar, embroidered with memories. This is precisely the kind of sensitive relationship between people and place that remained impossible in locations such as Tempelhof—partly due to the controls, partly due to the timescale, and partly due to the architecture. The inhabitants of Tempelhof never had a stable place in which to dwell because their status was so uncertain, their temporary homes too tightly controlled. This generated a tension in the aid world. Humanitarians wanted to control the shelters they were responsible for, but at the same time, they wanted to involve refugees, who they knew were lacking in power. Aid workers were pushed to negotiate these twin imperatives, retaining control as well as passing it onto recipients.

Shelter is a good illustration of these competing forces in the aid world. On the one hand, there is a pressure toward control, and on the other, there is a pressure toward participation.[34] The balance between the two is often mediated by timescale. In the early stages of an emergency, control can be crucial, usually framed as a way to ensure that the right aid reaches the right people when conditions are in flux. But as the situation begins to stabilize, there is more need for participatory approaches. Recipients expect to be involved, and there are calls for longer-term planning. The problem with the pragmatic approach to shelter in Berlin was that this timescale became compressed. All the attention was on the emergency phase even when, as time went on, these short-term shelters became completely unsuitable. One manager articulated this problem when she described how a pregnant woman had arrived at a shelter, and by the time she left, there was a child running around. "The shelter was meant to be open for three to six months, but we ended up having people live with us for over one and a half years," she said, describing the situation as "absurd."[35]

It is easy to forget that much of the refugee experience involves waiting, which goes on for weeks, months, and years as asylum applications are submitted and responses arrive, appeals lodged, and decisions finally communicated.[36] The scale of the arrivals in 2015 led to a backlog of applications and waiting times that were even longer than usual. Shelters that were meant to be temporary became permanent. Rules and regulations became a burden. Pragmatism, as an idea, should always be situated in relation to time. It is all about solving problems in the present, given constraints. Yet the future always lurks in the background, bringing the specter of failure. The inability to cook, to control the lighting, or to receive visitors started as simple inconveniences in Berlin, but eventually, they became a fiasco. As the circumstances changed, the pragmatism failed. The weeks turned to months, and the months turned to years until what first seemed pragmatic became profoundly damaging.

BUILDINGS THAT LEARN

It is by no means a new idea to adapt existing buildings. Since the 1960s, there has been a growing concern for the environment and much greater attention to the ecological cost of construction. In this context, "adaptive reuse" has become an important mantra.[37] The idea is simple: buildings do not need to be destroyed or left to rot once they become obsolescent; they can be reused and adapted instead. There is a traditionalist spirit at the heart of this idea, which moves beyond the notion of an omniscient, modernist designer trying to remake the world through a set of clear, precast visions about how a building should be used. Instead, the idea is that buildings can be organic; they can evolve. Buildings should be open to modification, shaped by each generation to meet their needs.[38]

It is only recently that the passing of time has become perceived as a threat to architecture.[39] Modernism solidified the notion that buildings should be designed and built as fixed manifestations of an architect's vision. For hundreds of years, however, architecture evolved more naturally. Medieval cathedrals were built as eternal testimonies to the human spirit, and they took decades—even centuries—to construct. No single overall designer could ever determine the final form as masons came and went, carpenters lived and died. The construction of such cathedrals became an ongoing, collaborative process in which time was not an obstacle but an integral part of building. This began to change in the fifteenth century when an Italian architect, Leon Battista Alberti, created blueprints for a final design.[40] The designer's plan became the idealized version of the final structure, fixed in time before construction had even begun. Time became the enemy. If construction dragged on, then the passing of time brought only problems, such as ballooning budgets, missed deadlines, deteriorating materials, and dead architects.

Modernism took the idea of fixing a building to its logical conclusion. Architects began to start trying to control everything right down to the arrangement of furniture and the shape of the cutlery in the kitchen. The ideal form of the modernist building was how it looked at the moment of its completion, when it could be photographed, pristine, with clean lines as vivid as the architect's drawings. From here on, everything was deterioration. Materials would erode, concrete became streaked by the rain, and inhabitants would make unauthorized adaptations. The building was unable to evolve.

Such an approach was always flawed because architecture does not end when people move into a building.[41] Buildings cannot exist frozen in time as sterile pieces of art; they should encourage inhabitants to etch lives into their surfaces and wear down their walls. The great triumph of refugee shelters in Berlin was to give monumental buildings a new life and embrace the passing of time. They looked to the future, reusing defunct spaces and drawing on the charms of a city whose attractions could always be found in the layers of history and decades of reuse and renewal. But these projects did not go far enough. Shelter in Berlin failed because it remained stuck in an emergency phase. The future was not fleshed out. There was no plan for development, no evolution of the building, no theory of social change. There was an irony, too, because the whole approach tried to recognize how buildings can have a new life, yet it did not consider how inhabitants also needed a future as well. The humanitarian focus was pragmatic in the short term, but it failed to look around the corner to the next obstacle, the subsequent life stage, the possibility of longer residence.

Humans cannot live when they're fixed in time, eating mass-catered food off silver trays. However, these shelters had to reckon with not only the future but the past as well. As people flowed into the dusty halls and corridors of the empty buildings, they disturbed memories and revived civic symbolism, which rose up like a cloud. The effects were far from benign. One of the refugee shelters in Berlin was created in the ICC, a vast spaceship of a building positioned by the autobahn in West Berlin. It was separated from residential areas by a network of access roads, which were hard to navigate even for local residents. The building had been completed in 1979 and was designed for fly-in, fly-out meetings by vehicle-bound international visitors rather than people searching for local shops and amenities. It had few windows and was all sleek gray surfaces in a high-tech modernist style. There was little ventilation and minimal natural light. Refugees slept in a huge plenary hall, again flimsily divided by drywall partitions and constantly illuminated by flickering fluorescent lights from above. In a juxtaposition that was startling even for Berlin, the enormous structure still had huge walk-in fridges for champagne, clearly labeled, and photos of lavish dinners next to the scuffed walls of temporary showers.

When fighting for the quickest-erected and most cost-effective shelter, it is hard to see history as important. Who can complain about historical residues when people have no roof over their head? Adaptation surely comes first—especially when there is no food and shelter—even if the symbolism of a building still matters. Yet structures like Tempelhof and the ICC were already embroiled in public debates about heritage and urban development when they were repurposed as refugee shelters. The symbolism and history mattered because a great deal of work had to be expended in convincing refugees and the wider public that such buildings, which were made for a very different purpose, could be adapted. Such issues drained the pragmatic approach of its former advantages.

6 | SHELTER AS POETICS

Social Furniture in Vienna

I BEGAN TO RECONSIDER my opinion of humanitarian architecture on a wet November day in Venice as rain lashed down on the city and darkness had just fallen. It was 2016, and the city had been hosting the Bienniale Architettura, a huge event with the theme and title *Reporting from the Front*. The phrase was chosen by the festival director to articulate how architecture should "tackle many fronts," working with the poor as well as the rich, providing basic shelter as well as fulfilling advanced human desires.[1] I had already heard a lot of enthusiastic commentary about this explicitly humanitarian event over the course of the previous summer and a great deal of excitement about "what design can do," but I remained skeptical of the triumphalism involved.[2] There seemed to be a lot of complacency in the exhibition, which involved architects celebrating a series of unrealistic schemes that had not been tested in practice.

During my first few days at the Bienniale, most of the exhibits sadly reaffirmed my suspicions. The scope of the event was huge, showing an almost limitless architectural imagination but very little in the way of pragmatism. There were proposals for huge residential blocks with "embedded refugee rooms," which could be made available in times of crisis.[3] There was a complete reimagining of the city as vertical towers of hybrid buildings, with space for refugees in layered and dense combinations.[4] There was a replicable design for drone ports that could be installed in camps and remote communities, promising a rapid way to deliver relief.[5] These ideas had a common theme: they were oriented more toward finding something novel to impress an architectural audience than actually being appropriate for solving real-world issues. Most of these designs were also top-down, showing no concern for representation from the communities that they were designed to assist. They made expansive humanitarian gestures but failed to grasp the nitty-gritty political predicaments that were causing so much suffering in the first place.

Walking through the halls and gardens of the Bienniale that year, it seemed to me that the event had floated free from its moorings. It came so soon after the 2015 refugee crisis, and as a result, it featured a range of exhibits on refugee shelter, but it seemed to contain very few workable proposals. It was also striking how few designers had recognized that the really big obstacles to building effective shelter were political. Among all that enthusiasm for "what design can do," it looked like many architects had failed to consider what design *cannot* do. Among other things, design cannot address the border regimes that cause so much suffering. Design cannot help to build legal frameworks needed to protect forced migrants. Design cannot challenge the discriminatory political discourse that blocks proper welfare for refugees—at least, design as understood in these exhibits. Such challenges demand a degree of modesty that seemed to be missing amid the fervent belief that design could remake the world.[6]

After several days wading through these technically unrealistic and politically limited proposals, I felt rather dejected. But on my final evening, as the darkness was closing in around the autumnal Venetian rains, I came upon three inspiring projects in the Austrian national pavilion. The exhibit was tucked away in a far corner of the Giardini, housed in a white, modernist pavilion that glistened through the leaves. Inside, there was a showcase for some practical architectural schemes that had been collected under the title "Places for People."[7] The walls of the bright-white pavilion were illustrated with simple photographs, and there were free newspapers stacked up in the corner that could be taken away to explain the idea in more detail. It was immediately clear that the projects were responding to a familiar situation from 2015—the use of inappropriate buildings as refugee shelters— but they showed a far more thoughtful approach to transformation through design.

There were three main projects on display here, each based on a similar idea. Their aim was not to construct new shelters but to improve the empty office buildings that lay empty across Vienna after the financial crash. The interventions used small, replicable objects, which had been chosen because they were cheap and could transform refugee shelters marked by the uninspiring aesthetics of a workplace. These buildings had thin carpet floor tiles, fluorescent strip lighting, and dropped ceilings. They had open-plan areas that offered no privacy. Refugees had been sleeping in such buildings for many months because the rent was cheap and the buildings were empty, but the residents had a familiar litany of complaints. The open spaces offered no comfort. The mealtimes were fixed and monotonous. There was particular dislike of the poor-quality lighting and fluorescent bulbs. Routines were fixed, with switches flicked on and off at fixed times each day.

Rather than proposing something structural and spectacular in response to this situation, the architects focused instead on the micro level. They added simple furnishings to the offices. They thought about how to create a more homely environment. The aim was to turn "nonplaces" into "places for people" through cheap and small-scale interventions.[8] The most striking of the three projects involved parasols as a deceptively simple motif. The parasol, these architects realized, could produce a more private and enclosed area in a wider office while filtering the harsh strip lighting that shone down from above. Working with a tight budget and limited timeframe, the architects purchased a large number of parasols from a garden supplier, which came with a heavy base and in an array of vibrant colors. They installed these throughout the open-plan areas, suspending large blankets around the edge of each parasol, which were clipped on with cable ties that had been fed through the fabric. In this way, they divided the large, shared space into something more intimate. The noises of neighboring residents became muffled through the fabric walls, and the parasol above diffused the fluorescent bulbs above into something softer. The light and sound were suddenly more controllable, and the gray office blocks were given a palette of color—all for a modest price.[9]

The intervention did not stop there. In addition to the parasol dividers, each resident was given cushions and a small lamp, which cast a cozy orange glow inside and meant that people could now control their environment even further. When the strip lights above were switched off at night, residents could read without disturbing their neighbors. In the daytime, dark blankets could cut out the overhead lights and allow people to sleep. The architects provided a potted plant for each resident and encouraged them to personalize their space, providing sewing machines and materials. When I visited the building later, I found thick rugs placed under parasols, rows of soft toys on the floor, photos pinned to fabric, and balloons suspended from umbrella supports. The architects topped this off by crafting old plastic bottles into a "doorbell" that could be rattled to alert the presence of someone outside.[10] This final, small addition kept the world at bay, creating a series of closed and controllable spaces within the impersonal environment of an office.

There was something distilled, almost poetic, about this scheme. It had been carefully pared back, and I later discovered that "poetics" was exactly what the designers in Vienna had in mind. They had been influenced by Gaston Bachelard, who wrote about the "poetics of space," and some of them had approached the problem through what they called "poetic analysis." This was a design whereby complex problems had been reduced to their simplest components. There was a focus on internal objects, the arrangement of space, and the power of small things. It was an unapologetically humanistic approach that tried to transform sterile buildings into suitable accommodation. Most radically, it looked beyond the structure to examine the interaction between people and their surroundings, raising important questions about the relationship between architecture and emergency housing. Are emotions important in the provision of shelter? Do architects

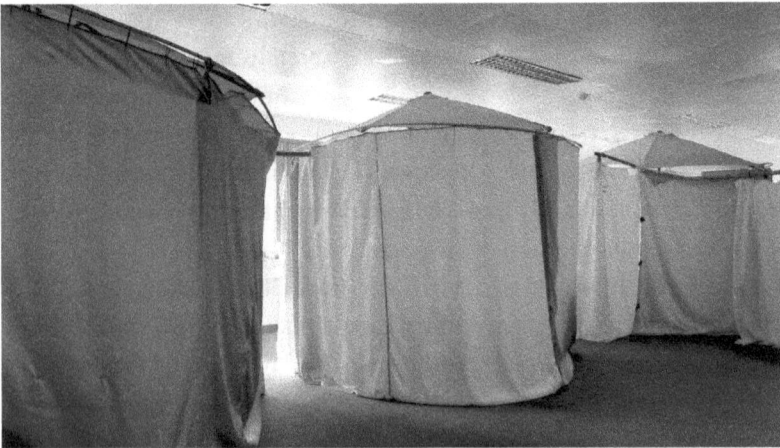

FIGURE 6.1. Parasol shelters erected to create private space in an office block on Pfeiffergasse. Vienna, Austria. © University of Oxford / Mark E. Breeze, 2017.

actually need to build concrete structures to have an impact? Should humanitarians and designers focus less on buildings and begin considering how places make people *feel*?

PLACES FOR PEOPLE

I traveled to Vienna to see how these schemes worked in practice, and when I arrived, I met the curators of the Bienniale exhibit. They explained how they had wanted to promote something realistic rather than purely imaginative. They had started by finding potential shelters in Vienna, and then they recruited architects to transform them. The Bienniale preparations in 2015 coincided with a rapid rise in refugee arrivals, and most aid agencies were struggling to think about anything other than the most urgent issues.[11] The charities running refugee shelters were spending much of their time managing short-term crises: finding space, negotiating rental agreements, and understanding the regulations that kept reshaping official policy. They did not have much time to think about architecture. It was a classic problem of mismatched expectations. The humanitarians viewed architecture as a profession geared toward high-end construction and lavish aesthetics, which they saw as expensive and irrelevant to the pressure of emergency conditions.[12] The first task for the Bienniale curators, therefore, was to convince humanitarians that architecture could be pragmatic, modest, and democratic. In the end, they found a partner in the aid agency Caritas, who ran a number of shelters in Berlin. As one of the curators put it to me, "It is often said, in emergency situations, that we don't need aesthetics. But architecture is a social discipline; ethics and aesthetics cannot be divided."[13]

Having selected three shelters, the curators appointed three design firms. Their work was all united by a shared approach. The idea was to spend money from the Bienniale exhibition on real-life projects, transforming shelters that already existed. The aim was to do something useful in the present rather than paying architects to draw utopian blueprints for the future. From the very start, the architects and humanitarians had to address practical concerns. As the Caritas project manager explained, the architects had to grasp the financial restrictions and regulations involved in running a refugee shelter. They had to become aware of their limitations. "The first step involved bringing all this information to the architects," he told me, "and showing them the constraints." From there, however, the ar-

chitects introduced a way of working that not just appealed to the aid workers at Caritas but had an impact on the residents as well. They showed how
architecture was not just about "rooms and walls and toilets and kitchens"
but also about "the social process itself—about how people interact."[14]

In each of the three buildings, the architects focused as much on process
as outcomes. They showed how architecture could involve participation and
consultation, which need not involve constructing buildings but could cre-
atively reshape internal spaces instead. These ideas aligned with those of
Alejandro Aravena, the director of the 2016 Bienniale, who became known
for the notion that architecture can be incremental. His most famous idea
was the "half house," a design that was literally half finished so that residents could adapt and finish their own homes. The idea emerged from
a crucial insight that buildings can adapt and change, but Aravena went
further. Rather than simply encouraging "adaptive reuse," he designed
flexibility into his buildings from the start. He advocated homes that were
deliberately incomplete. The half house had a full gable roof, which was only
half filled in below so the rest could be completed later. If one looked at the
building from the front and drew an imaginary vertical line down from the
apex of the roof, one would find that the building was only finished on one
side of this line. These half houses were first used in reconstruction after
earthquakes and were based on a fundamentally humanitarian calculation:
that if half a house costs half the money, it can help twice as many people.[15]

Aravena's half house proved that architects could make difficult sacri-
fices while ceding control and thinking about resident participation. The
Austrian projects had a similar approach, showing how architecture can
think *beyond* the provision of a complete house and the stereotypical four
walls and a roof. In the Viennese case, the architects worked directly with
Caritas to discuss the proposed changes. They consulted residents and were
always transparent about the costs and temporal limitations. The firm responsible for the parasol idea, for example, erected them in a large open-plan
building, with just €10,000 and three months to realize their vision. They
were dealing with a set of financial and temporal constraints that would
be familiar to many humanitarians, and they demonstrated how architectural thinking did not need to be grand and unrealistic. With around three
hundred people living in the building and less than fifty euros to invest
per person, their parasols offered a cost-effective, personal living space that
was focused particularly on the sensory aspects that might really improve

everyday life.[16] It was a clever idea not least because the whole arrangement was created from cheap materials available from builders' merchants and garden stores.

The budget, of course, excluded the labor costs, but the limitations also meant that the architects worked alongside refugees and could make use of their abilities. Many inhabitants had skills in sewing and construction, so their involvement created new ideas for how to create variation in the "rooms." The architects gave special thought to the color palette, which had a vibrancy through the different parasol materials, but the common colors in the blanket dividers—gold, white, and green—also gave the building a unifying feel. The parasols were used throughout, giving it a distinctive identity, and they could even be seen around picnic benches along the small open spaces outside. This made the building immediately recognizable as its boring white facade and barred rectangular windows were given a punch of color from the front. As the architects explained it, their role was to get things started, to give a little push, to suggest the overall plan, but ultimately, this was a process in which the inhabitants created configurations that worked for them. The architects' aim was to provide the basic materials, to suggest a few models, and to create small spaces of comfort and control before handing power to the inhabitants.[17]

This combination of small-scale suggestions and participatory implementation was a feature of all three of the projects. Each aimed to produce something practical yet nevertheless humanistic. As the leader of the parasol project explained, "Humanitarian action can be very bureaucratic; it's all about the square footage per person." The architects wanted to counteract this with "something playful," something that changed the quality of light, something that echoed not the tents of a refugee camp but the parasols of a beach.[18] The other projects showcased in Vienna, too, stressed how architecture should be *more* than just creating new buildings. Their inspiration came from various sources. First, there was Bernard Rudofsky, who suggested that architecture should transform everyday acts, like eating, washing, and sleeping.[19] Then, there was Victor Papanek, who advocated design for a better world.[20] Finally, hovering over this approach, was Bachelard, with his focus on how places make people feel.[21] Bachelard argued that buildings—and particularly homes—have great phenomenological significance. They have a profound subconscious influence on how we perceive the world, so it is particularly important to think about how people live in them, how they arrange them, and how they surround themselves with objects.

SOCIAL FURNITURE

The second of the three projects in Vienna was created in a building called Haus Erdberg. Before I even visited this place, I was warned that it was a "real monster," but even this did not prepare me for the reality.[22] The building stood along the street from the metro station, its streaked concrete facade dominating the street and its eight floors blocking out the sun. Even the long vertical windows seemed somehow apologetic amid the bulk of the building's vast edifice—a concession to the need for light coming from recesses carved into the rough walls. I approached the front door by passing underneath a huge arch and stepping up into a courtyard as the traffic rumbled behind me. After walking past the grimy fluorescent lamps of a nearby convenience store, I approached the dingy front door. Once inside, however, everything changed. The reception area contained an array of textures and colors with a bright-yellow desk and welcome signs pinned around that were made from the same luminescent formwork panels. Dotted around the building were other pieces of furniture, all brilliantly yellow. Chairs and benches stood in the hallways; cupboards and stools were placed in each room. These were all constructed from thickly stained plywood.[23]

The bright-yellow objects were known as "social furniture," and, like the parasols, they were part of an attempt to think about refugee shelter on a smaller and more human scale. They started from the view that the items populating a lived environment can have a huge impact on how it is felt. This was shelter distilled through objects, shelter as a form of poetics. The furniture in this building, like the parasols in the other scheme, gave a sense of life and unity that transformed its bureaucratic interior. The corridors of a gray and featureless space were given a common color and ethos—a bright yellow that was particularly welcome in this urban landscape of streaked, gray concrete.[24]

The designers of social furniture had set about trying to transform Haus Erdberg by working on two levels. To begin with, they had designed the objects themselves—eighteen pieces of furniture that were all marked with the same color and made from the same material. Some of these objects were oriented toward providing a more comfortable living space (includ-

FIGURE 6.2.   Haus Erdberg, Vienna, Austria. © University of Oxford / Mark E. Breeze, 2017.

ing stools, tables, and shelving units for bedrooms). Others were oriented toward helping people work (such as computer desks, bookcases, and workbenches). The most important objects were the bright-yellow kitchen units, which provided what so many shelters had lacked: communal spaces where people could cook familiar food for their families. The aim of these pieces of furniture was not just to improve daily life but also to bring people together.

Yet this scheme also operated on a second level as well since it was also about the *process* of construction. The designers believed that creating objects could make a more meaningful, shared life for everyone. Rather than asking external contractors to make furniture in fixed quantities, they tried to involve residents in an act of cocreation. They detailed the objects in an open-source catalog, with exploded-view line drawings showing how the parts were cut and assembled. They trained refugees to construct the furniture after providing wood, machinery, and tools. The refugees were given workshops in the basement of Haus Erdberg, which gave off sounds of sawing throughout the gray winter days. This provided more than just furniture, therefore; it also offered employment in a shared endeavor.[25]

I met the designers of this ambitious scheme in their industrial, starkly modern offices in Vienna and asked them to explain more about the idea of social furniture. A softly spoken man called Harald Gruendl described how the objects were really just a catalyst. "The idea of social furniture is to bring people together," he told me. "It is a catalyst for human interaction." Rather than slipping into the paternalistic act of giving charity to passive recipients, the idea was to create activities that unite people and build a community. The social aspect of the furniture could be seen in two different ways. First, the idea was that residents would build the furniture together. Second, the idea was that they would *use* it together. The end result was that Haus Erdberg aspired to become a new kind of community, a place where people made connections, created identities, and collaborated in improving their environment.[26]

I asked Harald about his favorite piece of furniture, and he replied by drawing my attention to the "pot commons." This was an object that encapsulated the whole approach. It was a large yellow board mounted on the wall above a kitchen worktop, which had space for a range of pots attached with magnets. It was meant to show how objects encourage people to interact, how objects can allow people to use spaces for social purposes. The central aim was to provide residents with shared tools to cook but also to encourage collaboration. People would come together in the kitchens, standing around the large yellow worktops, slicing ingredients, talking, and negotiating over the pots. This was the essence of social furniture. It was an idea of shelter that focused on the power of objects while also changing bureaucratic refugee shelters into places teeming with life.

Upon entering that that vast building, I began to understand the project in more detail. Each bedroom had cabinets, shelves, and chairs—cheerful storage that became layered with clothes and other belongings, supported by solid planks and screwed together. I wandered into the kitchens and saw how these had been converted from offices using simple worktops and cabinets, now thick with the smells of cooking. The yellow wood in these rooms seemed iridescent, attractively worn into lighter shades that had been repeatedly scrubbed clean. Some patches had been scored with navy blue knife lines where food had been cut and prepared, and the wood was stained in other places by the reds and yellows of a thousand sauces. Together, the furniture gave the whole place texture, color, and a unifying theme for the building.

The scheme was rooted in what the designers called "poetic analysis." This was an approach to design that involved reducing complex problems to their simplest components.[27] Just like written poetry, the idea was to create something dense and distilled. The sparse text of a poem obscures all the

FIGURE 6.3.   Office room converted into a kitchen by EOOS. Haus Erdberg, Vienna, Austria. © University of Oxford / Mark E. Breeze, 2017.

work and effort that goes into producing it, and similarly, the designers wanted to look at the central problem of shelter and address it through a series of simple interventions that did not fully show the work involved. Harald told me they had drawn on "images, myths, and rituals" to help generate ideas, themes that were "engraved in the human consciousness." He described how, in a previous design project, they had reimagined the modern kitchen by recalling the workshops of medieval craftsmen. Rather than starting with current kitchen arrangements—with fitted cupboards and multiple drawers liable to become cluttered—they had organized the kitchen instead around a solid simple workbench and an adjacent cabinet for implements. This became a model for social furniture—a bold proposal that sought ideas from the past while articulating the shared human problem of organizing tools for a common purpose.[28]

The "poetic analysis" that generated social furniture in Haus Erdberg drew on Thomas More's 1516 book, *Utopia*, which described a self-contained community where work was central to identity. Although it seems bizarre to relate a work of Renaissance satire to a gloomy concrete building for refugees on the outskirts of Vienna, the book stimulated an idea that work could be central to the construction of a new society. As Harald explained, he wanted to start with the idea that *work* is central to life. Work makes life meaningful, yet asylum seekers are too often reduced to a state of limbo, unable to work while their claims are heard. They may have had their necessities provided, but they were not able to earn—which was disempowering and led to inertia while wasting the skills refugees had gained.

Haus Erdberg, for example, had hairdressers, bakers, and programmers living within its walls. It had musicians, who could provide entertainment, and linguists, who could provide interpretation. Yet these people were stuck. They were waiting for their life to move on. They could not practice their crafts, so the designers of "social furniture" wanted to harness these skills and use them for the benefit of the whole.

It was an ambitious idea, which extended the scope of their intervention to the creation of a new community with its own currency. Manufacturing the furniture was the first step because it provided the environment for residents to start work and begin deploying their skills. The furniture included fittings for a hair salon, desks for a computer suite, and benches for a carpentry workshop. These all helped residents to do more and start to find meaning by returning to work. Yet the plan was to go further. The second stage was to introduce a new form of exchange, to create a sealed economy with tokens and some form of digital barter currency. This was meant to build a society without money—which asylum seekers were prohibited from earning—replacing the outside world from which residents had been barred. It was an "island" in Vienna, like Thomas More's Utopia.[29] It was not just about using objects to catalyze one-off relationships but also about leveraging them to construct a self-sufficient society.

In this way, the projects distilled ambitious visions into simple objects. They sought to transform human relations and bring new economies into existence. Did they succeed? Of course not, but these were projects with two sides: the practical and the idealistic. They showed that shelter can be ambitious but also focus on modest improvements. Haus Erdberg was previously a container for sleeping, but the project gave it a whiff of something more. The intervention had started small, with simple objects that could be easily constructed, but it had also thought big, encouraging everyone to contribute. It worked because these yellow-stained objects reappeared throughout the building, giving it coherence and a sense of community. It started to turn this monster of a building into an island of possibility. The fact that the new barter economy never took root will be unsurprising to economists, but the furniture itself endured as emblematic of a new approach.

SLEEPING PODS

Another street, another office block, another part of Vienna—the third project took place in a building that was less bulky than Haus Erdberg while equally isolated in feel. It was located in a 1980s structure—five floors of open-planned and gray-carpeted space that arched around a patch of scrubby grass. The long rows of red-fringed windows opened onto a featureless interior with vertical mullions resembling security bars and low ceilings covered by ugly deteriorating panels. Large communal rooms were punctuated by beds, which had been lined up against the wall. For years, businesses had rented this space, moving in and out before being replaced, and the bare bones of the building had elevators, noticeboards, and chunky pillars. Around this skeleton, you could still see the communicative flesh of administration—printers, workstations, and water coolers—and as people moved through, they barely left a mark. To use Marc Augé's words, these buildings were a nonplace, creating a feeling of being "always, and never, at home."[30]

How could this insipid and transient nonplace be turned into suitable accommodation? In this third example, the idea was to create a wooden pod, a "room within a room" that constituted a shelter in miniature. It was another distilled approach with the idea of creating intimacy within personal units—in this case, a module that closed up into a perfect cuboid. These pods were arranged at angles, with several in each room, and they had their own electricity supply with lights recessed into the walls. The modules contained various elements that could be shifted and arranged. There was a bed to sleep in, which could be completely surrounded when the wooden sides were folded down. There were drawers for clothing under the bed and a few shelves above. There was a retractable desk, and the whole unit could be shut off entirely and closed down by some pavilion-like doors that extended across the front. These doors had multiple hinges, which meant they could fold up and seal everything down or open up and envelop part of the surrounding office space to create a more private but larger area. Publicity shots for the scheme showed how the units offered a warm and glowing space, a striking contrast from the dark-gray, lightless offices.

I met the architects on site, and they explained that the idea was to create a shelter that appealed to young people, combining their need for private space with everything required for the most crucial tasks, such as learning, charging phones, and storing clothes and books. It was an idea not just for refugees but for students too, with everything important enclosed in a box, which one could close, lock, leave, or move to new locations. The architects were using the idea not just as a practical proposal in this particular location but as a way to ask wider questions about how we live in the city. They had observed that many young people embrace temporary living, moving from place to place every few years and existing in a more light and mobile style. With fewer possessions and fluctuating futures, these young people—whether refugees or not—occupy shared spaces but still need privacy. The proposal, in other words, allowed people to own a small pod that could be moved into featureless halls while also being able to close down and lock up if the need arose.

The units shared many features with the other schemes in this exhibition. There was a self-build element, because the pod—known as a Hawi—arrived in a kit that had to be assembled. There was an interest in the external space and landscaping as the designers also tried to open up the office building to the surrounding neighborhood by creating a walkway through the grounds. There was a commitment to transforming the feel of a building through carefully designed objects, with the idea of creating a more pleasant living environment. As the architects put it, the aim was to create enclosure and safety within the wider society: "It doesn't matter if you're in a bigger atmosphere because you have this privacy and warmth. It is a surrounding that holds you, that keeps you close." Indeed, the Hawi enveloped its inhabitants in such a way that they became more accepting of open and featureless buildings. The lead designer believed that there is "a big anxiety about emptiness," and the project tried to show that there can be beauty in the contrast between a featureless hall and the privacy of a pod.[31]

There seemed, at times, to be an almost obsessive interest in this aesthetic contrast between the nonplace of the office and the personal pods. This led to some striking photographs of the bare building punctuated by warmly lit modular units crammed with belongings. Yet the reality did not quite live up to the vision. In the office block, there were only a few Hawi units, and they did not seem particularly inviting. They stood surrounded by discarded office furniture in a drab medium-sized room. There was not enough money to install the units at scale, so the buildings felt unfilled yet also cluttered with other things. The purity of the architect's vision was compromised by circumstances, and the beauty of the photographs did not match the limited scale of the experiment and the imperfections of the site. There was perhaps a lesson here about cost and the importance of practical and small-scale interventions.

ARCHITECTURAL VISIONS

Architects often succumb to the temptations of large-scale transformation, the desire to reshape human relations as well as improve immediate surroundings. This might be seen as one of the most attractive things about the profession, although it also leads to suspicion. The "poetical" projects might be criticized for doing too much, tipping too far into the pit of over-complexity, but they tended to pack big dreams into small interventions. Across all three schemes, there was a hopeful expectation that inhabitants of emergency refugee shelters could transform the world—or, more prosaically, that they could have the time and inclination to get involved in construction and planning. The ethics of experimentation became an issue, too, as each intervention was driven by bigger ideals that ended up being tested on others who had to shoulder the burden of unrealistic expectations.[32] Yet none of this should detract from the concrete achievements of this Viennese example. These were pared-back interventions that contained depth and vision. The architects took a small budget and applied a large amount of creativity. They created a series of cheap interventions that transformed the experience of a space, and all of them were united by the idea that shelter does not purely reside in vast structures. This, in the end, is the essence of shelter as poetics: the idea that when we think of shelters, we may need to think small. Even modest items, such as umbrellas and blankets, can change the quality of everyday space. Crucially, these interventions can be planned in such a way as to leverage limited funds and at least *try* to give people greater control over spaces.

In his book *The Poetics of Space*, Bachelard draws our attention to our emotional response to buildings. He writes of how the house is a shelter for not just the body but also for memories and reveries, hopes and ideals. The house "shelters day-dreaming," he writes, "the house protects the dreamer, the house allows one to dream in peace."[33] Bachelard argues that our homes generate a sensory reaction that includes some kind of rootedness without which humans would be fragmented and dispersed. This is often forgotten in the provision of emergency shelter. The assumption seems to be that shelters have to be minimal because they are temporary, that shelters have to be unburdened by experiences, immediate in their aims and urgent in their construction. Yet it is not the case that shelter is *only* about protecting physical life. Shelters can *also* become places for daydreaming, furnished with the imaginative equipment Marina Warner so eloquently describes.[34]

The fact is people do not suspend their higher-order human ambitions just because they have to flee and end up living somewhere temporarily. If anything, these ambitions become more acute. "Whenever the human being has found the slightest shelter," Bachelard writes, "we see the imagination build walls of impalpable shadows."[35] This is one of his most striking insights—that wherever humans lie down, they begin a complex interplay between their minds and their surroundings. In the end, buildings are changed by this relationship too. "Faced with the bestial hostility of the storm and the hurricane, the house's virtues of protection and resistance are transposed into human virtues. The house acquires the physical and moral energy of a human body."[36] This idea may be extravagantly expressed, but it is certainly compelling. Bachelard reminds us that living in the most basic shelters can have a profound effect that aid workers need to take more seriously when providing relief.

7 | SHELTER AS AESTHETICS

The Yellow Bubble in Paris

ON MAY 31, 2016, the mayor of Paris, Anne Hidalgo, announced that a new humanitarian center would be opening in the north of
the French capital. The idea was to provide accommodation for migrants
who had been sleeping in increasing numbers on the streets of the city, often
under elevated metro tracks. The conditions in these camps were terrible—
cold, insecure, and insanitary—and Hidalgo considered the situation to
be a serious affront to the image of a progressive city. Her humanitarian
center was meant to solve the problem. Rather than sleeping on the streets,
the migrants would receive a bed, three meals per day, clean clothes, and
hot showers. The center had been designed to provide a safe and dignified
welcome for people arriving in Paris, expressing the city's Enlightenment
values.[1]

The project began soon after Hidalgo's announcement, and it was ex-
ecuted with impressive speed and efficiency. Within a few months, there
was an organization to manage the project and an architect appointed to
design it. A location was identified in an old railway depot near Porte de la
Chapelle at the northern fringes of the city, and the center was constructed
over the summer of 2016 with a colorful, playful design. Its most dramatic
feature was an enormous inflatable hall made from bright-yellow plastic
with gray-and-red detailing, which stood at the entrance to the site. This
"bubble," as it was known, became an emblem of the humanitarian center,
appearing as a logo on signs and leaflets. It could be seen for miles around,

rising over the tarmac of the abandoned industrial site and extending over eight hundred square meters.[2]

The so-called Yellow Bubble was intended to be a highly visible gesture of compassionate intent. For the mayor, it was meant to signal that Paris, the city of human rights, would welcome migrants in civilized conditions.[3] Hidalgo wanted to produce "a landmark, a signpost of humanity," which could be seen "from distant vistas in Paris."[4] Members of her administration proudly spoke of how they could see the flash of yellow from an airplane, from the Eurostar heading into Paris, and from the commuter lines connecting the city's suburbs. The bubble was visible from trains arriving at the Gare du Nord and from cars traversing the Boulevard Périphérique, the ring road that encircles the city.[5]

Such visibility was crucial to Hidalgo's plan, and it was defined by the inflatable structure. As one member of the mayor's team put it, the idea was to shelter migrants in a way that was characterized by "goodwill and beauty." It was meant to be a site with "a lot of humanity and a lot of sensibility."[6] The bubble itself—which was mainly a welcome and reception area—became so iconic that the whole center became known simply as la Bulle, or the Bubble. Its image appeared in stock photographs to illustrate articles about migration in France, and its distinctive outline of three intersecting curves could be found on promotional materials for the center. An image of the bubble even featured on the mayoral holiday card for the eighteenth *arrondissement*, where the center was based.[7]

When I began to spend some time in the bubble, however, it seemed that the symbolic emphasis was a problem. The design had been chosen for its aesthetic power, but the architecture was far from practical. The beauty of the design was directed outward, containing a message for political constituencies that were actually peripheral to the purpose of the building itself. The bubble did not seem to have the best interests of refugees at its heart, and it soon became embroiled in complex strategies of containment and control. This gave rise to big questions about shelter. Should beauty be important to refugee accommodation? What part do aesthetics play in the response to humanitarian emergencies? And when does a striking design actually end up disguising a place of misery, distracting from the failures of a given system?

FIGURE 7.1.   The Yellow Bubble at the Centre Humanitaire Paris-Nord. Porte de la Chapelle, Paris, France. © University of Oxford / Mark E. Breeze, 2017.

ARCHITECTURAL AIMS

The architect of the humanitarian center, Julien Beller, was part of a radical Parisian collective known as 6B. He was known in Paris for transforming postindustrial, gentrifying neighborhoods with ephemeral interventions and temporary designs. His studio, when I visited, was situated in a run-down building in the working-class suburb of Saint-Denis, peppered with murals, social enterprises, and youthful energy. When we sat down to talk, Beller expressed his vision in the clearest possible terms. "I think a city should be flexible. . . . A city should be alive, a city should evolve," he said. This emphasis on fast, mobile structures had previously led Beller to work with cultural installations at festivals and later with travelers and Romani people. His buildings expressed the language of impermanence, and he had a dynamic and rebellious image that became a crucial part of the project. The *New Yorker* reflected on his style: "Dressed in black, with a glinting nose stud and a terse yet thoughtful manner, he suggests less a Libeskind or a Piano than someone who might chain himself to a fence at a work site."[8]

Julien Beller's image certainly fit the municipal vision of this new humanitarian center, which had also been described as youthful, hip, and alternative.[9] As the city's architectural advisor explained, Mayor Hidalgo had insisted on "an extremely quick response but one that was also well thought out." She wanted the center to be flexible and short-term but also have a "powerful aesthetic sensibility." Temporality was, therefore, an important part of Beller's brief since the city had identified a site for the humanitarian center in an old railway depot, which was due to be turned into a university campus a few years down the line. Beller was also an ideal choice as architect because he was "outside the norms of the profession," and he had already demonstrated the ability to work on quick, temporary projects. Even critics received his involvement with enthusiasm as he had shown that architects could make short-term, low-budget interventions. As one commentator put it, this was "the first time a talented architect has been called upon to put together an encampment. . . . The first time that a public authority has equipped itself with the capabilities, with the talents of an architect who is really worthy of this title."[10]

After Mayor Hidalgo announced the project in May 2016, Julien Beller was brought on board in June. He had the summer to build the humanitarian center, and it opened for business in November, with a planned lifespan of just two years. Beller divided the site into two distinct halves. At the back of the site, he developed an empty, graffiti-ridden, and decrepit two-story, ten-thousand-square-meter railway warehouse into sleeping accommodation, which became known as la Halle, or the Hall. It was filled with eight "neighborhoods" of chipboard cabins, each with their own communal areas, shower block, and canteen. The aim, he told me, was to create shelter at a smaller and more human scale through the use of rough, new structures inside the site. This would ensure that people did not feel industrially housed in huge rooms, "like a camp [of] rabbits one next to the other."[11]

Beller also used scaffolding to elevate some of the rooms and to create new stairs, and he ensured that everything was removable (the building, after all, was due to be destroyed). He gave each neighborhood a distinctive color scheme, inviting artists to add sculptures and paint murals to the giant spaces. He ensured that each cabin only had four beds. This meant that, although the capacity of the hall could go up to four hundred people, inhabitants could live on a smaller, more human scale.

At the front of the site was the other half of Beller's plan: the inflatable structure known as la Bulle, or the Bubble. This was where the migrants and refugees were first received, and it was what most people saw from the street. The bubble was located on an old tarmac parking lot surrounded by a fence, accessed through a pair of turnstiles. It was so large that it loomed over its surroundings. It contained a waiting area and a bank of shipping-container offices that were stacked one on top of another. This was where new arrivals were registered and introduced to the facilities. Upon entering the bubble, the first thing you noticed was the strangely yellow hue. The sunlight filtered through the plastic walls, and the constant sounds of chatting and squeaking generated bizarre acoustic effects. Sound bounced off the irregular shape of the structure, and in summer, the space was also marked by heat and odor. With no insulation, it became sweltering, smelling of stale sweat from people who had been sleeping rough for weeks on end. Visually, the design of the interior was simple. Around the edge, there was seating. On the tarmac, there were games. Right in the middle, there were offices.

From outside, the bubble looked more impressive. It was tall, wide, and colored in intersecting yellow-and-gray stripes. The mayor's architectural advisor had wanted it to be a symbol, "a sign for the refugees," and the design was meant to indicate that Paris would "take on the responsibility to welcome and host migrants in good conditions." The bubble was meant to be "a sign of hope, of joy," as well as a message on coming development to local Parisians who lived in this poor area of the city. The structure aimed to allow

FIGURE 7.2.   Inside la Bulle. Porte de la Chapelle, Paris, France. © University of Oxford / Mark E. Breeze, 2017.

the residents of nearby tower blocks to "look onto a landscape that was a little less bleak [*misérabiliste*]. . . . An architecture that was a little less precarious, of a certain quality." The lively aesthetic of the bubble, I was told, could "speak to everyone" with its "bold colors and shapes." "When you enter into the bubble, it's pretty magical," one of the architectural advisors said. "It's like you're sheltered away from the world . . . like in a mother's womb."[12]

UTOPIAN SHELTERS

The design of the bubble was not actually created by Julien Beller himself. Beller had recruited someone else to set it up—an artist and engineer called Hans Walter Müller, who had been promoting inflatable architecture since the 1960s.[13] The collaboration was consistent with Beller's whole approach. As he explained it, "I don't want to be like God. I don't want to be the architect who decides everything. I want to bring people together with all the right skills."[14] This, again, reflected his commitment to the ethos of festivals and temporary installations, filling spaces with ideas made by many hands. In this spirit, Beller reached out to Müller, who was already known to Beller from the festival circuit and was now in his eighties. Originally from Germany, but a long-term resident in France, Müller had long been presenting these bubble-like structures as futuristic, ecological visions of life.

I heard that Müller was living in a bubble in the countryside south of Paris, so I set out with my colleagues to meet him.[15] On the journey out of the city, I began to think about the close relationship between shelter and utopianism, and the connections became clearer and clearer as I headed south. Finding Müller's home was not easy. After disembarking at a small, rural railway station, we had to walk along a country road through pine woodland to reach an isolated patch of forest where Müller had inflated his home. The address seemed to make no sense. Google was no help, and after getting thoroughly lost, we called for help. It turned out the inflatable home was hidden behind some rusting green gates in a densely wooded area nearby.

When we finally arrived, the house was as eerie as I had imagined. It looked like a bubble, a gently pulsating red-and-white plastic hemisphere emerging from a hollow in the ground. A barely audible hum indicated a distant motor pumping air inside, and through the broadleaf trees above, I could hear birdlife chirruping and squawking away. Hans Walter

Müller—an elderly German man in his eighties, dressed in a turtleneck and bright-red glasses—came out to greet me. He immediately invited us inside and offered a tour around his home. As I stepped inside, the sun illuminated the red-and-white stripes that curved far above us, giving the place a feeling of light and expansiveness. The sounds of woodland birds penetrated the thin synthetic walls, and our steps softly clunked around the wooden floor—beneath which lay Müller's darker, earthier sleeping quarters, which had been buried into the ground.

Müller sat down and offered us some wine. He began to talk about how it felt to live in this bubble and explain his idea of a lightweight form of living. Unlike traditional buildings, he said, inflatable architecture is alive. Like the birds outside, it wants to fly away. Most buildings push down into the earth with their solid mass of brick or concrete, but inflatable architecture is always pushed up by a small motor that constantly pumps air inside the plastic sheath of the bubble. To prevent the whole thing from becoming airborne, the sheath has to be lightly anchored around the periphery, which leaves the skin taut and pulsating. Müller described how this made his house feel like an organism. The motor is always working, he said, like "a heart that beats continuously." "Our bodies, too, are composed of fluids and tensions and pressures," Müller explained. He thought his home was similar. It was a "form built by nature." It was organic and ecological. He described how he had to check the pressure of his home, just like a doctor would monitor the pressure of blood to ensure good health. He also explained how he had to periodically change the plastic membrane, helping the house to shed its skin.[16]

Müller got up from his seat to turn off the pump, illustrating how his home relied on constant maintenance. The gentle hum of the motor ceased, and the outer sheath began to fall; without its heartbeat, the bubble would slowly deflate, the plastic creaking, folding, and wilting over our heads. Just as I began to fear for the bottle of wine, Müller turned the motor back on with a start, and his house returned to health. The plastic skin became tight again. This was Müller's dream, his utopia—a shelter so light it was almost ephemeral, an architectural form that was in tune with nature, a home he had to keep healthy, a home that felt like an organism, a home that was made from a foldable piece of plastic, which was easy to move and fast to erect.[17] It is unsurprising that Beller saw how this could be a symbol of weightlessness in our increasingly mobile world.

SPECTACLES OF SHELTER

Basic shelter is not, at first glance, a terrain in which utopias like this obviously loom large. When provided as a humanitarian gesture, emergency shelter is usually considered a short-term concern; it usually involves doing what one can, with limited resources, in constrained conditions. Shelter tends to be about defending a bottom line rather than pushing an upper ideal, focusing on immediate needs rather than expansive visions of society.[18] But from the very start of my research, I noticed that utopian proposals like this kept reappearing in the provision of emergency shelter, lying embedded in many designs. They could be seen in attempts to create "welcome neighborhoods" in large cities.[19] They were visible in schemes to manufacture tents from innovative "structural fabric."[20] They could be found in the design of flat-packed refugee shelters, in hexagonal structures, and in stackable homes.[21] More ambitious utopias, resembling Thomas More's original text, also appeared in concrete blocks in Vienna and proposed new islands in the Mediterranean.[22]

Müller's inflatable architecture was perhaps the most strikingly utopian proposal I came across in this research, which was probably no surprise because the whole approach to the Parisian Yellow Bubble was driven by aesthetics and symbolic power. Yet despite Müller's expansive vision and the ethereal world of his inflatable home, the utopian ideals seemed to dissipate as it was transferred from the rural pine woodland to the grimy streets of the inner city. When the birdsong was replaced by traffic and the slow-paced life of an octogenarian designer was switched for the screeches and chatter of a constantly fluctuating population of frustrated people, the design seemed less appropriate. That cool, earthy hollow beneath the broad-leaf trees had turned into a hot, plastic hemisphere on dark tarmac under the full power of the Parisian summer sun.

The result was—as anyone who spent any time in the bubble could tell you—a lot of heat, noise, and smell. The sounds of chattering and talking echoed incessantly around the structure. Sitting under the plastic sheath felt like being in a greenhouse. The manager of the center tried installing a sprinkler system to deal with the stifling heat, but this just produced fine sheens of water falling from perforated tubes, spraying around the plastic insides and turning a hot place into a hot and humid place. The situation was so bad that the site manager laughed indulgently when I asked about the design. "It's certainly original," he acknowledged, but "we're always immersed in noise, the brouhaha. . . . That can be exhausting by the end of the day when you've welcomed two hundred people."[23]

Müller's vision was not very practical for this purpose; it was a spectacle. Its protective skin, its organic layer, its very lightness and fragility made it symbolic rather than practical. But did that detract from its utopianism? The anthropologist Peter Redfield argues that utopia can be buried in many places, even in the most unlikely of designs. He makes this argument in relation to something called the iShack, an improved basic shelter developed for a South African township that first emerged in 2011.[24] The iShack was an enhanced version of the corrugated iron shacks that already populated such settlements, but it included improvements, such as a waste-compost system, a fireproof coating, and a photovoltaic panel. As Redfield points out, these improved shelters could be easily dismissed as measly and restricted, modest and limiting, but they incubated great hopes and ideals—something indicated by that small, lowercase prefix, that little *i* hinting at a "gleaming technological horizon." The iShack contained hopes of sustainability, of low carbon footprints, of improved lives, even if it did nothing to address the structures that caused people to live there in the first place.[25] This was utopia, Redfield argues, but a limited utopia. It was a utopia that existed within constraints.[26]

The Yellow Bubble can be seen in a similar way. It faced many constraints and had many limitations, but it nevertheless involved a utopia. It had been chosen as a symbol, something bright and recognizable, an object that indicated protection and lightness of touch. Müller had hoped that the bubble would "bring a little sunshine" and "a little joy" to those passing through. In the end, however, the architecture also had to negotiate not just with issues like heat and smell but also with the tense, taut, precarious practicalities of migration politics in France.

BEYOND A BED FOR THE NIGHT

"When we began the operation," I was told at city hall, "we only had one priority: to shelter the refugees so that they could have some calm after their long and exhausting trip." The idea was to create a space where people could "eat, sleep, and have some administrative support," a place where people could receive an "unconditional welcome" in Paris. This was crucial to Mayor Hidalgo's vision. "It's extremely important for the mayor," one of her advisors told me, "that everyone, absolutely without distinction, will be welcomed on this site."[27] It was a laudable idea that drove the whole project, but it soon had to engage with some hard political realities. In order to get the project off the ground, the city had to partner with the state in order to share the cost of running the center, and it soon turned out that the Ministry of the Interior did not agree on the idea of an unconditional welcome. The bubble became a space where residents would enter into a contract. In return for their shelter, they had to visit the police, register their information, and enter the formal system of asylum.[28]

This was, perhaps, inevitable. Humanitarianism always has to reckon with politics because it is bound up in decisions about who gets access to resources.[29] In the case of the Yellow Bubble, this generated important questions: How would the center be financed? Would migrants be permitted to stay as long as they wished? And if they were ejected, where would they go? Before long, it was clear that the mayor's original vision of an unconditional welcome was not sustainable. The center provided only four hundred beds, which was a tiny number given the extent of the need. Meanwhile, the flow of new arrivals kept increasing. If no one moved out of the center, then nothing more could be done for the thousands of other people arriving in the city every month. But if, alternatively, people were only allowed to stay for a limited time—say, a week or two—something needed to happen to them afterward. They could hardly be thrown back out on the streets since that would leave them barely better off than they were when they entered the bubble two weeks previously. But they couldn't stay in the bubble indefinitely.

The result was a classic humanitarian dilemma, which concerned how an emergency project like this has to engage with long-term issues.[30] It was now clear that an unconditional welcome could only ever be extended to a very small number of people, leaving many more people unassisted. It was also clear that providing comfortable accommodation did not solve any long-term questions of status. A conditional welcome, in contrast, would end up compromised by political realities, leaving humanitarianism just an arm of the government. These tensions between short-term needs and longer-term implications are very common in humanitarian relief, but here, the stakes were even higher because the site was so visible. The project had always wanted to send a prominent message to the world about the compassionate values of Paris, and so the inevitable compromises became even more awkward due to the scale of the publicity surrounding them.

When the center finally opened, the rules of entry stipulated that people were only allowed to stay for a limited period before being processed by the state or ejected back on the streets. Before long, the center became known as a "platform for dispatching" migrants to other places. The phrase was part of the official discourse, and I heard it regularly in the mayor's office. A disillusioned member of staff on the ground put things more vividly. The place had become a "postbox," he said. Migrants were posted in, registered, and then carried off for delivery elsewhere. When a migrant entered the revolving doors of the Yellow Bubble, in other words, they immediately made a pact. In return for two weeks of comfort, they agreed to visit the local *préfecture de police*, where they would register and give up their fingerprints. Their fingerprints would then be checked against the European database, leaving them subject to deportation if they had been registered elsewhere. Finally, the individual was transferred out of the center on a scheduled bus that left Paris to one of the many state-run Reception and Orientation Centers around France.[31]

I spent some days observing this process in the bubble, where the contract was explained. As the manager of the bubble put it to me, "when people arrive, they have to sign a contract, where they commit to respecting the different appointments we're going to organize." This included the appointment with the police, the appointment to have fingerprints taken, and the appointment to be transferred out of the center on a bus after a period of five to ten days. "If the person doesn't present themselves for these administrative appointments," he went on, "they've broken the contract." They are then ejected from the center. To use the formal, administrative language, they are "APEC-ed: given a notice entitled 'Arrêt de prise en charge.'"[32] This notice says to them, "We're obliged to mark the end of our care." They are then put back on the streets with the telephone number of a homeless service.

Legal activists condemned this practice on the grounds that the deal was not clear at the beginning, that, in some sense, it was a forced choice. Certainly, it was explained very quickly in the registration process, but there was a simple, visual equation that appeared on posters throughout the rooms and halls, its brutal clarity making any question of misinterpretation impossible. It was an image of a fingerprint printed next to an image

FIGURE 7.3. Logo and information board, Centre Humanitaire Paris-Nord. Porte de la Chapelle, Paris, France. © University of Oxford / Mark E. Breeze, 2017.

of a bed with a simple equal sign between them. The message was clear: biometric data was required if you wanted shelter. From the perspective of the manager, this deal was necessary to keep the system functioning. "If you don't respect the process," he told me, "there's a grain of sand in the gears. That means that everything else gets jammed and we can no longer welcome new people." The center, in other words, relied on people moving smoothly through the "sorting and dispatching process."[33] This was a long way from Hidalgo's vision of unconditional hospitality. Refugees and other migrants had to surrender to the system that had so often alienated them, and if they wished to take up the offer of humanitarian assistance, they had to be registered and processed by the state.

CLEARING THE STREETS

The legal activists I spoke to were quite clear that this sorting-and-dispatching feature was related to the other key purpose of the bubble: the political imperative to get migrants off the streets. This, of course, was not conspiracy or speculation; it was the whole aim of the center itself. As Mayor Hidalgo had put it at the very beginning of the project, the idea was to replace the terrible living conditions on the streets with something more dignified and humane.[34] It would be naïve, however, to suppose that this was only ever in the interest of migrants. It was also an electoral strategy. Clearing camps from the Parisian streets, after all, was a response to ordinary voters who found them ugly and threatening. As the architect of the center put it when I asked him, the project is "not only humanitarian, it's also [about] taking care of the city, security problems, and hygiene problems."[35] The informal camps were perceived as unhygienic and unsafe. Many voters were concerned about the very existence of the camps, combined with a sense of embarrassment that Paris, this cradle of Western culture and civilization, could not find a way to manage the large and visible population of homeless migrants sleeping on its streets.

The humanitarian center, therefore, was consistent with a long tradition of policies that tried to deal with migration and homelessness. Then president François Hollande had already instigated a "zero-tolerance" policy on informal camps after the growth of the Calais Jungle, which had led the police to disperse and destroy informal settlements in an ever-more aggressive manner. Accusations of brutality were common. The police were blamed for driving people into the countryside, leaving them without possessions, stealing blankets in the middle of winter, and arriving in the dead of night to bulldoze any tents and possessions on the streets.[36] Early one morning, I went to a large street camp near Porte de la Chapelle to witness a clearance that was rumored to happen that day. Although I was blocked from witnessing the actual evacuation, it was possible to follow the aftermath: teams of policemen and refuse workers in hazmat suits working their way through the detritus. It was a clear, crisp summer dawn, and the roads were strangely quiet. Hundreds of people had been sleeping under bridges, slip roads, and underpasses just an hour previously, but their poignant remnants were now being collected with rubber gloves and scissor tongs. Cheap tents, identification documents, sleeping bags, and groceries were all being picked up and taken to the dump.

I heard later from many people subjected to these forced removals that the humanitarian center was making police action more acceptable. It enabled the government to say to migrants that they have somewhere to go, that they have no reason to be on the streets. A legal activist made this point particularly clearly when she told me that the center "legitimizes violence toward refugees." "Before the creation of the center," she said, "there were already a lot of roundups, arrests, checks, teargassing by the police. . . . [But] since the opening of this center, we have seen police repression become more and more significant." The center, she continued, is an opportunity for the police to say that "if you are not registered, then you have no right to stay outside." The camp helped disperse and remove people.[37]

This echoed Georges-Eugène Haussmann's cleansing of Paris in the 1850s and 1860s, when hovels and the homeless were swept aside on the grounds of hygiene and rationalization. It was a point also underlined by an architectural critic I interviewed, who sketched out how design contributed to this system. The mechanisms for clearing the streets, he said, were part of the Yellow Bubble's design. "The space we are discussing is not solely the space that is marked on the map as being the humanitarian center," he said. It's also "the barbed wire, the barriers, the four and a half kilometers of fences in the city of Paris, the rocks that are put around the center to prevent people from setting up there . . . all of that is a whole." This assemblage of objects, he told me, was all part of the mise-en-scène: the arrangement of props, scenery, and backdrops where the theater of humanitarianism combined with the theater of clearance and control. The design of the humanitarian center was crucial here, he said, with its symbolism playing an important role.[38]

As the bubble went up, the tents came down. The center created an authorized version of encampment, which replaced the eyesores under metro tracks with a pretty symbol of the city's compassion. There was a fascinating reversal going on here, too, as the attempt to make street camps invisible was challenged by activists, who wanted even greater visibility of the shocking conditions on the streets. Fellow citizens could only be made to think about migration, they argued, by *seeing* the dirty consequences of state migration policy. These issues were easier to ignore after the Yellow Bubble started hiding migrants behind its taut yellow skin.[39] There was an irony here, too, because this was a highly visible statement of benevolent intent. The declaration of compassion actually made compassion more difficult as it hid the real problem of migrant homelessness. In the end, French citizens would find fewer informal camps on their streets because the migrants were being sorted and dispatched elsewhere.[40]

Nowhere was this dynamic of visibility and invisibility clearer than in the fence that surrounded the humanitarian center. This tall, chain-link barrier was turned into a canvas for an art installation. At the request of Julien Beller, a pair of visual designers wove colorful, adhesive, insulating tape through the wire. The artists, known as *les soeurs Chevalme*, aimed to transform the barrier into a pleasant, joyful pattern, which was meant to resemble Islamic latticework or the bright geometric motifs on a mosque. It was another of Beller's collaborations—a simple, cheap, and clever intervention that was meant to produce, in the architect's words, something less "carceral."[41] The aim was to make the center more secure while also permeating it with an artistic sensibility. The mayor's architectural advisor also praised this move, explaining how it was integral to the center's vision. "This fencing was really something very, very important for us," she said. "Once again, we wanted to approach this in a Parisian manner, signaling that, yes, this is a fence, but it can be a kindly [*bienveillant*] fence ... a frame for an artistic intervention."[42]

As critics would later put it, this fence was part of the mise-en-scène for the whole shelter. It was part of a landscape of "hostile urban design," or "defensive architecture," which prevented people from finding an informal bed on the streets of Paris. The most common examples of defensive architecture are park benches designed to disrupt sleeping bodies and the subtle use of spiky surfaces under sheltered areas of the pavement.[43] In French, this is known as "bristling" (*se hérisser*) the city streets. The streets around the bubble were bristled in many places, particularly in the form of rocks and barbs across the pavements and roads. One morning, for example, a

FIGURE 7.4.   Perimeter fence with art installation. Porte de la Chapelle, Paris, France. © University of Oxford / Mark E. Breeze, 2017.

collection of "antimigrant boulders" appeared on a prominent traffic island to stop migrants from sleeping rough while they waited for a place in the bubble. They were spaced precisely so that a single sleeping body could not fit between them. The boulders were subtler than the bristles—they aspired to be humanitarian architecture, not just defensive architecture—but they had a similar effect. Julien Beller was asked to turn them into another artistic intervention, but this time he refused. As he recalled, "I said 'no, *please*, I have enough work inside; I won't decorate your stones to say they are nice stones.'"[44]

Hostile architecture like this does not stand in contradiction with the symbolic hospitality of the bubble, however. The two are closely related. To use Derridean language again, such hostility and hospitality are locked together. There is a kernel of hostility lying in every hospitable encounter.[45] What made this example distinctive, however, was the role of symbolism and aesthetics. Many of my interviewees described how the Yellow Bubble provided a welcome for migrants while also forcing them to engage in hostile political processing, but the architecture pushed this tension beneath the surface. The center aspired to be fast and symbolic, proclaiming benevolence without acknowledging politics. Yet it showed only one side of the dyad of hospitality. It revealed the beauty while failing to recognize the pain.

ARCHITECTURAL DILEMMAS

Over the last two decades, many scholars have noticed a decline in the ability of humanitarians to make a real and lasting impact in many spheres of life along with a related rise in doctrines that emphasize self-help through entrepreneurship and resilience.[46] Small-scale humanitarian designs often reflect this new environment, indicating a neoliberal move away from top-down assistance and toward the idea that people should help themselves.[47] In this context, humanitarian *performances* have become more important. As professional aid workers become squeezed by political encroachments and the rise of the private sector, humanitarianism has often become focused on theatricality and aesthetics.[48] Architecture is a crucial part of this process.

Through bright, optimistic detailing, new designs like the Yellow Bubble can add a veneer of humanitarian legitimacy to repressive situations. Many of the people I interviewed made this point particularly colorfully. "For the refugees, I think it's a big fucking lie," one activist told me. "This looks like the entrance to Disneyland," he continued, but the reality is very different. There was a central irony, this interviewee said, that a so-called "signpost of humanity," a hypervisible symbol of compassion, was actually making the violence of the state *less* visible.[49] A legal activist agreed, expressing frustration at the way the design had attracted so much attention from the Parisian middle classes. "Frankly, it does not interest me at all whether it is beautiful," she told me. "What counts is sheltering people, and that is not at all what is being done."[50]

The case of the Yellow Bubble speaks to this difficulty of acting effectively in a politically hostile world, a context that is often illuminated through the quandary of the camp doctor. This is best described as the situation a physician might find themselves in when they have to work in a highly coercive environment, such as a detention center, internment camp, or some other location where people are neglected, confined, or transported against their will. Here, the camp doctor's role is to heal people, treating the worst cases of suffering, but they have little power to address the root causes of such distress except through high-profile refusal. Their role is to provide care but in terrible situations, and they ultimately have to release people, who become exposed again to mistreatment and coercion. The problem is not just that the camp doctor is powerless to change the structures of oppression but also that their presence ends up serving and legitimizing these structures. In the end, the camp doctor makes the camp itself somehow more acceptable.[51]

Like the camp doctor, the camp architect faces a dilemma. Architecture can succeed in making a camp more pleasant and colorful, and this is certainly important. Despite the legal activist saying that it does not interest her whether or not a camp is beautiful, it would certainly be of concern if the camp had been actively ugly. Imagine the critical reaction if a camp only provided a grim, gray, concrete environment.[52] Yet although architecture can improve spaces such as refugee camps, there is always a suspicion that such interventions are a form of window dressing.[53] The Yellow Bubble shows how designs can be driven by the need to communicate a political message rather than by the interests of inhabitants. There is always an element of design that turns outward rather than inward like this, containing a message for wider constituencies—in this case, voters and citizens of Paris—rather than working to improve the environment of those living inside.

On March 31, 2018, the Yellow Bubble center finally closed. The structure was deflated and packed away, and the railway yard where it had been located was prepared for demolition.[54] Visitors walking around the site could still find remnants. Colorful murals still flashed on broken walls, and peeling stencils were brightly illuminated by the spring sunshine beyond the fence. Some parts, however, were clearly decaying. The delicately woven strips of insulation tape, which had been formed into Islamic patterns around the outside fence, were now turning to shreds. They had gradually been picked away by bored residents over many months, their ends left fluttering in the breeze. Soon after the closure, another huge street camp was evacuated and destroyed at nearby Porte de la Villette, showing how the underlying system of managing migration was left unchanged. The "kindly" fence had become just another fence, serving to block a new area of the city from migrants, who had become quite familiar with attempts to restrict their access and send them away from the city streets.

CONCLUSION

We lost our home, which means the familiarity of daily life. We lost our occupation, which means the confidence that we are of some use in this world. We lost our language, which means the naturalness of reactions, the simplicity of gestures, the unaffected expression of feelings.

—*Hannah Arendt, The Jewish Writings*

THIS BOOK BEGAN WITH A puzzle in two parts. The first involved deconstruction, exploring how we might define shelter as a basic human need and starting with the bottom line. What is the essence of shelter? I asked. How can we encapsulate our common human requirements? The second puzzle involved reconstruction, asking: How have humanitarians provided shelter in practice? What works, what fails, and what is the role of design?

In this conclusion, I pull together the threads in order to provide an answer to these questions while also making a proposal of my own. In order to respond to these fragments of shelter, I suggest, we need to think about the principle of autonomy. At its heart, I argue, shelter should be a place that people can control, a place where people can pick up the pieces of their lives and make choices about what comes next. This should be seen as an exercise in design, like those that I have explored in this book. "We lost our home, which means the familiarity of daily life," wrote Hannah Arendt.[1] The fundamental task of shelter is to restore that familiarity. Given that shelter is so fragmented, so indeterminate and contextual, the most important thing is that humanitarians allow inhabitants as much power as possible over their daily existence—however limited that may be.

SEVEN SHELTERS IN PRACTICE

The first chapter of this book set out the central problem of emergency shelter by examining a project that sought to mass-produce a flat-pack home. Known later as the Better Shelter, this was a rudimentary structure delivered in two boxes that contained literally hundreds of components: small pieces of shelter that could be reconstructed in emergencies. The IKEA shelter was an attempt to capture the essence of shelter, but it demonstrated what happens when we try to articulate some common ground: shelter has a tendency to splinter into pieces, shattering into parts with no single definition. There were disputes about how "basic" this shelter was and long lists of elements that it neglected. It became clear that the shelter was culturally and politically situated, and it did not translate very well to other places. The central lesson of this chapter was that attempts to produce a universal basic shelter will always flounder. It would be better to give refugees greater power to shape its final form and, rather than seeking a model that could be used anywhere, to encourage refugees to define what they need given the peculiarities of their situation and the country in which they live.

The second chapter turned away from the idea of a bare, basic shelter to focus instead on more expansive and comprehensive settlements. It focused on two large refugee camps in Jordan called Za'atari and Azraq, which were defined through comprehensive metrics. The aim in these cases was not to design a single unit but rather to create whole towns shaped by minimum standards. This was a story in two parts. In Za'atari, the camp inhabitants managed to wrest back some control over the rigid plan by moving shelters and filling the gaps between them, establishing family compounds and a multitude of shared social spaces. In Azraq, however, shelters were fixed, detailed rules were established, and surveillance extended across the whole site. This resulted in a place that stifled self-sufficiency and individual flourishing. The lesson of this case was that greater autonomy in places like Za'atari can produce a more pleasant living environment by allowing refugees to serve their own needs and build social and cultural lives.

Chapter 3 examined a very different approach to shelter, which was characteristic of Athens in Greece. Focusing particularly on a squat called Hotel City Plaza, this chapter examined how shelter could become a springboard for bigger ideological debates about borders and states. Hotel City Plaza was founded by a group of activists in an empty hotel, where they established a self-governing community for refugees. The activists pointed out that shelter is always engaged in politics and that any attempt to be neutral will become blown off course by the prevailing winds of state power. They wanted to create a place where everyone took equal part in decision making, but critics argued that they could never operate at scale and that they would end up excluding certain people on the basis of their political opinions. Shelters like this were fighting for a world without borders, but as a result, they offered little for people who actually *wanted* to live in a nation-state or who preferred to build their own lives rather than commit to cohousing.

Chapter 4 demonstrated the limitations of the activist vision by turning to the case of Lebanon. Here, it was possible to see what happened when a state prevented the centralized provision of shelter and proceeded without a coordinated plan. The result was that refugees were left in an assortment of substandard shelters, often at the mercy of landlords who sold them spaces in factories, farms, and half-built warehouses. The humanitarian interventions revolved around the piecemeal improvement of these shelters, but it was difficult to change such poor conditions without a wider strategy. The result was shelter as a form of tactics. It unfolded in a fragmented, haphazard manner and tended to benefit those with preexisting advantages, such as landlords. Refugees ended up making choices within a limited range of options, and they were forced by circumstance to inhabit unsuitable buildings with insufficient support.

Chapter 5 turned to Germany, which took a different approach to shelter. After welcoming large numbers of refugees, the authorities in many cities designated huge empty buildings to be used as housing, and in Berlin, the most famous was Tempelhof Airport, which had been built under Nazi rule in the 1930s. Such locations seemed deeply inappropriate, but they represented a fundamentally pragmatic response to the problem, which aimed to prevent vulnerable people from sleeping on the street. In some respects, the approach succeeded. Shelters like Tempelhof provided basic protection and three meals a day, but life in these shelters became peppered with intricate constraints. Even simple things like noise, food, and lighting were subject to small-scale bureaucratic restrictions. Often, it seemed like the things refugees *could* have been given power over were being deliberately taken away, such as what they ate, when they woke, and with whom they lived. The inhabitants of these shelters were already living in a state of great existential uncertainty, and so it was even more damaging when they lost control over the rhythms of daily life.

Chapter 6 turned to a more participatory shelter in Vienna, which tried to address such problems. Vienna had transformed a number of empty buildings—mostly vast and soulless office blocks with open-plan floors and institutional fittings—into refugee accommodation. Like in Berlin, life inside these shelters involved a succession of tiny hardships: poor catering, harsh lighting, and the inability to shape daily routine. After a group of architects got involved, however, the buildings were given a low-cost but sensitive transformation through objects and "social furniture." This changed the experience of what were previously grim surroundings. The interventions included blankets to dampen the communal noise, fabric to filter the harsh light above, and dividers to create a more personal space. The architects worked with refugees to install these features while also experimenting with larger items of furniture that could bring people together through construction. The Viennese interventions were creative and contextual, emerging from the character of the office blocks, the needs of refugees, and conversations about priority. This shows what can be achieved from an approach to shelter that thinks carefully about autonomy, producing enclaves of control in a wider environment of restriction.

The seventh and final chapter turned to Paris, where the Yellow Bubble illustrated the role of large-scale symbolism in design. The mayor of Paris had chosen this hemispherical architectural feature as a "signpost of humanity," a mark of compassionate intent, but despite such benevolent intentions, the design had many drawbacks—both practical and political. Practically, the use of inflatable architecture created an uncomfortable space that was noisy and poorly insulated. Politically, too, the design became compromised, ending up as a "sorting-and-dispatching" center for the state. The most crucial problem, however, was that the aesthetics did not serve the inhabitants. The striking design had been chosen for political reasons and did not make the shelter any better for the people inside. This was, in the end, a space where migrants would receive a few nights of warmth in return for registration, restriction, and rapid processing. It did not offer a chance for them to control their immediate environment or create solid foundations for their future. It primarily served a political imperative: the need to get rough sleepers off the streets of Paris and control the political narrative about migration.

These seven fragments of shelter each show how there is a fundamental imprecision at the heart of this basic human need. They also show, perhaps most significantly, some common failings. The lesson from each chapter might be summarized as the need to take autonomy more seriously as a principle of design—a principle that allows refugees to decide what to prioritize while also addressing the humanitarian tendency toward paternalism. Autonomy is best described as the ability to act on one's own terms and without undue influence from others. To be autonomous is to shape one's own life— even in small matters—rather than have decisions imposed from on high.[2]

This matters because it makes shelter more appropriate. Facilitating autonomy can help refugees respond to local conditions and the particularities of their own situation rather than the problems imagined by distant planners. Yet autonomy also has a deeper and more fundamental value because it is based on respect for all people. We need to take autonomy more seriously, in short, because it is central to acknowledging our equal moral standing and the capacity of refugees to be authors of their life. Joseph Raz defines autonomous persons as "those who can shape their life and determine its course."[3] This has the benefit of clarifying the stakes. Autonomy is about the ability to govern ourselves, carving our own path through the world and making decisions about how to live. Violating autonomy, in turn, alienates us from ourselves, cutting us off from the ability to define value and compromising our standing as a human.

AUTONOMY AND POLITICAL THEORY

The great irony of humanitarianism is that, while it is a sector ostensibly committed to the equal moral worth of all people, it often undermines this in practice. Many scholars have shown how the aid industry perpetuates inequalities in a way that contradicts its own principles—something Didier Fassin calls the "politics of life."[4] In the shelter sector, there are many small but significant ways in which this type of politics plays out. To understand how this can happen, just think of your daily routine. If the lights had been automatically turned on in your bedroom at six o'clock this morning, if you were not able to decide the food you ate for breakfast, if strangers were coming and going from your home all day without your knowledge, then the cumulative effect of this could be more damaging than being restricted in bigger decisions. We often expect the large things in life to lie outside our direct control, but we can feel demeaned and violated if we cannot control more quotidian matters.

Having power over our schedule, when we wake in the morning, and even how much salt to put in our food is not just important to our wellbeing and mental health; it gets to the core of our very humanity.[5] Aid agencies can cause a great deal of harm by making these small decisions on behalf of others—decisions that may seem individually inconsequential but that soon add up.[6] Autonomy can stand as a protection against this harm. It is not, of course, a traditional humanitarian principle. Nor is it held up as an ideal in the aid world—except insofar as it connects to the related but distinctive idea of participation or self-reliance. But it is important to take seriously because it resonates with the embedded liberalism that underpins so much humanitarian work. Despite certain concerns about its origins— which I will tackle below—autonomy can orientate humanitarian relief in a way that recognizes the imperfect and highly constrained circumstances in which it takes place, remaining consistent with liberal traditions and addressing the destructive tendency toward top-down decision making that remains one of the most intractable problems of aid work today.

To illustrate this, let us consider how the idea of autonomy might be applied. What does it mean to reframe shelter as a way to expand autonomous action? Some of the case studies in this book show how humanitarians have begun to consult refugees. The makers of the IKEA-funded Better Shelter, for example, conferred with refugees in Ethiopia before launching their design. The architects in Vienna worked with refugees to construct social furniture. The activists in Athens developed an even more radical approach, which tried to break down hierarchies and create participatory assemblies in self-governing shelters. Yet all these approaches had limits. In Vienna, participation was restricted to a single moment: the consultation or construction of a shelter. In Ethiopia, the team at Better Shelter only consulted with refugees after the major design decisions had been made. In the Greek example, it was impossible to shake off the effect of more subtle power relations. These projects chose participation rather than autonomy, focusing on particular moments of consultation rather than devolving decision making from the start.

This an important difference because participation easily becomes a token gesture. It can be reduced to a check-box consultation, a one-off meeting, or the offer of limited choices from a preapproved range of options.[7] Autonomy, in contrast, is a substantive and thicker concept. It extends far beyond a simple involvement in the administration of a shelter, and it requires both substantive power and meaningful choice. It is important to remember that refugees always engage in participatory processes from a position of weakness. They are already facing narrow options, forced choices, and constrained power. What is needed, therefore, is a thicker concept of autonomy that affects enduring circumstances of life rather than just encouraging participation at a particular moment in time.

Political theorists highlight two main conditions for autonomous action. The first is a requirement of meaningful choice. For autonomy to have any meaning, the argument goes, we need a palette of options, a range of paths open to us. If we are boxed in by physical constraints, fixed expectations, or a lack of resources, then we are not truly autonomous. The second condition relates to power, and it is a harder one to measure. In order to effectively choose between the various options open to us, the argument goes, we need to be free from coercion. We need the ability to seize options without being pressured, manipulated, or misled.[8]

It is easy to see how these conditions might be lacking in refugee shelter. The requirement of sufficient power, for example, is rarely met for noncitizens, who are reliant on others for their shelter. Even where there are ample opportunities for participation, as in the case of Hotel City Plaza in Athens, there remain subtle hierarchies that can influence what is said and done. The same is true for the requirement of meaningful choice. Providing a range of *significant* options means having a variety of paths that lead to considerably different outcomes, but too often, choices are limited, offering small variations in design, as in the IKEA case. A fuller idea of autonomy would try to correct this, enhancing options and transferring power to those that need it most. This should generate two central questions that might be asked at the outset of any project. First, does this proposal offer a chance for refugees to truly control their daily conditions and routines? And second, does this shelter maximize the ability of inhabitants to choose between different futures and carve out a distinctive life of their own?

Starting with these questions would be a considerable change from the way that shelter is usually imagined. We too often see shelter as an issue of protection, which is an approach that becomes paternalistic and hard to contain. It is certainly understandable that shelter is framed in this way, not least because it involves specialists tasked with providing for a comprehensive package of human needs that—as we saw in the introduction—end up being recast as part of shelter. The result is that humanitarians and designers become compelled to do more and more, protecting a group of people deemed temporarily restricted in their ability to provide for themselves. When shelter is conceived in this way, humanitarians—limited as they are by restricted funds and urgent timeframes—can only select and emphasize some of these aspects of shelter at the expense of others. This becomes frustrating, imperfect, top-down, and fragmented.

The alternative is to see shelter through the lens of autonomy. This changes the terms of debate. Instead of asking what humanitarians should provide, it asks what inhabitants can do. Instead of deciding what shelter *means*, it allows people to define it for themselves. Instead of seeing shelter as an opportunity to provide protection, it sees shelter as an opportunity to provide much-needed autonomy. This may seem like a small shift of emphasis, but it leads to a completely new starting point. To return to the words of Raz, it means that designers must first and foremost consider whether a shelter allows its inhabitants to shape their life and determine its course. Humanitarians would need to break down what is needed to foster autonomy, focusing particularly on the two conditions discussed above: options and power. The aim would be to encourage as much autonomy as possible for people living in circumstances that seem deliberately designed to deny it. Faced with the choice of either reproducing or resisting the paternalistic restrictions faced by refugees in wider society, shelters could create spaces of control and independence instead.

AUTONOMY AND DESIGN

To understand how this might work, let us begin by considering what one might do if led by the principle of autonomy. When faced with a wave of new refugee arrivals, a humanitarian or government official might consider the unconditional transfer of cash directly to forced migrants. This would maximize both options and choice. Cash could provide refugees with a range of options about where to live—a convertible medium of exchange that could be used to pay rent, buy building materials, contract laborers, or offer compensation to friends or host families. Cash would also give more power to refugees, allowing them to make choices and gain power as clients with consumer rights.[9] The more money that was made available, too, the more choices and power they would have. Yet despite these advantages, there are many obstacles to cash-based assistance.

The key issue would be that it requires the complete devolution of control and the perceived undermining of expertise. Cash may mean fewer opportunities to monitor vulnerable populations, who are in effect required to care for themselves with the money provided. It could also lead to anxieties about control on the part of governments, who, at the very least, seek to monitor migration and incentivize certain kinds of action. A brave and principled politician might be able to fund unconditional cash transfers to asylum seekers on the basis of general taxation, but to be meaningful, these transfers would need to be sufficiently high to pay for market rents in urban areas. This would be unlikely to happen, producing a negative response from domestic voters. Expert shelter specialists, too, may feel their knowledge is being undermined if the act of finding shelter becomes managed without their input.

There are alternative approaches that might place autonomy more firmly at the heart of shelter. Shelters might be offered with fewer rules and greater freedoms. Aid agencies could provide more generous financial allowances and transfer funds directly to refugees. Focusing on autonomy might also involve providing better services inside the shelter itself. The best shelters offer detailed advice and information, with access to a team of social workers, legal caseworkers, and administrators to help people settle and integrate. The principle of autonomy could demand even more assistance in this area, helping inhabitants to develop their options and providing more meaningful choices when it comes to longer-term accommodation and employment. Enhancing options and power can certainly be pursued in this way; after all, autonomy is not an all-or-nothing affair. It can take place incrementally, expanding opportunities for control over the rhythms of daily life and freeing up routines or curfews, even if the broader political context remains largely restrictive.

The central challenge of emergency shelter is to provide more than just a fragment of home. Ideally, homes are places of security and stability. They are places where we have some control. They are places where we arrange things on our own terms rather than on the terms of others. Making a home is all about building a social and cultural environment that is indisputably ours. Homes, in short, are a place where one can build an autonomous life.[10] Refugees will always try to create islands of such autonomy when they arrive in temporary accommodation, which we can see clearly from the courtyards in Za'atari camp and the private parasols of Viennese office blocks.[11] But the key thing is for humanitarians to think about ways to expand autonomy from the start, to find strategies for turning emergency shelters from a mere fragment into something closer to the *ideal* of a fully rounded home.[12]

This means asking refugee inhabitants what they need rather than trying to imagine human requirements in the abstract. As one of my interviewees put it, architects dealing with humanitarian situations often fall into the trap of designing shelters for themselves: "They don't really understand the context that they're designing for . . . [and] their tendency is to design for a problem that lives in their own imagination." As this interlocutor put it, there is an "inward-looking utopianism" in so much architectural engagement, which generates a desperate need for more feedback. "A really good architect should know how to observe and how to listen and how to question. If you are designing shelter for a population or a culture that you don't understand, then your first job is to understand that culture. If you skip that step, you're only designing for yourself."[13]

One could go further. Humanitarian design arguably needs more than a feedback loop. It needs a complete change of perspective. The problem with "feedback" is the same as participation: it can be thin, it can be selective, and it involves little transfer of power. The alternative is to look for a more fundamental shift in emphasis, minimizing or even eliminating the role of architects and humanitarians by allowing inhabitants to make decisions. This is not as radical as it sounds. One aid worker told me that emergency shelter should always involve stepping back and *resisting* the urge to be involved. The task, he said, is not to understand everything and then come up with an inspired design but rather to empower and facilitate people to find their own solutions.[14] It should not be hard for architects to do this given that they are experts in process. The whole point of good architecture is to understand the context before putting pen to paper—to understand how people live, to learn about the needs of the client, and then balance this with the constraints of materials, planning, and the site itself. Humanitarian architecture fails when this process becomes obscured by the desire to make a flashy product. It has become a cliché to say that shelter is a process not a product, but it remains a lesson not fully absorbed.[15]

As suggested above, one way to inoculate against this tendency is to turn refugee inhabitants more clearly into clients, giving them money and greater power. This could help architects navigate the complicated landscape of situations in which the client is often confused or unclear. The client of a shelter project is rarely seen as the final user of the structure—that is, the refugee. More often, it is the aid agency that commissions it or the donor who is paying for it. Refugees' perspectives tend to get lost and end up at the bottom of clamoring imperatives. Thinking of shelter through the lens of autonomy may be a way to change this dynamic.

HUMANITARIAN IMPLICATIONS

Autonomy is not just important for shelter; it is important for humanitarians more broadly. Despite attempts over the past few decades to reorient the aid industry around the idea of human rights, the sector remains grounded on the notion of meeting needs. This leads to two recurring problems. First, there is the issue of precision—a question of how to define these needs. Second, there is the issue of paternalism—a question of how to meet these needs without exerting unconscionable power and influence over a group of vulnerable people. In this book, I have shown how these problems of precision (defining shelter) and paternalism (avoiding top-down provision) hold back many designs in practice. But this does not mean abandoning the framework of needs entirely. The great attraction of human needs is that they can be a unifying force. We live in a world of profound divisions, but we all know what it feels like to lack a basic need. We can empathize with people who are hungry, cold, or thirsty. Our needs bring us together as they are something shared, visceral, and strongly felt.[16]

This framework has the benefit of great simplicity and power, but when humanitarians actually set about meeting human needs, two issues arise. The first is the difficulty of coming to a common agreement about the scope and extent of basic needs. What is a genuine human need? How can we measure that need? When is a need actually satisfied? The second emerges as a result, capturing the difficulty of defining human needs without exerting unacceptable levels of power. How can humanitarians avoid imposing their own definition of needs when so much is culturally contingent? How do they prevent their work from becoming cumbersome and bureaucratic? And how can they act quickly in emergency conditions without invasively poking about in people's lives?

These questions occur in many humanitarian operations, but they recur in the academic literature too. Despite the powerful moral case for meeting human needs, there are many political philosophers who argue that needs are not a solid foundation for theories of justice.[17] The problem of precision, for example, is more than just a practical challenge because everyone has a different idea about which needs are important and under what circumstances they might be considered satisfied. It is hard to argue that needs should take priority when there is so much that can be included. The idea of human needs easily becomes a bottomless pit, which is a serious problem in a world of scarce resources.

The second obstacle arises as a consequence of the first because paternalism is a common result. Even if one *could* define needs without the imposition of a common standard, the act of actually meeting those needs usually requires a large and cumbersome bureaucracy. To ensure fair treatment, a single agency would have to measure people and compare their situations before even getting to the stage of determining how best those needs might be met. The complexities and pitfalls of this approach have led many political philosophers to focus instead on the distribution of primary goods or capabilities, which allow people to decide on their own priorities.[18] Others have focused on a further end that seems to lie behind the satisfaction of basic needs, such as the way this can contribute to happiness or protect liberty or avoid harm.[19] But these ideas are hardly open to humanitarians, for whom the notion of human needs is central to identity and important as a unifying force.[20] The task, instead, is to retain the rhetorical power of human needs while addressing the problems of imprecision and paternalism. The best way to do this is to move away from the idea that humanitarians should be providing needs directly and embrace the idea that they are a precondition for social existence instead.

There are various theories one could draw on here, but the most important are those that show how needs are crucial in order to participate fully in social life. David Braybrooke, for example, argues that the satisfaction of human needs should focus on enabling people to carry out four specific roles in society: those of the citizen, parent, householder, and worker.[21] David Miller suggests that basic needs are important because they allow a person to avoid harm and live a minimally decent life within a particular context.[22] Len Doyal and Ian Gough propose that needs are crucial for enabling nonimpaired participation in collective existence, whatever culture one is from.[23] These theories emphasize how human needs are not just physiological; they also include an array of nonmaterial issues such as self-determination, self-reliance, and cultural identity.[24] Autonomy, in particular, is often included in such needs, enabling people to function in society by capturing that crucial ability to govern oneself. It has been emphasized specifically in the theory of Doyal and Gough, who suggest that physical health and autonomy are the two pillars on which all theories of need should stand.[25] This could become an important theoretical foundation for the application of autonomy as a humanitarian principle and a straightforward way of integrating it into existing practices of aid.

The importance of autonomy derives from its position as a foundation for action. Without autonomy, we could not act, even though autonomy is not the same as freedom—one can have autonomy without being completely free. In fact, autonomy often exists within constraints, and it can always be advanced in stages. Some humanitarians may be reluctant to talk about autonomy because it seems like an excuse for *in*action. It can resemble the conservative appeal for vulnerable people to pull themselves up by their bootstraps rather than expecting assistance from others. This is certainly a valid concern, but the whole idea of prioritizing autonomy in relief is *not* to disengage but rather to use aid in a different way. The idea is to put recipients in control, allowing them to develop their longer-term plans with support and investment from others.

Another reason humanitarians may be reluctant to acknowledge autonomy is because the concept seems so saturated by a rationalist and Eurocentric history.[26] There are again grounds for this concern since the notion of autonomy is rooted in Western political philosophy, and at times, it has been associated with unhelpfully rationalistic models of human behavior. In the Kantian tradition, for example, it has been presented as the ability to make choices that are unclouded by emotion, desire, or cultural pressures.[27] Autonomy often appears highly individualistic, overlooking the importance of social relationships and communal life. Other approaches, however, present a different view. John Stuart Mill, for example, sees autonomy as a matter of control rather than rationality. He frames autonomy as being free from the power of others, which could mean acting *precisely* according to our emotions, desires, and cultural values if that is what is important.[28] This is the tradition in which I use the word—seeing no antagonism between social ties, cultural practices, and the ability to decide a course of action. When defined in this way, the principle of autonomy has a number of advantages as it allows choices to be shaped by culture, it guards against paternalism, and it frees people to follow what they think gives life meaning rather than being subjected to instructions in the name of their best interests.

Finally, autonomy can be pursued in steps, which makes it a pragmatic principle. It can lead to greater control over small, everyday matters. This makes particular sense in the aid world, where humanitarians often have limited power. Shelter specialists, for instance, cannot address the legal restrictions affecting refugees. They cannot change the lack of political representation in a host state. They cannot award final citizenship or provide an ultimate solution to refugee status. Yet none of this detracts from the importance of promoting autonomy over more mundane issues. Indeed, humanitarian shelter should focus on giving refugees greater say over daily matters *precisely* because they face bigger constraints. Recognizing autonomy over the small things helps to underline the equal moral worth of all people, even if political rights are slow to catch up.

AMONG THE RUINS

W. G. Sebald writes of how "outsize buildings cast the shadow of their own destruction before them and are designed from the first with an eye to their later existence as ruins."[29] The shelters in this book tended to be more ephemeral and so will leave no lasting ruins.[30] Some remain in place. Azraq camp, for example, is still open as evidence of the flaws of approaching shelter as metrics. The IKEA Better Shelter remains in production, demonstrating the limitations of reducing shelter to its most basic form. Tempelhof Airport remains host to refugees, although the huge hangars are no longer used, and refugees are housed instead in temporary units on the tarmac outside. Many other shelters, however, have disappeared. The Yellow Bubble was deflated in 2018, and the site turned into a new university campus. Hotel City Plaza closed in 2019 when a right-wing government took power in Greece. The informal structures of Lebanon have been renewed many times since 2015, but the fundamental precariousness of their inhabitants remains unchanged.

The Calais Jungle, too, was destroyed in 2016, but this did not end the story. Many refugees simply melted into the countryside. Pursued by the police, they began a less visible existence, moving from place to place and dismantling each camp by day so that they could then return at night. The anthropologist Maria Hagan describes the situation in Calais as a "contingent camp": a form of shelter that leaves virtually no material trace.[31] It involves small groups of people sleeping in bushes and meeting in fields, creating social structures that can be easily hidden. They socialize in the long grass, drink tea in the hidden dips of sand dunes, and pray in a woody glade—a place they call their "invisible church." Meanwhile, the physical structures of the former Jungle have long been buried and its site repurposed as a reserve for migratory birds—a shift that is laden with irony.[32]

Despite the years that have passed since 2015—with all the money spent, asylum claims heard, and shelters closed—there are new generations of forced migrants that remain in perilously insecure forms of accommodation. Since I began work on this book, there have been many more types of refugee shelter appearing and disappearing; to take just one example, the current media interest in Britain is concentrated on an enormous offshore barge to house asylum seekers on the sea.[33] It seems that humanitarians still have insufficient influence and resources to provide decent accommodation at scale, and they are always struggling to respond to the political and cultural circumstances of each crisis. The analysis in this book suggests that a new approach is needed. The central purpose of refugee shelter should be shifted to enable displaced people to find their own solutions, to give them as much control as possible over their immediate circumstances. For humanitarian designers, this means greater humility, learning that the best approach to solving shelter—ironically—may be not to build anything at all.

There are many ways to avoid the temptation to build. Humanitarians might focus on cash, or they could invest in hosting schemes. Architects might first decide to adapt what is there, helping people transform what they have. Designers can also shift from buildings to objects and furniture, and it is surely not a coincidence that some of the best examples in this book have involved pausing, learning, and doing something other than building a shelter. Focusing on autonomy can produce even better results, increasing the freedom of people living through a period of constraint. This can have a positive impact on mental health, and it acknowledges the shared humanity that lies at the heart of the humanitarian encounter. Refugee shelters are, by definition, imperfect and impermanent, but they might nevertheless become places where people can make plans, live according to their own values, and have some freedom to act—even if this is only over the smallest of daily decisions.

Bachelard writes of how "a house that is final, one that stands in symmetrical relation to the house we were born in, would lead to thoughts—serious, sad thoughts—and not to dreams. It is better to live in a state of impermanence than in one of finality."[34] This may seem glib—even the response of someone who has never lived in true impermanence—but it contains a kernel of truth. A shelter that is presented with finality has no room for the future, no room for people to change that shelter, to transform it and dream of a better life. As Bachelard puts it, "maybe it is a good thing for us to keep a few dreams of a house that we shall live in later."[35] Maybe we need that flexibility, that sense of progression, that idea of a positive future. This is a hard lesson to integrate into humanitarian relief given the many constraints of the aid world, but for that reason, it is all the more important that we try.

Notes

Introduction

1. Dan Hicks and Sarah Mallet, *Lande: The Calais 'Jungle' and Beyond* (Bristol: Bristol University Press, 2019), 1–18.

2. Michel Agier, *The Jungle: Calais's Camps and Migrants* (Medford: Polity, 2018); Oli Mould, "The Calais Jungle: A Slum of London's Making," *City* 21, no. 3–4 (2017): 388–404.

3. This particular building became more widely known in the United Kingdom when it featured in an edition of the television program *Songs of Praise*.

4. Oli Mould, "The Not-So-Concrete Jungle: Material Precarity in the Calais Refugee Camp," *Cultural Geographies* 25, no. 3 (2018): 393–409. Everything was temporary because the police surrounded the camp and prevented any permanent building materials from being brought in—stone and steel were banned.

5. Elisa Sandri, "'Volunteer Humanitarianism': Volunteers and Humanitarian Aid in the Jungle Refugee Camp of Calais," *Journal of Ethnic and Migration Studies* 44, no. 1 (2018): 65–80.

6. The official name for this container camp was the Centre d'Accueil Provisoire (Provisional Reception Center). For more on the use of shipping containers for refugee shelter, see Hanna Baumann, "Moving, Containing, Displacing: The Shipping Container as Refugee Shelter," in *Structures of Protection? Rethinking Refugee Shelter*, ed. Tom Scott-Smith and Mark E. Breeze (Oxford: Berghahn Books, 2020), 15–29. See also Miriam Ticktin, "Calais: Containment Politics in the 'Jungle,'" *Funambulist Magazine* 5 (2016): 29–33.

7. Cannelle Gueguen-Teil and Irit Katz, "On the Meaning of Shelter: Living in Calais's Camps de la Lande," in *Camps Revisited: Multifaceted Spatialities of a Modern Political Technology*, ed. Irit Katz, Diana Martín, and Claudio Minca (London: Rowman and Littlefield, 2018), 83–86; Irit Katz, "Between Bare Life and

Everyday Life: Spatializing Europe's Migrant Camps," *Architecture_MPS* 12, no. 2 (2017): 4.

8. The walled municipal summer camp was officially called the Jules Ferry Centre but informally known as Al-Salaam. It was located on the edge of the Jungle and run by a French organization called la Vie Active. This was another more formal part of the humanitarian provision, providing showers and free supplies to residents.

9. These centers were widely known by the initialism CAO. For more on the peculiarities of humanitarianism and asylum in France, see Miriam Ticktin, "Where Ethics and Politics Meet: The Violence of Humanitarianism in France," *American Ethnologist* 33, no. 1 (2006): 33–49; Miriam Ticktin, *Casualties of Care: Immigration and the Politics of Humanitarianism in France* (Berkeley: University of California Press, 2011). The final clearance and removal of the Jungle began on October 24, 2016.

10. For a powerful article and photo collection showing the destruction of the Jungle, see Alan Taylor, "France Dismantles 'the Jungle' in Calais," *The Atlantic*, October 26, 2016.

11. Mahmoud Darwish, *A River Dies of Thirst*, trans. Catherine Cobham (New York: Archipelago Books, 2009), 12. The poem from which these lines are taken is entitled "The House as Casualty." The poignancy of the objects left buried in the ruins of the Jungle led many activists and artists to collect them for exhibitions and installations. See, e.g., Gideon Mendel, *Dzhangal* (London: GOST Books, 2017); Hicks and Mallet, *Lande*, 77–78.

12. At the time, Za'atari was in its infancy, but it would soon become one of the largest refugee camps in the world.

13. Svenja Schurade, "Writing a History of the 'Long Summer of Migration,'" *Journal Blog, Public Anthropologist*, August 3, 2021, https://publicanthropologist .cmi.no/2021/08/03/writing-a-history-of-the-long-summer-of-migration -reflections-on-activist-academic-practices/.

14. The term "refugee crisis" is unpopular with many scholars who prefer to frame this as a "refugee reception crisis" or "hospitality crisis." See Seth Holmes and Heide Castañeda, "Representing the 'European Refugee Crisis' in Germany and Beyond: Deservingness and Difference, Life and Death," *American Ethnologist* 43, no. 1 (2016): 12–24.

15. Florian Trauner and Jocelyn Turton, "'Welcome Culture': The Emergence and Transformation of a Public Debate on Migration," *Austrian Journal of Political Science* 46, no. 1 (2017): 33–43. The three-year funding for this research was secured in 2016 from the Arts and Humanities Research Council and the Economic and Social Research Council of the United Kingdom (grant ES/P005004/1). For a critical take on the relationship between crisis and research grants, see Heath Cabot, "The Business of Anthropology and the European Refugee Regime," *American Ethnologist* 46, no. 3 (2019): 261–75.

16. My attitude at the time is summarized in Tom Scott-Smith, "Humanitarian Neophilia: The 'Innovation Turn' and Its Implications," *Third World Quarterly*

37, no. 12 (2016): 2229–51. For more critical literature on humanitarian design, see Stephen Collier et al., eds., "Little Development Devices / Humanitarian Goods," special issue, *Limn* 9 (2017). For some intellectual foundations, see Jamie Cross and Alice Street, "Anthropology at the Bottom of the Pyramid," *Anthropology Today* 25, no. 4 (2009): 4–9; Peter Redfield, "Bioexpectations: Life Technologies as Humanitarian Goods," *Public Culture* 24, no. 1 (2012): 157–84.

17. For more on these designs, see Tom Scott-Smith, "Places for People: Architecture, Building, and Humanitarian Innovation," *Journal of Humanitarian Affairs* 1, no. 3 (2019): 14–22. An overview of recent design in the shelter sector can be found in Esther Ruth Charlesworth, *Humanitarian Architecture: 15 Stories of Architects Working after Disaster* (London: Routledge, 2014). For further background, see Tom Scott-Smith, "Places of Partial Protection: Refugee Shelter since 2015," in *Structures of Protection? Rethinking Refugee Shelter*, ed. Tom Scott-Smith and Mark E. Breeze (Oxford: Berghahn Books, 2020), 1–12.

18. Liisa Malkki, *The Need to Help: The Domestic Arts of International Humanitarianism* (Durham: Duke University Press, 2015); Peter Redfield, *Life in Crisis: The Ethical Journey of Doctors without Borders* (Oakland: University of California Press, 2013). Other notable examples include literature on "aidland," including David Mosse, ed., *Adventures in Aidland: The Anthropology of Professional International Development* (Oxford: Berghahn Books, 2011); Heather Hindman and Anne-Meike Fechter, eds., *Inside the Everyday Lives of Development Workers: The Challenges and Futures of Aidland* (Sterling: Kumarian, 2011); Silke Roth, *The Paradoxes of Aid Work: Passionate Professionals* (London: Routledge, 2015).

19. For some classic texts on the relationship between shelter and society, see Bernard Rudofsky, *Architecture without Architects: A Short Introduction to Nonpedigreed Architecture* (Albuquerque: University of New Mexico Press, 1964); Paul Oliver, *Shelter and Society* (New York: Praeger, 1969); Paul Oliver, *Dwellings: The House across the World* (Oxford: Phaidon, 1987); Amos Rapoport, *House Form and Culture* (Englewood Cliffs: Prentice Hall, 1969); Marcel Vellinga, "The End of the Vernacular: Anthropology and the Architecture of the Other," *Etnofoor* 23, no. 1 (2011): 171–92.

20. This approach has been particularly influenced by the work of Tim Ingold. E.g., see Tim Ingold, "That's Enough About Ethnography!," *HAU: Journal of Ethnographic Theory* 4, no. 1 (2014): 383–95; Tim Ingold, "Anthropology Contra Ethnography," *HAU: Journal of Ethnographic Theory* 7, no. 1 (2017): 21–26.

21. Daniel Bradburd, *Being There: The Necessity of Fieldwork* (Washington: Smithsonian Institution Press, 1998).

22. During this period, with my collaborator Mark E. Breeze, I also made a film, from which the images in this book are drawn. For the final multipart documentary, see the webpage "Shelter without Shelter," Refugee Studies Centre, University of Oxford, accessed November 26, 2023, https://www.rsc.ox.ac.uk/shelter-without-shelter.

23. Abraham Maslow, "A Theory of Human Motivation," *Psychological Review* 50 (1943): 370–96.

24. I am indebted to Peter Redfield for this thought. For many years, blankets were central to emergency shelter: in 1978, Oxfam estimated that 66 percent of their shelter aid was in the form of blankets. See Jim Howard and Robert Mister, "Lessons Learnt by Oxfam from Their Experience of Shelter Provision 1970–1978," *Disasters* 3, no. 2 (1979): 136–44. For a particularly fascinating anthropological study, see Lucy Norris, "Economies of Moral Fibre? Recycling Charity Clothing into Emergency Aid Blankets," *Journal of Material Culture* 17, no. 4 (2012): 389–404.

25. For a reflective history of the 3.5-square-meter guidance, see Jim Kennedy and Charles Parrack, "The History of Three Point Five Square Metres," in *Shelter Projects 2011–2012*, ed. Joseph Ashmore (Geneva: IFRC and UNHCR, 2013), 109–10.

26. Tom Corsellis and Antonella Vitale, *Transitional Settlement: Displaced Populations* (Oxford: Oxfam, 2005), 11, 411. Emphasis mine. Thanks to Jennifer George at the University of Cambridge for sharing her record of definitions in the shelter sector. This has subsequently appeared as Jennifer Ward George, Peter Guthrie, and John Orr, "Redefining Shelter: Humanitarian Sheltering," *Disasters* 47, no. 2 (2023): 482–98.

27. UN-Habitat, *Multilingual Glossary of Human Settlements Terms* (Nairobi: United Nations Centre for Human Settlements, 1992), 121.

28. Enrico Quarantelli, "Patterns of Sheltering and Housing in US Disasters," *Disaster Prevention and Management: An International Journal* 4, no. 3 (1995): 43–53. See also Jennifer Ward George, "Humanitarian Sheltering: Analysing Global Structures of Aid" (PhD diss., University of Cambridge, 2023).

29. For an example, see Esther Schroeder Goh, "Structures to Shelter the Mind: Refugee Housing and Mental Wellbeing in Berlin," in *Structures of Protection? Rethinking Refugee Shelter*, ed. Tom Scott-Smith and Mark E. Breeze (New York: Berghahn Books, 2020), 175–84.

30. Ian Davis, "What Have We Learned from 40 Years' Experience of Disaster Shelter?," *Environmental Hazards* 10, no. 3–4 (2011): 193–212; Ian Davis, *Shelter after Disaster* (Oxford: Oxford Polytechnic Press, 1978).

31. Gaston Bachelard, *The Poetics of Space* (Boston: Beacon Press, 1969), 6.

32. Marina Warner, "Report: Bearer-Beings and Stories in Transit / Storie in Transito," *Marvels and Tales* 31, no. 1 (2017): 149–50.

33. John Berger, *And Our Faces, My Heart, Brief as Photos* (London: Bloomsbury, 2014), 56.

Chapter 1: Shelter as Basics

1. For an overview of some recent shelter designs like these, see Dima Albadra, David Coley, and Jason Hart, "Toward Healthy Housing for the Displaced," *Journal of Architecture* 23, no. 1 (2018): 115–36. Technical details for a range of designs can also be found in UNHCR, *Shelter Design Catalogue* (Geneva: UNHCR, 2016).

2. This account is based on a series of visits to AidEx, "the world's leading humanitarian aid and disaster relief event," between 2016 and 2019. (This description of AidEx can be found on their website: "Home," AidEx, accessed November 21, 2023, https://www.aid-expo.com.) For many years, this event took place at the Brussels Ex-

hibition Centre at the Heysel Plateau in Laeken, but it now has a regular home at Palexpo in Geneva. There are many other humanitarian trade fairs, too, including the Dubai International Humanitarian Aid and Development Conference (DIHAD) and the Humanitarian Networks and Partnerships Week (HNPW) in Geneva.

3. Interview with Johan Karlsson, Stockholm, May 19, 2017. Gaston Bachelard writes that "all great, simple images reveal a psychic state . . . [and] many children draw a house spontaneously while dreaming over their paper and pencil. . . . Asking a child to draw his house is asking him to reveal the deepest dream. . . . If he is happy, he will succeed in drawing a snug, protected house which is well built on deeply-rooted foundations." Bachelard, *Poetics of Space*, 92. Perhaps Karlsson's point was that a five-year-old is best placed to sketch out a dream of safety, but this seems too much of a positive gloss on what might otherwise be described as a failure of design.

4. Beazley, "Flat-Packed Refugee Shelter Named Best Design of 2016," news release, Design Museum, London, January 26, 2017, https://www.beazley.com/news/2017/winners_beazley_designs_of_the_year.html. For more on the reception of the IKEA Better Shelter, see Tom Scott-Smith, "Beyond the Boxes: Refugee Shelter and the Humanitarian Politics of Life," *American Ethnologist* 46, no. 4 (2019): 509–21; Elisa Pascucci, "Refugee Shelter in a Logistical World: Designing Goods for Supply-Chain Humanitarianism," *Antipode* 53, no. 1 (2021): 260–78.

5. Liz Stinson, "IKEA Develops a Smart Flat-Pack Shelter for Disaster Refugees," *Wired*, July 10, 2013.

6. Interview, Karlsson.

7. Footage taken by Mark E. Breeze for the film *Shelter without Shelter*, which accompanies this research project.

8. Tents never last much longer than a year, especially when exposed to a lot of sun, and according to one oft-cited statistic, refugees live in camps for an average of seventeen years. This factoid was often used in the development of the Better Shelter, but it is based on an old, flawed report. See Xavier DeVictor, "How Long Do Refugees Stay in Exile? To Find Out, Beware of Averages," *Development for Peace* (blog), *World Bank Blogs*, December 9, 2019, https://blogs.worldbank.org/dev4peace/2019-update-how-long-do-refugees-stay-exile-find-out-beware-averages. Benjamin Thomas White, "17 Years in a Refugee Camp: On the Trail of a Dodgy Statistic," *Singular Things* (blog), July 4, 2015, https://singularthings.wordpress.com/2015/07/04/17-years-in-a-refugee-camp-on-the-trail-of-a-dodgy-statistic/.

9. Interview, Karlsson.

10. Interview, Karlsson.

11. For more on the idea of transitional shelter, see Sam Collins, Tom Corsellis, and Antonella Vitale, *Transitional Shelter: Understanding Shelter from the Emergency through Reconstruction and Beyond* (London: ALNAP, 2010); Tom Corsellis, *Transitional Shelter Guidelines* (Geneva: International Organization for Migration, 2012).

12. Interview with Olivier Delarue (founder of UNHCR Innovation), Geneva, September 18, 2017.

13. As Karlsson put it, the concern was "transition into what? What should this transition to?" Interview, Karlsson. This tied into a long-standing division between humanitarianism and development work. For more on the long history of this tangled relationship, see Tom Scott-Smith, "Paradoxes of Resilience: A Review of the World Disasters Report 2016," *Development and Change* 49, no. 2 (2018): 662–77.

14. Interview, Karlsson.

15. Interview, Karlsson.

16. Rudofsky, *Architecture without Architects*; Rapoport, *House Form and Culture*.

17. Janet Carsten and Stephen Hugh-Jones, eds., *About the House: Lévi-Strauss and Beyond* (Cambridge: Cambridge University Press, 1995). For a classic article on this topic, see Pierre Bourdieu, "The Berber House or the World Reversed," in *Rules and Meanings: The Anthropology of Everyday Knowledge*, ed. Mary Douglas (Harmondsworth: Penguin Education, 1973), 98–110.

18. Interview with Märta Terne, Stockholm, May 20, 2017.

19. Interview with Vinay Gupta, London, August 9, 2017.

20. See Marc-Antoine Laugier, *An Essay on Architecture; in Which Its True Principles Are Explained, and Invariable Rules Proposed, for Directing the Judgement and Forming the Taste of the Gentleman and the Architect, with Regard to the Different Kinds of Buildings, the Embellishment of Cities* (London: Osborne and Shipton, 1755). This is the English version; Laugier's essay was first published in French in 1753. I am indebted to Mark Breeze for introducing me to this foundational essay in architectural theory and for discussions on its relevance to the Better Shelter.

21. Laugier, *Essay on Architecture*, 10–11.

22. Laugier, *Essay on Architecture*, 11. Laugier argues that all forms of human art are born in this way: inspired by nature. It is to "the imitation of her proceedings," he explains, "to which art owes its birth." Ibid.

23. Pauline Garvey, *Unpacking IKEA: Swedish Design for the Purchasing Masses* (London: Routledge, 2017); Keith Murphy, *Swedish Design: An Ethnography* (Ithaca: Cornell University Press, 2015).

24. Interview, Gupta.

25. Interview, Karlsson.

26. What "better" meant for the shelter, therefore, was driven more by logistics than by comfort. For more on this notion, see Pascucci, "Refugee Shelter."

27. Interview, Terne.

28. Interview with Dennis Kanter, Stockholm, May 18, 2017.

29. Interview, Karlsson.

30. For more on the relationship between security, aid, and research, see Mark Duffield, "Challenging Environments: Danger, Resilience and the Aid Industry," *Security Dialogue* 43, no. 5 (2012): 475–92; Ruben Andersson, *No Go World: How Fear Is Redrawing Our Maps and Infecting Our Politics* (Oakland: University of California Press, 2019).

31. Oliver Wainwright, "IKEA Brings Flatpack Innovation to Emergency Refugee Shelters," *Guardian*, July 2, 2013.

32. Maureen Pao, "New Kind of IKEA Hack: Flat-Packs Head to Refugee Camps,"

NPR, July 2, 2013, https://www.npr.org/sections/parallels/2013/06/27/196356373/new
-kind-of-IKEA-hack-flat-packs-head-to-refugee-camps.

33. Interview, Terne.

34. In fact, the shelter had never been formally called the IKEA Shelter. As a prototype, it had been previously known as the Refugee Housing Unit, or RHU, before being rebranded.

35. "Flat-Pack Accounting," *Economist,* May 11, 2006, https://www.economist
.com/business/2006/05/11/flat-pack-accounting.

36. Interview, Karlsson.

37. I am grateful to Mark E. Breeze for outlining these critiques, which he develops more in Mark E. Breeze, "Towards Better Shelter: Rethinking Humanitarian Sheltering," in *Structures of Protection? Rethinking Refugee Shelter,* ed. Tom Scott-Smith and Mark E. Breeze (New York: Berghahn Books, 2020), 287–300.

38. Interview, Karlsson.

39. This idea was originally proposed in Davis, *Shelter after Disaster,* 33, and quoted directly in UNDRO, *Shelter after Disaster: Guidelines for Assistance* (Geneva: Office of the UNDRO, 1982), iii. See also Davis, "What Have We Learned," 193–212.

40. This idea of balance can be seen as a wider characteristic of Swedish design. See Murphy, *Swedish Design,* 69–70. The idea of *lagom* also appeared in an IKEA advertising campaign around that time, entitled Live Lagom.

41. For more on the political circumstances in Lebanon and the distinctive approach to shelter in that country, see chapter 4.

42. Norimitsu Onishi, "Lebanon Worries that Housing Will Make Syrian Refugees Stay," *New York Times,* December 11, 2013; Aryn Baker, "After a Long Delay, Lebanon Finally Says Yes to IKEA Housing for Syrian Refugees," *Time,* December 16, 2013; interview with anonymous UNHCR shelter specialist, Amman, May 23, 2017.

43. Interview, Karlsson.

44. Interview, Karlsson.

45. Interview with Tim de Haas, Stockholm, May 18, 2017.

46. Paul Turner, "Romanticism, Rationalism, and the Domino System," in *The Open Hand: Essays on Le Corbusier,* ed. Russell Walden (Cambridge: MIT Press, 1977), 14–41.

47. Alvar Aalto, "Emergency Housing: Emergency Housing for Refugees and in Solution of Immediate Post-war Housing Problems," *Journal of the Royal Institute of British Architects* 48, no. 7 (1941): 119–21.

48. Alejandro Aravena and Andrés Iacobelli, *Elemental: Incremental Housing and Participatory Design Manual* (Ostfildern: Hatje Cantz, 2016). For a critical view of this approach, see Camillo Boano and Francisco Vergara Perucich, "Half-Happy Architecture," *Viceversa* 4 (2016): 59–81.

49. Shigeru Ban and Riichi Miyake, *Shigeru Ban: Paper in Architecture* (New York: Rizzoli International Publications, 2009).

50. Interview with Jana Scholze, Design Museum, London, April 25, 2017.

51. Jana Scholze, quoted in Beazley, "Flat-Packed Refugee Shelter."

Chapter 2: Shelter as Metrics

1. Known confusingly as "transitional shelters," or "T-shelters," these dwellings had been designed to last longer than a strictly emergency structure like the tent, but they did not fit the organic and adaptable intentions of Shelter Centre's original model (discussed in chapter 1, endnote 11). For more on the challenges of temperature in this place, see Dima Albadra et al., "Thermal Comfort in Desert Refugee Camps: An Interdisciplinary Approach," *Building and Environment* 124 (2017): 460–77. For more on transitional shelters as a concept, see Collins, Corsellis, and Vitale, *Transitional Shelter*.

2. For an interesting account of another "model camp," see Mac McClelland, "How to Build a Perfect Refugee Camp," *New York Times*, February 13, 2014. For more on ideal camps, see Ayham Dalal et al., "Planning the Ideal Refugee Camp? A Critical Interrogation of Recent Planning Innovations in Jordan and Germany," *Urban Planning* 3, no. 4 (2018): 64–78. It is important to clarify that the majority of refugees in Jordan were not living in camps, yet the country became known for these huge examples in the desert. The camp was often described as meeting all the most important, basic needs, but some scholars point out that many needs were not met in practice and certain services—such as electricity—did not arrive until several years after the camp was formally opened. See Melissa Gatter, *Time and Power in Azraq Refugee Camp: A Nine-to-Five Emergency* (Cairo: American University in Cairo Press, 2023).

3. Elizabeth Cullen Dunn and Martin Demant Frederiksen, "Uncanny Valleys: *Unheimlichkeit*, Approximation and the Refugee Camp," *Anthropology Today* 34, no. 6 (2018): 21–24.

4. Like in the case of robots, the artificial precision of camps is what becomes so unnerving. This idea of the uncanny, developed in Dunn and Frederiksen, "Uncanny Valleys," comes originally from an essay by Masiko Mori, published in Japanese in 1970. For a translation of this essay, see Masahiro Mori, "The Uncanny Valley," trans. Karl MacDorman and Norri Kageki, *IEEE Robotics and Automation Magazine*, June 2012, 98–100.

5. For more on this "bureaucratic modality" of humanitarianism, see Elizabeth Cullen Dunn, *No Path Home: Humanitarian Camps and the Grief of Displacement* (Ithaca: Cornell University Press, 2018), 64–90.

6. Interview with Vincent Dupin, Amman, May 24, 2018. Since 2014, the idea of camps as a last resort has been official policy at the UN Refugee Agency, as set out in UNHCR, *Policy on Alternatives to Camps* (Geneva: UNHCR, 2014).

7. See, e.g., Hanno Brankamp, "Camp Abolition: Ending Carceral Humanitarianism in Kenya (and Beyond)," *Antipode* 54, no. 1 (2022): 106–29.

8. For more on the background to this situation, see Dawn Chatty, *Displacement and Dispossession in the Modern Middle East* (New York: Cambridge University Press, 2010); Dawn Chatty, *Syria: The Making and Unmaking of a Refuge State* (London: Hurst and Company, 2018).

9. It is important to emphasize that 84 percent of refugees in Jordan still lived in host communities even after this policy was implemented. See Chatty, *Syria*, 227–28.

10. A brief account of this visit is provided in the introduction to this volume.

11. These communal blocks did not last long. When I spoke to the head of the UNHCR technical unit, he considered them to be of a "high standard," but refugees wanted their own private spaces for bathrooms and kitchens, and with no ownership, these shared facilities were not being cared for. Eventually the blocks were destroyed after becoming dirty and unsafe. As the head of the technical unit later reflected, "We obviously lost some time and obviously we lost some money . . . everything invested in these communal facilities was basically lost." Interview, Dupin.

12. Mohamed Dualeh, "Letter: Do Refugees Belong in Camps?," *Lancet* 346, no. 8986 (1995): 1369. This article went on: "There are political, social and environmental factors upon which governments base their decisions for hosting large numbers of refugees and these are often beyond the control or influence of the international community. UNHCR's mandate is to protect and assist refugees. We never choose to house large numbers of refugees in camps. But when this has been necessary, our policy is to urge governments to keep the size of camps to manageable numbers." Ibid.

13. UNHCR, *Policy on Alternatives*, 4. Despite this policy, the UN Refugee Agency still describes camps as "an essential part of UNHCR's operational response, particularly during emergencies." Ibid.

14. Michal Givoni, "Beyond the Humanitarian/Political Divide: Witnessing and the Making of Humanitarian Ethics," *Journal of Human Rights* 10, no. 1 (2011): 63. Other scholars describe camps similarly as "one of the most poignant manifestations of humanitarian space." Maja Janmyr and Are Knudsen, "Introduction: Hybrid Spaces," *Humanity: An International Journal of Human Rights, Humanitarianism, and Development* 7, no. 3 (2016): 391.

15. Jeff Crisp and Karen Jacobsen, "Refugee Camps Reconsidered," *Forced Migration Review*, no. 3 (December 1998): 27–30. As some writers put it, "Camps replicate an entire support system." See Corsellis and Vitale, *Transitional Settlement*, 115. For a good summary of this debate, see Stefaan van der Borght and Mit Philips, "Letter: Do Refugees Belong in Camps?" *Lancet* 346, no. 8979 (1995): 907–8. In chapter 4, I explore the implications for humanitarian aid when refugee camps are not possible.

16. As Mohamed Dualeh of UNHCR put it years ago, "Huge influxes of refugees can completely overwhelm the capacity of the local population and the infrastructure, wreaking havoc on the environment and socioeconomic system. Thus, local authorities sometimes have no choice but to seek separate sites for the refugees." Dualeh, "Letter," 1369.

17. In other words, the attraction of camps for host governments is that they assist in "preventing the local integration of exiled populations, in facilitating the early and organised repatriation of refugees, and in attracting international assistance through the creation of very visible refugee settlements." Crisp and Jacobsen, "Refugee Camps Reconsidered," 28.

18. The dilemmas and complexities of "refugee-warrior communities" have been extensively documented since they were first articulated in Aristide Zolberg, Sergio

Aguayo, and Astri Suhrke, *Escape from Violence: Conflict and the Refugee Crisis in the Developing World* (Oxford: Oxford University Press, 1989), 275–78. See, in particular, Fiona Terry, *Condemned to Repeat? The Paradox of Humanitarian Action* (London: Cornell University Press, 2002); Sarah Kenyon Lischer, *Dangerous Sanctuaries: Refugee Camps, Civil War, and the Dilemmas of Humanitarian Aid* (Ithaca: Cornell University Press, 2005); Kirsten McConnachie, "Rethinking the 'Refugee Warrior': The Karen National Union and Refugee Protection on the Thai–Burma Border," *Journal of Human Rights Practice* 4, no. 1 (2012): 30–56.

19. On the use of Goffman to analyze the refugee camp, see Liisa Malkki, *Purity and Exile: Violence, Memory and National Cosmology among Hutu Refugees in Tanzania* (Chicago: University of Chicago Press, 1995), 237; Carol Mortland, "Transforming Refugees in Refugee Camps," *Urban Anthropology* 16, no. 3/4 (1987): 388, 396.

20. On the application of Agamben's ideas to the camp, see Jenny Edkins, "Sovereign Power, Zones of Indistinction, and the Camp," *Alternatives: Local, Global, Political* 25, no. 1 (2000): 3–25; Bülent Diken and Carsten Bagge Laustsen, "The Camp," *Geografiska Annaler Series B-Human Geography* 88, no. 4 (2006): 443–52. The application of Agambenian theory to this area also has its critics. See, e.g., Adam Ramadan, "Spatialising the Refugee Camp," *Transactions of the Institute of British Geographers* 38, no. 1 (2013): 68; Patricia Owens, "Reclaiming 'Bare Life': Against Agamben on Refugees," *International Relations* 23, no. 4 (2009): 567; Kim Rygiel, "Politicizing Camps: Forging Transgressive Citizenships in and through Transit," *Citizenship Studies* 16, no. 5–6 (2012): 808–11.

21. See, e.g., Jennifer Hyndman, *Managing Displacement: Refugees and the Politics of Humanitarianism* (Minneapolis: University of Minnesota Press, 2000); Peter Nyers, *Rethinking Refugees: Beyond States of Emergency*, Global Horizons Series (London: Routledge, 2006). See also Simon Turner, *Politics of Innocence: Hutu Identity, Conflict, and Camp Life*, Studies in Forced Migration (Oxford: Berghahn Books, 2010), 8–9.

22. Richard Black, "Putting Refugees in Camps," *Forced Migration Review*, no. 2 (August 1998): 4–7; Crisp and Jacobsen, "Refugee Camps Reconsidered," 27–30. For more on this debate on the nature of power in refugee camps, see Emma Larking, "Are Refugee Camps Totalitarian?," *Arendt Studies* 2 (2018): 243–52.

23. The last part of this formulation is the more controversial one. It is fashionable to say that care is a form of control but less common to point out that controlling can enable care. Yet this is all part of humanitarianism's long-standing paternalistic streak, which is often praised. See, e.g., Michael Barnett, *Empire of Humanity: A History of Humanitarianism* (Ithaca: Cornell University Press, 2011), 12. For a detailed historical example of the relationship between control and care, see Tom Scott-Smith, *On an Empty Stomach: Two Hundred Years of Hunger Relief* (Ithaca: Cornell University Press, 2020), 90–105.

24. As Kirsten McConnachie puts it, "Every camp is a complex governance environment in its own right, the product of pluralistic legal and political interactions and of extensive historical and cultural influences." Kirsten McConnachie, "Camps

of Containment: A Genealogy of the Refugee Camp," *Humanity: An International Journal of Human Rights, Humanitarianism, and Development* 7, no. 3 (2016): 399.

25. See, e.g., Ilana Feldman, "What Is a Camp? Legitimate Refugee Lives in Spaces of Long-Term Displacement," *Geoforum* 66 (2015): 244–52; Ilana Feldman, *Life Lived in Relief: Humanitarian Predicaments and Palestinian Refugee Politics* (Oakland: University of California Press, 2018); Kirsten McConnachie, *Governing Refugees: Justice, Order and Legal Pluralism*, Law, Development and Globalization (Abingdon: Routledge, 2014); Dunn, *No Path Home*; Nando Sigona, "Campzenship: Reimagining the Camp as a Social and Political Space," *Citizenship Studies* 19, no. 1 (2015): 1–15; Victoria Redclift, "Abjects or Agents? Camps, Contests and the Creation of 'Political Space,'" *Citizenship Studies* 17, no. 3–4 (2013): 308–21.

26. There can be a Foucauldian tinge to some of this literature, too, with the production of new identities seen as a function of power—all part of showing how power is productive, not just controlling or repressive.

27. With no one inside, a line of tents could fly away if the wind got underneath, and they were impossible to seal from the encroachment of sand. The camp planners spent much of their time trying to deal with the dust in this area by compacting roads and ordering gravel, using chemicals to coagulate the dust into something more like soil. There was a serious health reason for this as the sand irritated the skin and eyes and it was inhaled deep into lungs, causing respiratory conditions.

28. For a detailed description of Za'atari's caravans, see Ayham Dalal, *From Shelters to Dwellings: The Zaatari Refugee Camp* (Bielefeld: Verlag, 2022), 77–79, 154–72.

29. REACH, *Al Za'atari Refugee Camp Shelter Assessment* (Geneva: REACH Initiative, 2014).

30. Interview with Mais al-Suradi, Amman, May 28, 2018.

31. Interview, Dupin. This rearrangement often took place at night, under cover of darkness, but the movement was captured on aerial video footage. "It was extremely funny," said one of the aid workers monitoring the situation on the ground, "because, from above, it looked like the houses were moving." Interview with Elias Jourdi, Amman, May 25, 2018. For a more thorough account of these vernacular adaptations, see Dalal, *From Shelters to Dwellings*.

32. For more on these adaptations and the sheer variety of forms in the camp, see Kamel Doraï and Pauline Piraud-Fournet, "From Tent to Makeshift Housing: A Case Study of a Syrian Refugee in Zaatari Camp," in *Refugees as City-Makers*, ed. Mona Fawaz et al. (Beirut: American University of Beirut, 2018), 136–39. See also Jason Hart, Natalia Paszkiewicz, and Dima Albadra, "Shelter as Home? Syrian Homemaking in Jordanian Refugee Camps," *Human Organization* 77, no. 4 (2018): 371–80.

33. This was sometimes rendered humorously as the "Shams-Élysées," a play on the word *Shams*, the Arabic word for Levant.

34. Interview with anonymous UNHCR official, Amman, May 26, 2018.

35. James Scott, *Seeing like a State: How Certain Schemes to Improve the Human Condition Have Failed* (London: Yale University Press, 1998).

36. As I argue elsewhere, this desire for effective humanitarian control can be

realized through "stickiness" in material designs. See Tom Scott-Smith, "Sticky Technologies: Plumpy'nut®, Emergency Feeding and the Viscosity of Humanitarian Design," *Social Studies of Science* 48, no. 1 (2018): 3–24.

37. Interview, Dupin.

38. As one shelter specialist put it, the infrastructure had become "a labyrinth" where "it was impossible to pass a pipe in." Interview, Jourdi.

39. The conditions were particularly difficult because Za'atari had become so large and maintaining its constantly shifting infrastructures was time consuming and expensive. The ideal camp size, according to humanitarian guidelines, is ten thousand people, but Za'atari was forced to accommodate over one hundred thousand refugees, primarily due to political pressure, and it had been laid out in a rush.

40. Interview, Al-Suradi.

41. For the guidelines that stipulate this notion of the ideal, see UNHCR, *Handbook for Emergencies*, 3rd ed. (Geneva: UNHCR, 2007); Sphere Project, *The Sphere Handbook: Humanitarian Charter and Minimum Standards in Humanitarian Response*, 4th ed. (Rugby: Sphere Association, 2018); NRC, *The Camp Management Toolkit* (Oslo: NRC, 2008).

42. The metric actually specifies 4.5–5.5 square meters of living space per person in cold climates or urban settings. The 3.5-square-meter guideline excludes cooking space, a bathing area, and sanitation facilities, and an internal floor-to-ceiling height of 2.6 meters is stipulated for hot climates. See UNHCR, *Handbook for Emergencies*, 221.

43. Sphere Project, *Sphere Handbook*, 250

44. This is based on the assumption that the water flow is 7.5 liters per minute. Sphere Project, *Sphere Handbook*, 106; UNHCR, *Handbook for Emergencies*, 236–59.

45. NRC, *Camp Management Toolkit*, 23.

46. For more on this process of measurement, see Albadra, Coley, and Hart, "Toward Healthy Housing," 115–36. For more on the notion of "trust in numbers," see Theodore Porter, *Trust in Numbers: The Pursuit of Objectivity in Science and Public Life* (Princeton: Princeton University Press, 1995); Sally Engle Merry, *The Seductions of Quantification: Measuring Human Rights, Gender Violence, and Sex Trafficking* (Chicago: University of Chicago Press, 2016).

47. For more on humanitarian "adhocracy," see Elizabeth Cullen Dunn, "The Chaos of Humanitarian Aid: Adhocracy in the Republic of Georgia," *Humanity: An International Journal of Human Rights, Humanitarianism, and Development* 3, no. 1 (2012): 1–23.

48. Interview with Jalal Al Husseini, Amman, May 23, 2018. To be clear, my interlocutor here was summarizing the vision rather than endorsing it, arguing instead that camps are often where rights are violated rather than protected. See also Maja Janmyr, "Spaces of Legal Ambiguity: Refugee Camps and Humanitarian Power," *Humanity: An International Journal of Human Rights, Humanitarianism, and Development* 7, no. 3 (2016): 413–27.

49. Dunn and Frederiksen, "Uncanny Valleys," 22. For more on these abstractions, see Scott-Smith, *On an Empty Stomach*, 176; Joël Glasman, *Humanitarianism*

and the Quantification of Human Needs: Minimal Humanity (New York: Routledge, 2020). Arguably, the abstraction of people into numbers is the only way that humanitarian agencies can respond to so much suffering with so few resources.

50. Dalal et al., "Planning the Ideal," 69.

51. Sophia Hoffmann, "Humanitarian Security in Jordan's Azraq Camp," *Security Dialogue* 48, no. 2 (2017): 104–5.

52. Dalal, *From Shelters to Dwellings*, 201–2. See also Gatter, *Time and Power*.

53. Interview, Al Husseini.

54. Interview with anonymous resident, Azraq camp, May 22, 2018.

55. For a thorough exploration of such dynamics, see Paolo Boccagni and Sara Bonfanti, eds., *Migration and Domestic Space: Ethnographies of Home in the Making* (London: Springer, 2023); Paolo Boccagni, *Migration and the Search for Home: Mapping Domestic Space in Migrants' Everyday Lives* (New York: Palgrave Macmillan, 2017). A classic if limited account of homemaking in relation to internal and external space can be found in Bourdieu, "The Berber House," 98–110.

56. Dalal, *From Shelters to Dwellings*, 201. See also Gatter, *Time and Power*.

57. See also Hoffmann, "Humanitarian Security," 97–112.

58. Refugees were placed in Village Five if they emerged as a threat and were stuck there until cleared and released back into camp or deported back to Syria. A rare and compelling account of Village Five can be found in Melissa Gatter, "Preserving Order: Narrating Resilience as Threat in Jordan's Azraq Refugee Camp," *Territory, Politics, Governance* 11, no. 4 (2023): 695–711. I cannot think about Village Five without also recalling the film *District 9* (dir. Neill Blomkamp, 2009), a dystopian thriller about alien asylum seekers from outer space.

59. Brian Keenan, *An Evil Cradling* (London: Vintage, 1993), 68–70.

60. Or, to use the Vitruvian language introduced in chapter 1 of this book, they need *venustas* as well as *firmitas* and *utilitas*.

61. Talia Radford, "Refugee Camps are the 'Cities of Tomorrow,' Says Humanitarian Aid Expert," *Dezeen*, November 23, 2015; interview with Kilian Kleinschmidt, Vienna, February 11, 2017.

62. Kakuma in Kenya is a good example of this type of transformation, which can also be seen in Palestinian refugee camps throughout the Middle East. For more on the Kakuma example, see Bram Jansen, *Kakuma Refugee Camp: Humanitarian Urbanism in Kenya's Accidental City* (London: Zed Books, 2018).

63. Robert J. Gordon, *The Rise and Fall of American Growth: The U.S. Standard of Living since the Civil War* (Princeton: Princeton University Press, 2016), 126–7.

64. One of the first academic journal articles on refugee-camp planning made this point back in 1977, suggesting that shelters need to be considered in terms of everything "found in a town," such as "water, sewers, roads, clinics, fire protection, garbage disposal, parks, [and] schools." See Frederick Cuny, "Refugee Camps and Camp Planning: The State of the Art," *Disasters* 1, no. 2 (1977): 127. This article grew into the first version of the UNHCR handbook, which appeared in 1981 and remains one of the key documents specifying metrics and minimum standards for shelter in camps today.

65. Scott, *Seeing like a State*. Perhaps the most famous example of this failure was the destruction of the Pruitt-Igoe housing complex in 1972—a moment that has been used to mark the end of modernity itself. Charles Jencks, *The Language of Postmodern Architecture* (London: Academy Editions, 1978), 22–23; Fredric Jameson, *Postmodernism, or, the Cultural Logic of Late Capitalism* (London: Verso, 1991), 41–50.

66. Manuel Herz, "Refugee Camps—or—Ideal Cities in Dust and Dirt," in *Urban Transformation*, ed. Ilka Ruby and Andreas Ruby (Berlin: Ruby, 2008), 283.

67. Herz, "Refugee Camps." For more on high modernism, see Scott, *Seeing like a State*.

68. Kilian Kleinschmidt, "Cities of Tomorrow: From Temporariness to Inclusion," Blox Hub, May 24, 2019, https://bloxhub.org/urban-resilience/cities-of-tomorrow-from-temporariness-to-inclusion. Although Kleinschmidt likes to suggest that all cities began like refugee camps—as places of protection where people would gather together—the term "camp" actually derives from the Latin *campus* referring to a field or open space *outside* of town—a place that was distinct from the town. For more, see McConnachie, "Camps of Containment," 399.

69. Paul Collier, "A Jobs Solution to the Migration Crisis," *World Bank Blogs*, September 9, 2015, https://blogs.worldbank.org/jobs/jobs-solution-migration-crisis. Collier refers to an "economy-in-exile which, once peace is restored, could return and speed recovery." As he puts it, "Camps, instead of being the repositories of human tragedies, should be the job havens that incubate the future economy." See also Alexander Betts and Paul Collier, *Refuge: Transforming a Broken Refugee System* (London: Allen Lane, 2017).

70. Simon Turner, "What Is a Refugee Camp? Explorations of the Limits and Effects of the Camp," *Journal of Refugee Studies* 29, no. 2 (2015): 139–48; McConnachie, "Camps of Containment." The UN, of course, has a more practical definition: "A camp is any purpose-built, planned and managed location or spontaneous settlement where refugees are accommodated and receive assistance and services from government and humanitarian agencies." UNHCR, *Policy on Alternatives*, 12.

71. Louis Wirth, "Urbanism as a Way of Life," *American Journal of Sociology* 44, no. 1 (1938): 1.

72. Interview, anonymous UNHCR official.

73. To use Michel De Certeau's term—which we will return to in chapter 4—cities are places where people can engage in "tactics."

74. This distinction between camp and city is reminiscent of that well-known ethnographic study of camps and towns in Malkki, *Purity and Exile*.

75. Felix Bender, "Should Refugees Govern Refugee Camps?," *Critical Review of International Social and Political Philosophy* (2021): 1–24, https://doi.org/10.1080/13698230.2021.1941702.

76. Dalal, *From Shelters to Dwellings*. Dalal's idea of appropriation could be rolled out not just at the level of the individual building but also across whole cities. See John Turner and Robert Fichter, eds., *Freedom to Build: Dweller Control of the Housing Process* (New York: Macmillan Press, 1972).

77. Brankamp, "Camp Abolition."

Chapter 3: Shelter as Politics

1. The occupation, which began on April 22, 2016, was led by a group of left-wing activists calling themselves the Solidarity Initiative for Political and Economic Refugees. Hotel City Plaza is located at 78 Acharnon, Athens, which has been closed since 2010. Its owner was the stage actress Aliki Papahela. For more details, see Aryn Baker, "Greek Anarchists Are Finding Space for Refugees in Abandoned Hotels," *Time*, November 3, 2016. A good summary of the foundation of City Plaza from the inside can be found in Olga Lafazani, "Intervention—1.5 Year City Plaza: A Project on the Antipodes of Bordering and Control Policies," Antipode Online, November 13, 2017, https://antipodeonline.org/2017/11/13/intervention-city-plaza/.

2. Óscar García Agustín and Martin Bak Jørgensen, *Solidarity and the 'Refugee Crisis' in Europe* (Basingstoke: Palgrave Macmillan, 2018), 60.

3. Interview with Nasim Lomani, Athens, April 21, 2017.

4. Agustín and Jørgensen, *Solidarity*, 52; Loukia Kotronaki, "Outside the Doors: Refugee Accommodation Squats and Heterotopy Politics," *South Atlantic Quarterly* 117, no. 4 (2018): 914–24. City Plaza hosted a number of events with prominent leftist intellectuals, from Judith Butler to Angela Davis and David Harvey to Alain Badiou. See "39 Months City Plaza: The End of an Era, the Beginning of a New One," City Plaza, accessed May 16, 2022, https://best-hotel-in-europe.eu.

5. Agustín and Jørgensen, *Solidarity*, 49–72.

6. Interview, Lomani. He was paraphrasing the words of a former resident.

7. Harold Lasswell, *Politics: Who Gets What, When, How* (New York: Peter Smith, 1950).

8. Lafazani, "Intervention."

9. As Rancière puts it, "Politics exists when the natural order of domination is interrupted by the institution of a part of those who have no part." See Jacques Rancière, *Disagreement: Politics and Philosophy*, trans. Julie Rose (Minneapolis: University of Minnesota Press, 1999), 11. The connection between City Plaza and Rancière's understanding of politics is made particularly explicit in Agustín and Jørgensen, *Solidarity*, 53–60.

10. Heath Cabot, "The European Refugee Crisis and Humanitarian Citizenship in Greece," *Ethnos* 84, no. 5 (2018): 747–71. I am also grateful to Daniel Howden for sketching out the history of this crisis in such a clear manner, which I draw on here. His account can be seen in the film accompanying this research, *Shelter without Shelter*. For more on the citizen response, see Katerina Rozakou, "Crafting the Volunteer: Voluntary Associations and the Reformation of Sociality," *Journal of Modern Greek Studies* 34, no. 1 (2016): 79–102.

11. Leonidas K. Cheliotis and Sappho Xenakis, "What's Left? Political Orientation, Economic Conditions and Incarceration in Greece under Syriza-Led Government," *European Journal of Criminology* 18, no. 1 (2021): 90.

12. Daniel Howden, "Moria: Anti-shelter and the Spectacle of Deterrence," in *Structures of Protection? Rethinking Refugee Shelter*, ed. Tom Scott-Smith and Mark E. Breeze (New York: Berghahn Books, 2020), 59. See also John Borton and Sarah

Collinson, *Responses to Mixed Migration in Europe: Implications for the Humanitarian Sector* (London: Overseas Development Institute, 2017), 11.

13. It is instructive that the Greek government only opened one small camp to accommodate refugees that summer of 2015 despite tens of thousands of people moving through the country every week. This was Eleonas refugee camp, which had a capacity of just a few hundred people.

14. The northern border was closed on March 9, 2016, and the EU-Turkey deal was agreed upon soon after, on March 18, coming into effect on March 20. For more on the context, see Kim Rygiel, Feyzi Baban, and Suzan Ilcan, "The Syrian Refugee Crisis: The EU-Turkey 'Deal' and Temporary Protection," *Global Social Policy* 16, no. 3 (2016): 315–20.

15. Amnesty International, *Trapped in Greece: An Avoidable Refugee Crisis* (London: Amnesty International Publications, 2016). During this period, gates E1, E2, and E3 of the port became overcrowded, temporary shelters for thousands of people.

16. Giorgos Maniatis, "From a Crisis of Management to Humanitarian Crisis Management," *South Atlantic Quarterly* 117, no. 4 (2018): 906–8.

17. Daniel Howden and Apostolis Fotiadis, "The Refugee Archipelago: The Inside Story of What Went Wrong in Greece," *New Humanitarian*, March 6, 2017. This situation emerged because the government wanted to avoid having megacamps, such as those in Jordan, but the result was more camps dispersed over a wider area. As this article puts it, "No one is certain exactly how many refugee camps there are in Greece. . . . Migration Ministry bulletins list 39 camps . . . the UNHCR said there were more than 50, but did not give a specific number." See also Nikos Belavilas and Polina Prentou, "The Typologies of Refugees Camps in Greece" (keynote address, Autonoma: International Conference on Urban Autonomy and the Collective City, Athens, Greece, July 1, 2016).

18. Belavilas and Prentou, "Typologies of Refugees Camps." Skaramangas started operating on April 11, 2016, to rehouse people who had been living in the informal camps of Piraeus Port. See also Tineke Strik, *Refugees at Risk in Greece* (Strasbourg: Council of Europe, 2016), 11.

19. Teresa Thornhill, *Hara Hotel: A Tale of Syrian Refugees in Greece* (London: Verso, 2018), 320; Patrick Kingsley, "'Prisoners of Europe': The Everyday Humiliation of Refugees Stuck in Greece," *Guardian*, September 6, 2016. See also Daniel Howden and Apostolis Fotiadis, "Where Did the Money Go? How Greece Fumbled the Refugee Crisis," *Guardian*, March 9, 2017. Softex was located outside Thessaloniki.

20. Annabell Van den Berghe, "These Refugees Escaped War. Now They're Freezing in Greece's Migrant Camps," *Washington Post*, January 28, 2017. See also Liz Alderman, "Wintry Blast in Greece Imperils Refugees in Crowded Camps," *New York Times*, January 11, 2017; Helena Smith, "Greece: Severe Weather Places Refugees at Risk and Government Under Fire," *Guardian*, January 10, 2017.

21. This fieldtrip was taken with Rachael Kiddey and Mark E. Breeze, to whom I am indebted for organization, support, and countless stimulating conversations.

22. The area had the seemingly appropriate name of Klafthmonos, or the Square of Tears, named for the tearful appeals of fired civil servants who were known to congregate in the square. This interview and subsequent trips to the camps were organized by Mark E. Breeze, to whom I am indebted.

23. This camp was called Eleonas, and it was the first to open on mainland Greece during the summer of migration in 2015. The government preferred it to be known as an "open center." See Angeliki Dimitriadi, *Irregular Afghan Migration to Europe: At the Margins, Looking In* (London: Palgrave Macmillan, 2018), 180.

24. In 2005, a competition to regenerate and transform the area was won by David Serero, Elena Fernandez, and Philippe Coignet.

25. Three camps were set up in this location between November 2015 and February 2016. One was in the Olympic hockey stadium (Elliniko I), one was in the arrivals' terminal of the unused airport (Elliniko II), and one was on the Olympic baseball field (Elliniko III). See Amnesty International, *Trapped in Greece*, 22–23. For more information, see Maria Petrakis, "In Athens, Former Olympic Venues Now Play Host to Refugees," *Los Angeles Times*, November 12, 2015.

26. Interview with Dimitra Mouteveli, Ministry of Migration, Athens, April 3, 2017.

27. Viktoria Square, in particular, became a locus for these citizen efforts in Athens. See Berna Turam, "Refugees in Borderlands: Safe Places versus Securitization in Athens, Greece," *Journal of Urban Affairs* 43, no. 6 (2021): 764–67. For context, see Agustín and Jørgensen, *Solidarity*, 58.

28. For more on the "solidarity economy" in this period, see Theodoros Rakopoulos, "Resonance of Solidarity: Meanings of a Local Concept in Anti-austerity Greece," *Journal of Modern Greek Studies* 32, no. 2 (2014): 313–37; Rozakou, "Crafting the Volunteer," 79–102. See also Sarah Green and Patrick Laviolette, eds., "The Other Side of the Crisis: Solidarity Networks in Greece," special section, *Social Anthropology* 24, no. 2 (May 2016).

29. Giorgos Serntedakis, "'Solidarity' for Strangers: A Case Study of 'Solidarity' Initiatives in Lesvos," *Etnofoor* 29, no. 2 (2017): 83–98; Borton and Collinson, *Responses to Mixed Migration*, 21–23. For more on the political makeup of the movement involved in occupying City Plaza, see Loukia Kotronaki, Olga Lafazani, and Giorgos Maniatis, "Living Resistance: Experiences from Refugee Housing Squats in Athens," *South Atlantic Quarterly*, 117, no. 4 (2018): 892–95; Lafazani, "Intervention."

30. Heath Cabot, "'Contagious' Solidarity: Reconfiguring Care and Citizenship in Greece's Social Clinics," *Social Anthropology* 24, no. 2 (2016): 152–66; Katerina Rozakou, "Solidarity #Humanitarianism: The Blurred Boundaries of Humanitarianism in Greece," *Etnofoor* 29, no. 2 (2017): 99–104; Dimitrios Theodossopoulos, "Philanthropy or Solidarity? Ethical Dilemmas about Humanitarianism in Crisis-Afflicted Greece," *Social Anthropology* 24, no. 2 (2016): 167–84. See also Sotiris Chtouris and DeMond Miller, "Refugee Flows and Volunteers in the Current Humanitarian Crisis in Greece," *Journal of Applied Security Research* 12, no. 1 (2017): 61–77.

31. Interview with Daniel Howden, Oxford, July 18, 2018. The fact that Greece was relatively safe meant that the international-volunteer phenomenon was even more pronounced.

32. Interview, Howden. Again, I am grateful to Daniel Howden for putting this so clearly in the interview referenced above. There was a compelling convergence here, too, of radicalism and neoliberalism, with both standing opposed to faceless bureaucracies and large organized systems.

33. Borton and Collinson, *Responses to Mixed Migration*, 17. As Katerina Rozakou also puts it, "the solidarians acquired a central role in organizing reception for border-crossers, in rescue operations, in providing services and goods." Rozakou, "Solidarity #Humanitarianism," 102.

34. Interviews with anonymous activists, Athens, March 29, 2017. For more on this fascinating relationship between activists and NGOs, see Armine Ishkanian and Isabel Shutes, "Who Needs the Experts? The Politics and Practices of Alternative Humanitarianism and Its Relationship to NGOs," *Voluntas: International Journal of Voluntary and Nonprofit Organisations* 33 (2021): 397–407.

35. The EU-Turkey deal came into effect on March 20, 2016, and the City Plaza building was occupied on April 22, 2016. The statements issued by the collective indicate clearly that the EU-Turkey deal was the trigger.

36. Among the anarchist squats in Athens were Notara 26 and Themistokleus 58. The seemingly refugee-run squats included 5th School, and the feminist squats included Strephi. For more on the landscape of occupied buildings in Athens, see Rachael Kiddey, "Reluctant Refuge: An Activist Archaeological Approach to Alternative Refugee Shelter in Athens (Greece)," *Journal of Refugee Studies* 33, no. 3 (2020): 599–621; Agustín and Jørgensen, *Solidarity*, 59; Kotronaki, "Outside the Doors," 924. One of the few books on this fascinating topic is Pierpaolo Mudu and Sutapa Chattopadhyay, eds., *Migration, Squatting and Radical Autonomy* (London: Routledge, 2016).

37. Agustín and Jørgensen, *Solidarity*, 61. Compared to the other squats in Athens, permission to conduct research in City Plaza was straightforward, and there was distinctly less suspicion toward outsiders.

38. This campaign had the memorable tagline "No pool, no minibar, no room service, but still the best hotel in Europe." See City Plaza, "39 Months City Plaza." A full list of public events run in City Plaza can be found in Kotronaki, "Outside the Doors," 919–20. See also Leandros Fischer and Martin Bak Jørgensen, "'We Are Here to Stay' vs. 'Europe's Best Hotel': Hamburg and Athens as Geographies of Solidarity," *Antipode* 53, no. 4 (2021): 1062–82.

39. This was a very different idea of "the city" than the one taken by camp planners as discussed in the last chapter. The activist argument was not that cities were entrepreneurial spaces but instead that they were places of political struggle and solidarity. In other words, rather than looking to transform camps into cities, the activists showed how the two categories were incompatible. This perspective echoes the work of Warren Magnusson, who has written about "seeing like a city" as a

contrast to James Scott's top-down modernist strategies in "seeing like a state." See Warren Magnusson, *Politics of Urbanism: Seeing like a City* (London: Routledge, 2011).

40. This characterization is also reminiscent of the key distinction made between camps and towns in Malkki, *Purity and Exile*.

41. Often this narrative came directly from city mayors. For example, in 2015, a joint statement from the mayors of two of Europe's largest cities articulated how only cities (as opposed to states) can offer deeper forms of sanctuary and shelter: "States grant asylum, but it is the cities that provider shelter." See Susanne Soederberg, "Governing Global Displacement in Austerity Urbanism: The Case of Berlin's Refugee Housing Crisis," *Development and Change* 50, no. 4 (2019): 924. See also Jonathan Darling, "Forced Migration and the City: Irregularity, Informality, and the Politics of Presence," *Progress in Human Geography* 41, no. 2 (2017): 178–98.

42. Robert Ezra Park and Ralph Turner, *On Social Control and Collective Behavior: Selected Papers* (Chicago: University of Chicago Press, 1967), 3. See also Magnusson, *Politics of Urbanism*, 32.

43. Olga Lafazani, "Homeplace Plaza: Challenging the Border between Host and Hosted," *South Atlantic Quarterly* 117, no. 4 (2018): 896.

44. This text also appeared on the City Plaza Facebook page and in City Plaza, "39 Months City Plaza."

45. Lafazani, "Homeplace Plaza," 898.

46. Lafazani, "Homeplace Plaza," 897.

47. Lafazani, "Homeplace Plaza," 899. Lafazani goes on to clarify: "Of course, this is a broad generalization and does not apply to everyone. For instance, the Kurds of Rojava or Turkey or the politicized Turkish refugees who have had similar experiences understand the project of City Plaza much better." Ibid.

48. Lafazani, "Homeplace Plaza," 900.

49. Interview with NGO staff, Athens, March 27, 2017. The anarchist position, this interviewee argued, originated primarily from people who had enough comfort to refuse the documents that had already provided them with advantages.

50. Interview, Howden.

51. For a recent discussion of classical humanitarianism and varieties of more politicized relief, see Miriam Bradley, "Five Shades of Grey: Variants of 'Political' Humanitarianism," *Disasters* 46, no. 4 (2022): 1027–48.

52. Interviews with anonymous activists, Athens, April 2, 2017. Their view was also reflected in a powerful stencil, daubed on walls throughout Exarcheia, which described NGOs as part of a "three in one": an existential enemy that stood in the way of radicalism along with its bedfellows, "racists and cops." See also Ishkanian and Shutes, "Who Needs the Experts?"

53. Robin Vandevoordt, "Subversive Humanitarianism: Rethinking Refugee Solidarity through Grass-Roots Initiatives," *Refugee Survey Quarterly* 38, no. 3 (2019): 245–65; Rozakou, "Solidarity #Humanitarianism," 99–104; Anne-Meike Fechter and Anke Schwittay, "Citizen Aid: Grassroots Interventions in Development and

Humanitarianism," *Third World Quarterly* 40, no. 10 (2019): 1769–80. Other terms for this phenomenon are "vernacular humanitarianism," "demotic humanitarianism," and "volunteer humanitarianism."

54. So despite the insistence of some activists that they were "solidarians" rather than "humanitarians," these ideas have a longstanding and close relationship. Indeed, solidarity itself is a central humanitarian principle with a long history. For more, see Hugo Slim, "Relief Agencies and Moral Standing in War: Principles of Humanity, Neutrality, Impartiality and Solidarity," *Development in Practice* 7, no. 4 (1997): 342–52; Thomas Weiss, "Principles, Politics, and Humanitarian Action," *Ethics and International Affairs* 13, no. 1 (1999): 1–22. For the idea of solidarity in faith-based NGOs, see Andrea Paras and Janice Gross Stein, "Bridging the Sacred and the Profane in Humanitarian Life," in *Sacred Aid: Faith and Humanitarianism*, ed. Michael Barnett and Janice Gross Stein (Oxford: Oxford University Press, 2012), 218.

55. This division between a professional, apolitical version of humanitarianism and a more amateur, activist type goes back a long way in humanitarian history. It was at the root of a famous split within Médecins Sans Frontières (MSF) and can be seen in the evolution of many other aid agencies as well. For more on the MSF story, see Redfield, *Life in Crisis*.

56. One squat I visited—in a former school—had terrible conditions, with dirty mattresses lined up on the floor, smashed windows, and what looked like drug deals taking place in the corner. No one would talk to me without the approval of an absent "boss," and some refugees admitted privately that they were scared to say anything. This highlights the dangers of domination and abuse in an unregulated landscape. For more on the material dimensions of shelter in Greece, see Nada Ghandour-Demiri and Petros Passas, "Materiality, Agency and Temporariness in Camps in Greece," in *Material Culture and (Forced) Migration: Materializing the Transient*, ed. Friedemann Yi-Neumann et al. (London: UCL Press, 2022), 282–304.

57. It is hard to get firm figures, but it is likely that no more than one or two thousand refugees were living in city squats at the height of the refugee crisis in Greece—not a large number given that around sixty thousand needed accommodation at the time. The activists responded by pointing to the thousands of empty buildings that could be claimed, but this did not take into account the intense labor required to establish the squats and live alongside refugees. Kiddey, "Reluctant Refuge," 604.

58. Interview with anonymous activist, Hotel City Plaza, March 25, 2017.

59. According to some calculations, the response to refugees in Greece became "the most expensive humanitarian response in history . . . when measured by the cost per beneficiary." For some excellent investigative journalism on this topic, see Howden and Fotiadis, "Where Did the Money."

60. City Plaza, "39 Months City Plaza."

61. City Plaza, "39 Months City Plaza."

62. City Plaza, "39 Months City Plaza." Some may argue that there is indeed exaggeration in this statement, but it nevertheless stands as a succinct summary of the overall aims.

63. Molly Crabapple, "The Attack on Exarchia, an Anarchist Refuge in Athens," *New Yorker*, January 20, 2020.

64. Baker, "Greek Anarchists." See also the Maria Margaronis, "Greece's Haven Hotel," *Crossing Continents*, BBC World Service, BBC Radio 4, April 5, 2018.

65. Interview, Lomani.

Chapter 4: Shelter as Tactics

1. Lebanon's power-sharing arrangements were revised at the end of the civil war through the 1989 Taif Accords. Fear for the maintenance of this negotiated peace has been widely reported, although some scholarship offers a more nuanced account of sectarianism. See, e.g., Ussama Makdisi, "Reconstructing the Nation-State: The Modernity of Sectarianism in Lebanon," *Middle East Report* 200 (1996): 23–30.

2. For more on the dynamics of displacement in the history of the Middle East, see Chatty, *Displacement and Dispossession*. For more on the history of camp forms and their transformation over time, see Are Knudsen, "Camp, Ghetto, Zinco, Slum: Lebanon's Transitional Zones of Emplacement," *Humanity: An International Journal of Human Rights, Humanitarianism, and Development* 7, no. 3 (2016): 443–57.

3. Simon Haddad, "The Origins of Popular Opposition to Palestinian Resettlement in Lebanon," *International Migration Review* 38, no. 2 (2004): 470–92; Maja Janmyr, "No Country of Asylum: 'Legitimizing' Lebanon's Rejection of the 1951 Refugee Convention," *International Journal of Refugee Law* 29, no. 3 (2017): 438–65.

4. Palestinian autonomy has grown in Lebanon since the late 1960s, especially after the 1969 Cairo Accords gave provisions for the presence of Palestinian military groups in the country. For more on this history, see Yezid Sayigh, *Armed Struggle and the Search for State: The Palestinian National Movement 1949–1993* (Oxford: Clarendon Press, 1997).

5. These are the words of Makram Malaeb of the Lebanese Ministry of Social Affairs, as quoted in Onishi, "Lebanon Worries." For more on *tawteen*, or *tawtin*, see Daniel Meier, "Al-Tawteen: The Implantation Problem as an Idiom of the Palestinian Presence in Post-civil War Lebanon (1989–2005)," *Arab Studies Quarterly* 32, no. 3 (2010): 145–62; Fida Nasrallah, "Lebanese Perceptions of the Palestinians in Lebanon: Case Studies," *Journal of Refugee Studies* 10, no. 3 (1997): 349–59; Andrew Arsan, *Lebanon: A Country in Fragments* (London: Hurst and Company, 2018), 264–65.

6. Population statistics on Lebanon are complex and disputed, but there is little doubt about the scale of the refugee population. In 2015, UNHCR had over one million refugees in its records, and most estimates of the country's population come in at around five million people.

7. For an overview of the no-camp policy and its implications, see Romola Sanyal, "A No-Camp Policy: Interrogating Informal Settlements in Lebanon," *Geoforum* 84 (2017): 117–25.

8. The notion of this as a "policy of no policy" is articulated most clearly in Sally Abi Khalil, *Lebanon Looking Ahead in Times of Crisis: Taking Stock of the Present*

to Urgently Build Sustainable Options for the Future (Beirut: Oxfam, 2015), 11–15. For more on how government inaction shaped accommodation policy, see Lama Mourad, "'Standoffish' Policy-Making: Inaction and Change in the Lebanese Response to the Syrian Displacement Crisis," *Middle East Law and Governance* 9, no. 3 (2017): 249–66; Estella Carpi, "Winking at Humanitarian Neutrality: The Liminal Politics of the State in Lebanon," *Anthropologica* 61, no. 1 (2019): 83–96.

9. For a detailed account of the dynamics of humanitarianism in Lebanon, see Estella Carpi, *The Politics of Crisis-Making: Forced Displacement and Cultures of Assistance in Lebanon* (Bloomington: Indiana University Press, 2023).

10. For more on the planning sector in Lebanon and the role of refugee self-reliance in finding accommodation for refugees, see Mona Fawaz, "Planning and the Refugee Crisis: Informality as a Framework of Analysis and Reflection," *Planning Theory* 16, no. 1 (2016): 99–115; Lewis Turner, "Explaining the (Non-)Encampment of Syrian Refugees: Security, Class and the Labour Market in Lebanon and Jordan," *Mediterranean Politics* 20, no. 3 (2015): 386–404.

11. This terminology is often in flux, but the three categories emerged from interviews with Ahmad Kassem (shelter coordinator), UNHCR Lebanon, Beirut, March 2 and April 10, 2018. For an overview, see United Nations, *Lebanon Crisis Response Plan 2017–2020* (Beirut: United Nations, 2019), 169–187; Nasser Yassin et al., *No Place to Stay? Reflections on the Syrian Refugee Shelter Policy in Lebanon* (Beirut: UN-Habitat, 2015). For more on collective shelters, see UNHCR, *Guideline for Collective Shelter and Small Shelter Units in Lebanon* (Beirut: UNHCR, 2012).

12. For another, more complicated humanitarian attempt to categorize the shelters in Lebanon, see the UNHCR, "Shelter Typologies," accessed January 16, 2024, https://data.unhcr.org/en/documents/download/62289.

13. Known as the Nazih Karami Warehouse, this shelter was located in the village of Miriata to the east of Tripoli. Over forty refugee households were living around the warehouse, sharing very basic facilities.

14. The Waha Complex, or Al-Waha arcade, was up on a hillside on the outskirts of Tripoli. It housed over 120 households and had the dubious distinction of being featured in a sympathetic article in the British *Daily Mail*. See Paul Donnelley, "Inside the Abandoned Lebanese Shopping Centre That Is Now Home to More than 1,000 Syrian Refugees," *Daily Mail*, June 18, 2014.

15. For more on the dynamics of the labor migration between Lebanon and Syria, see John Chalcraft, *The Invisible Cage: Syrian Migrant Workers in Lebanon* (Stanford: Stanford University Press, 2009).

16. Interview with Mona Harb, Beirut, April 13, 2018.

17. Interview, Harb.

18. For more on the differences between different municipal responses in Lebanon, see Alexander Betts, Fulya Memisoglu, and Ali Ali, "What Difference Do Mayors Make? The Role of Municipal Authorities in Turkey and Lebanon's Response to Syrian Refugees," *Journal of Refugee Studies* 34, no. 1 (2020): 491–519.

19. Interview with anonymous refugee family, informal tented settlement near

Bar Elias, April 17, 2018. I am grateful to Mark E. Breeze for conducting this interview.

20. Interview, anonymous refugee family.

21. Interview, Kassem, April 10, 2018. As another shelter specialist put it, improving informal settlements involves "a constant struggle with the authorities because they do not want to see the use of permanent materials." Interview with Nick Harcourt, Norwegian Refugee Council, Beirut, April 13, 2018.

22. An intermediary called the *"shaweesh"* was crucial to these relationships as they managed the recruitment of laborers and the relationship with farm owners. See Faten Kikano, Gabriel Fauveaud, and Gonzalo Lizarralde, "Policies of Exclusion: The Case of Syrian Refugees in Lebanon," *Journal of Refugee Studies* 34, no. 1 (2021): 422–52.

23. For more on the legal status of Syrian refugees in Lebanon, see Maja Janmyr, "Precarity in Exile: The Legal Status of Syrian Refugees in Lebanon," *Refugee Survey Quarterly* 35, no. 4 (2016): 58–78. For more on the *kafala* system, see Amrita Pande, "'The Paper That You Have in Your Hand Is My Freedom': Migrant Domestic Work and the Sponsorship (Kafala) System in Lebanon," *International Migration Review* 47, no. 2 (2013): 414–41.

24. Based on interviews in 2018, the ground rent for an informal tented settlement could be as little as fifty US dollars per year. This is compared to $600–$2000 for space in a collective shelter and upward of $5,000 for a private rented apartment.

25. "Occupancy free of charge," or OFC, was the term given to the scheme by the Norwegian Refugee Council (NRC). At UNHCR, a similar scheme was called "small shelter units," or SSUs. In October 2018, the NRC released an impact evaluation: NRC, *An Evaluation of the NRC Shelter Occupancy Free-of-Charge Modality in Lebanon* (Beirut: NRC, 2018).

26. Interview, Harcourt.

27. Interview, Harcourt.

28. The scheme worked by making Syrian families more attractive as tenants, but it also produced an incentive for uncontrolled development. Developers were building skeletons of buildings and then applying for funding through the program in order to finish them off; in effect, the scheme offered a subsidy for continued sprawl.

29. Interview, Harcourt.

30. For more on self-reliance and its history, see Claudena Skran and Evan Easton-Calabria, "Old Concepts Making New History: Refugee Self-Reliance, Livelihoods and the 'Refugee Entrepreneur,'" *Journal of Refugee Studies* 33, no. 1 (2020): 1–21.

31. Interview, Harcourt.

32. This point has been developed particularly clearly in Kikano, Fauveaud, and Lizarralde, "Policies of Exclusion," 447, which argues that the result of shelter policies in Lebanon was "concealed ghettos, producing the very outcome that Lebanon was trying to avoid when it banned camps."

33. As the deputy representative at UNHCR put it, "If, as a refugee, you cross a checkpoint and you don't have your residency permit, they will arrest you. Simple as that." Interview with Emmanuel Gignac, UNHCR Lebanon, Beirut, April 13, 2018. For more on checkpoint dynamics, see Lama Mourad, "Brothers, Workers or Syrians? The Politics of Naming in Lebanese Municipalities," *Journal of Refugee Studies* 34, no. 2 (2021): 1387–99.

34. Michael Walzer, *Spheres of Justice: A Defence of Pluralism and Equality* (Oxford: Robertson, 1983), 39.

35. UNHCR, *Policy on Alternatives.*

36. Interview, Gignac. Emphasis mine.

37. Interview, Gignac.

38. Humanitarianism is meant to act as a safety net, they argue, designed to kick in and save lives when bigger systems and structures break down. The classic argument for this kind of minimalist, "classical" humanitarianism can be found in David Rieff, *A Bed for the Night: Humanitarianism in Crisis* (London: Vintage, 2002).

39. Some aid agencies in Lebanon took this view, such as Oxfam's "one-programme" approach.

40. Interview with anonymous aid worker, Amman, May 23, 2018.

41. Interview with Mona Fawaz, American University of Beirut, Beirut, April 14, 2018.

42. An engaging account of one meeting during which the idea of camps was thrown back on the table can be found in Fawaz, "Planning," 99.

43. Interview, Fawaz.

44. Mona Fawaz et al., eds. *Refugees as City-Makers* (Beirut: Issam Fares Institute, 2018). See also Mona Fawaz, "An Unusual Clique of City-Makers: Social Networks in the Production of a Neighborhood in Beirut (1950–75)," *International Journal of Urban and Regional Research* 32, no. 3 (2008): 565–85.

45. Michel De Certeau, *The Practice of Everyday Life* (Berkeley: University of California Press, 1984). As one scholar puts it, tactics allow the weak to break free from constraints, offering a chance for "redemption from the overbearing panopticism of modern society." See Jon Mitchell, "A Fourth Critic of the Enlightenment: Michel De Certeau and the Ethnography of Subjectivity," *Social Anthropology* 15, no. 1 (2007): 99.

46. True, refugees were trying to work around constraints by acting opportunistically, occupying spaces that could be found in empty shopping malls, at the edge of fields, in unfinished buildings, and so on. Yet to interpret this in De Certeau's terms would mean suggesting it was a form of subversion or resistance, which would both misunderstand the nature of power in Lebanon and idealize the refugees' position of weakness.

47. Jordan offers a good example of this ineffective governmental control. The aid agencies in the camps of Azraq and Za'atari seemed, at first glance, to be purveyors of order and control, but even in this case, they were being led by government policy and they had limited power in practice.

48. There has been a tendency in recent scholarship to treat aid workers as if they are the "the most powerful pacific weapons of the new world order." See Michael Hardt and Antonio Negri, *Empire* (Cambridge, MA: Harvard University Press, 2000), 36. In reality, humanitarians do not wield totalizing power but are highly restricted in what they do—and they are always at risk of being ejected from a country.

49. This is a point made particularly clear by Jon Mitchell, who also notes that there is an antimodern attitude at play here, "a theology of the human spirit as redemptive counterpoint to the [perceived] moral bankruptcy of modernity." Mitchell, "A Fourth Critic," 103.

50. On the idea of "alchemical" humanitarianism, see Barnett, *Empire of Humanity*, 39–40.

Chapter 5: Shelter as Pragmatics

1. The phrase came from a federal press conference on August 31, 2015, quoted and discussed in Trauner and Turton, "Welcome Culture," 33–43; Billy Holzberg, "'Wir Schaffen Das': Hope and Hospitality beyond the Humanitarian Border," *Journal of Sociology* 57, no. 3 (2021): 743–59.

2. Interview with Uwe Wilhelms, Berlin, October 25, 2017.

3. Interview with Sascha Langenbach, Berlin, October 23, 2017.

4. Interview, Wilhelms.

5. Interview with Maria Kipp, Berlin, March 27, 2018; interview, Wilhelms.

6. Friederike Windel, Arita Balaram, and Krystal M. Perkins, "Discourses of the *Willkommenskultur* (Welcoming Culture) in Germany," *Critical Discourse Studies* 19, no. 1 (2022): 93–116; Trauner and Turton, "Welcome Culture."

7. Justin Huggler, "Berlin Turns Stasi Headquarters into Refugee Shelter," *Daily Telegraph*, November 23, 2015.

8. Holly Young, "Life in the Aluminium Whale: A Study of Berlin's ICC Shelter," in *Structures of Protection? Rethinking Refugee Shelter*, ed. Tom Scott-Smith and Mark E. Breeze (New York: Berghahn Books, 2020), 163–73.

9. For a comprehensive overview of refugee accommodation in Germany during this period, see Peter Cachola Schmal, Oliver Elser, and Anna Scheuermann, *Making Heimat: Germany, Arrival Country* (Berlin: Hatje Cantz Verlag, 2016). This book describes itself (on the title page) as an "Atlas of Refugee Housing."

10. The forced labor camp at Tempelhof was known as Columbia-Haus, the only SS concentration camp in Berlin. For more on this history, see Susan Pollock and Reinhard Bernbeck, "A Gate to a Darker World: Excavating at the Tempelhof Airport," in *Ethics and the Archaeology of Violence*, ed. Alfredo Gonzalez-Ruibal and Gabriel Moshenska (London: Springer, 2015), 137–52; Maria Theresia Starzmann, "Excavating Tempelhof Airfield: Objects of Memory and the Politics of Absence," *Rethinking History* 18, no. 2 (2014): 211–29; Toby Parsloe, "Arriving through Infrastructures: Berlin's Institutional Shelters for Refugees 2015–2019" (PhD diss., University of Cambridge, 2021).

11. For more on Welthauptstadt Germania (World Capital Germania), see

Jochen Thies, Ian Cooke, and MaryBeth Friedrich, *Hitler's Plans for Global Domination: Nazi Architecture and Ultimate War Aims* (New York: Berghahn Books, 2012); Colin Philpott, *Relics of the Reich: The Buildings the Nazis Left Behind* (Barnsley: Pen and Sword, 2016).

12. Interview with Kerstin Meyer, Berlin, March 27, 2018. See also Clare Copley, "Curating Tempelhof: Negotiating the Multiple Histories of Berlin's 'Symbol of Freedom,'" *Urban History* 44, no. 4 (2016): 698–717.

13. In 2014, a citizen referendum was held, which suggested preserving the entire space of the park and prohibiting development by law. The proposal was passed, and the story of Tempelhof moved into a new phase. It had been a symbol of totalitarianism and then a symbol of openness. The airfield now represented something different: the city's resistance to gentrification and opposition to the enclosure of this important public space.

14. Randy Malamud, "The New Psychogeography of Tempelhof Airport, Once a Nazi Landmark," *The Atlantic*, December 23, 2013.

15. Malamud, "The New Psychogeography." See also Nick Foster, "Berlin Neighborhood Thrives at Edge of Old Airport," *New York Times*, August 8, 2013.

16. Interview, Kipp. The facility inside Tempelhof was run by Tamaja, whose director, Michael Elias, was interviewed in the *New York Times*. See Alison Smale, "Tempelhof Airport, Once a Lifeline for Berliners, Reprises Role for Refugees," *New York Times*, February 10, 2016.

17. Interview, Langenbach.

18. Ayham Dalal, Aline Fraikin, and Antonia Noll, "Appropriating Berlin's Tempohomes," in *Spatial Transformations: Kaleidoscopic Perspectives on the Refiguration of Spaces*, ed. Angela Million et al. (London: Routledge, 2022), 285–93.

19. Interview, Kipp.

20. Interview with anonymous resident, Tempelhof, October 22, 2017.

21. Interview with anonymous resident, Tempelhof, March 28, 2018.

22. Toby Parsloe, "From Emergency Shelter to Community Shelter: Berlin's Tempelhof Refugee Camp," in *Structures of Protection? Rethinking Refugee Shelter*, ed. Tom Scott-Smith and Mark E. Breeze (New York: Berghahn Books, 2020), 275–86.

23. Interview with Christiane Beckmann, Berlin, October 24, 2017.

24. Interview with anonymous resident, Tempelhof, March 27, 2018.

25. Goh, "Structures to Shelter," 175–84.

26. Interview with Jenny Rumohr, Berlin, October 24, 2017.

27. Interview, anonymous resident, March 27, 2018. For more on the longer-term implications of this shelter, see Parsloe, "Arriving through Infrastructures"; Baumann, "Moving, Containing, Displacing," 15–29.

28. Interview, Rumohr.

29. Interview with Holly Young, Berlin, October 23, 2017.

30. Jacques Derrida, *Of Hospitality* (Stanford: Stanford University Press, 2000); Michael Herzfeld, "'As in Your Own House': Hospitality, Ethnography, and the Stereotype of Mediterranean Society," in *Honor and Shame and the Unity of the Mediterranean*, ed. David D. Gilmore, (Washington, DC: American Anthropolog-

ical Association, 1987), 75–89; Andrew Shryock, "Breaking Hospitality Apart: Bad Hosts, Bad Guests, and the Problem of Sovereignty," *Journal of the Royal Anthropological Institute* 18, no. 1 (2012): S20–S33.

31. As Jacques Derrida argues, hospitality is, in many ways, inseparable from hostility. Offering someone a bed for the night requires mastery over a space, and we can only extend hospitality from a position of control. Derrida shows how the two words "host" and "hostile" are etymologically connected since the word *hostis* (which means an enemy or "hostile stranger" in Latin) is related to the term *hospes* (which means a guest or "welcome stranger"). In order to meaningfully offer hospitality, in other words, we need the ability to exclude others and control the place from which we welcome. Derrida, *Of Hospitality.* For more on the dynamics of hospitality, see Matei Candea and Giovanni Da Col, "The Return to Hospitality," *Journal of the Royal Anthropological Institute* 18 (2012): S1–S19; Andrew Shryock, "Thinking about Hospitality, with Derrida, Kant, and the Balga Bedouin," *Anthropos* 103, no. 2 (2008): 405–21. For more on hospitality specifically in relation to forced displacement, see Catherine Brun, "Hospitality: Becoming 'IDPs' and 'Hosts' in Protracted Displacement," *Journal of Refugee Studies* 23, no. 3 (2010): 337–55; Jonathan Darling, "Becoming Bare Life: Asylum, Hospitality, and the Politics of Encampment," *Environment and Planning D: Society and Space* 27, no. 4 (2009): 649–65.

32. Interview, Rumohr.

33. The essay was entitled *Building Dwelling, Thinking*, originally published in 1954. It has been reprinted in Martin Heidegger, *Poetry, Language, Thought* (New York: Harper and Row, 1971), 141–163. For the application of this idea to housing, see Hazel Easthope, "A Place Called Home," *Housing, Theory and Society* 21, no. 3 (2004): 128–38.

34. Humanitarian emergencies have recently generated a range of new technologies and objects that are specifically designed to help balance these two imperatives. Scott-Smith, "Sticky Technologies," 3–24.

35. Interview, Rumohr.

36. The asylum process in Germany involved moving through many different stages and related accommodation. First, there was police registration at a designated first-arrival point (*Ankunftszentrum*). Next, the asylum seeker was allocated to one of the federal states through a national distribution system called König-steiner Schlüssel, which shared allocations according to population size and gross domestic product. Once they arrived in the state, asylum seekers had to reside first in official emergency accommodation (*Notunterkünft*) while their asylum case was processed, which could take up to two or three years. Sometimes, they were be moved to collective accommodation centers (*Gemeinschaftsunterkünft*), and only after the asylum status was clarified did refugees have the right to choose their own accommodation—although many stayed in state-run facilities if they did not have the means to move.

37. Liliane Wong, *Adaptive Reuse: Extending the Lives of Buildings* (Basel: Birkhäuser, 2016).

38. As Stewart Brand puts it, buildings can learn. The problem with modernist architecture, Brand suggests, is it has so often been driven by the grand visions of an expert designer who focused on producing finished blueprints and plans that were not open to adaptation or truly responsive to the needs of inhabitants. See Stewart Brand, *How Buildings Learn: What Happens after They're Built* (London: Viking, 1994). A similar line of argument also emerges in the work of John Turner, who advocates the importance of placing dwellers in control. See John Turner, "Housing as a Verb," in *Freedom to Build: Dweller Control of the Housing Process*, ed. John Turner and Robert Fichter (New York: Macmillan Press, 1972), 148–75.

39. This paragraph is strongly informed by Níall McLaughlin, "Six Pockets of Time" (lecture, University College London, London, England, March 20, 2019).

40. Marvin Trachtenberg, *Building-in-Time: From Giotto to Alberti and Modern Oblivion* (New Haven: Yale University Press, 2010).

41. Brand, *How Buildings Learn*.

Chapter 6: Shelter as Poetics

1. Alejandro Aravena, *Reporting from the Front: Biennale Architettura 2016, Venice*, 2 vols. (Venezia: Marsilio, 2016), 1:3–4.

2. What Design Can Do (WDCD) is one of many events and organizations promoting the power of social design. For a foundational text, see Cameron Sinclair and Kate Stohr, eds., *Design like You Give a Damn: Architectural Responses to Humanitarian Crises* (London: Thames and Hudson, 2006).

3. Milja Lindberg, "We House Refugees" (Finland), assisted by Christopher Erdman. Listed in the official catalog of the fifteenth Biennale Architettura. See Aravena, *Reporting from the Front*, 2:42–43.

4. Harri Ahokas, Tomi Laine, Akseli Leinonen, Pia Rautiainen, Nikolai Rautio, and Matias Saresvuo, "Helsinkikasbah" (Finland), assisted by Pekka Huima. Listed in the official catalog of the fifteenth Biennale Architettura. Aravena, *Reporting from the Front*, 2:42–43.

5. Norman Foster Foundation, "Making the Droneport Prototype" (Britain). Listed in the official catalog of the fifteenth Biennale Architettura. Aravena, *Reporting from the Front*, 1:364. The Bienniale contained many other examples of refugee housing, including a large number just within the German pavilion. For an overview, see Schmal, Elser, and Scheuermann, *Making Heimat*. For a brief listing within the exhibition catalogue, see Aravena, *Reporting from the Front*, 2:46–47.

6. Scott-Smith, "Humanitarian Neophilia," 2229–51. In relation to humanitarian architecture specifically, see Tom Scott-Smith, "The Humanitarian-Architect Divide," *Forced Migration Review* 55 (June 2017): 67–68; Scott-Smith, "Places for People," 14–22.

7. Elke Delugan-Meissl, Sabine Dreher, and Christian Muhr, *Reports and Stories from 'Places for People'* (Venice: Biennale Architettura, 2016).

8. Marc Augé, *Non-places: Introduction to an Anthropology of Supermodernity* (London: Verso, 1995).

9. The location of this building was Pfeiffergasse 1150 in central Vienna. The

building dates from the 1990s and was formerly the headquarters of an information-technology company.

10. The idea of the bottle doorbell connects with the concern with "knockiness" in chapter 1—that is, the need for a way for visitors to indicate their presence when it was impossible to knock on canvas or blankets.

11. In the autumn of 2015, 788,000 refugees passed through Austria, and three hundred thousand through the city of Vienna. Around ninety thousand applied for asylum in Austria in 2015. Figures cited in Delugan-Meissl, Dreher, and Muhr, *Reports and Stories*, 9.

12. Scott-Smith, "The Humanitarian-Architect Divide."

13. Interview with Sabine Dreher, Vienna, February 13, 2017. More about this project can be found in Delugan-Meissl, Dreher, and Muhr, *Reports and Stories*.

14. Interview with Clemens Foschi, Vienna, February 14, 2017.

15. Some dismissed Aravena's idea as a gimmick, arguing that they were trying to convince people that "less is enough," which became an elaborate architectural excuse for substandard accommodation in the poorest communities. See, e.g., Boano and Perucich, "Half-Happy Architecture," 59–81. Perhaps this is a little unfair, however, as the "half house" was not really about getting people to accept less, but rather allowing them to do more.

16. Delugan-Meissl, Dreher, and Muhr, *Reports and Stories*, 21–23.

17. Interview with Gunter Katherl, Vienna, February 9, 2017. The project leader even spent time living under a parasol installation to get a sense of the limitations of this concept.

18. Interview with Martin Haller, Vienna, February 8, 2017.

19. Rudofsky, *Architecture without Architects*.

20. Victor Papanek, *Design for the Real World: Human Ecology and Social Change* (St. Albans: Paladin, 1974).

21. Bachelard, *Poetics of Space*. These influences are all documented in Delugan-Meissl, Dreher, and Muhr, *Reports and Stories*.

22. Interview with anonymous aid worker, Vienna, February 9, 2017.

23. The furniture was made from plywood boards that were used for casting concrete in large building projects. They were known as Doka boards, and they had already been stained yellow before being donated to the project by the Austrian firm Umdasch.

24. This project was located at Erdbergstraße, in a 68,000-square-meter building complex, partly managed by Caritas and Arbeiter-Samariter-Bund. It had previously been a training school for customs officers and border guards, part of the state apparatus to defend national borders.

25. The labor was permitted under asylum regulations, which allowed a limited amount of remuneration for community work.

26. Interview with Harald Gruendl, Vienna, February 10, 2017.

27. EOOS, *Meet EOOS*, pamphlet (Vienna: EOOS, June 2014), 22. See also EOOS, *The Cooked Kitchen: A Poetical Analysis* (Vienna: Springer, 2006).

28. Interview, Gruendl.

29. Delugan-Meissl, Dreher, and Muhr, *Reports and Stories*, 26–28.

30. Augé, *Non-places*, 109.

31. Interview with Marie-Therese Harnoncourt-Fuchs, Vienna, February 9, 2017.

32. Refugees were sharing vast buildings with people they barely knew, and for good reason, many of them preferred to focus on their own preoccupations rather than participating in an ambitious scheme for human improvement. The less successful elements of these projects were, therefore, those that tried to reshape human relations, build new communal forms, and placed unreasonable burdens on the inhabitants. The idea of an alternative economy in Haus Erdberg, e.g., struggled due to lack of time and the problems of creating a digital currency. The idea of forging a close-knit community through social furniture was hampered by the preference of refugees to *leave* the building rather than stay within its walls. The idea of kitchens as communal hubs never quite worked because residents seldom lingered in the common areas and rarely shared their food with others. Some of these issues could later be solved through more clever design (in the case of the kitchens, e.g., the team behind the social furniture created some ingenious cabinets on wheels to link public and private space), yet the bigger visions led to disappointment, even when channeled through smaller steps.

33. Bachelard, *Poetics of Space*, 6.

34. Warner, "Report," 149–50.

35. Bachelard, *Poetics of Space*, 5.

36. Bachelard, *Poetics of Space*, 46.

Chapter 7: Shelter as Aesthetics

1. Maryline Baumard, "Des Villes Refuges Pour Migrants," *Le Monde*, June 20, 2016; Maryline Baumard, "Paris Aura un Camp Humanitaire Pour Accueillir les Réfugiés," *Le Monde*, May 31, 2016. Drawing attention to Paris's history as a beacon of the Enlightenment, the deputy mayor for urban planning said to me, "If we cannot organize a decent way of welcoming these people, well, where are our values?" Interview with Jean-Louis Missika, Paris, May 29, 2017.

2. The formal name for this shelter, situated at Porte de la Chapelle, was the Centre Humanitaire Paris-Nord.

3. Interview with Maryline Baumard, Paris, June 1, 2017.

4. Interview, Missika.

5. Interview with Michèle Zaoüi, Paris, May 29, 2017.

6. Interview, Zaoüi.

7. I am indebted to Zoey Poll for pointing this out, as well as for her work on the bubble and assistance in Paris. See also Zoey Poll, "Bursting the Bubble: A Critical Examination of Hospitable Paris" (master's thesis, University of Oxford, 2017).

8. Lauren Collins, "Paris's First Official Refugee Shelter," *New Yorker*, November 7, 2016.

9. Jean-Laurent Cassely, "Le Paris d'Anne Hidalgo: Les Bobos, C'est Fini, Voici les Sosos," *Slate France*, June 28, 2013.

10. Interview with Cyrille Hanappe, Paris, June 2017.

11. Interview with Julien Beller, Saint-Denis, May 31, 2017.

12. Interview, Zaoüi; interview, Missika.

13. Marc Dessauce, *The Inflatable Moment: Pneumatics and Protest in 1968* (New York: Princeton Architectural Press, 1999).

14. Interview, Beller.

15. I was accompanied on this trip by Zoey Poll and Mark E. Breeze, to whom I am indebted for organizational support, interpretation, and countless conversations on ephemeral architecture.

16. Interview with Hans-Walter Müller, la Ferté-Alais, May 11, 2017. Here, Müller sounded like Claude Lévi-Strauss: "The house is an extension of the person; like an extra skin, carapace or second layer of clothes, it serves as much to reveal and display as it does to hide and protect." Quoted in Janet Carsten and Stephen Hugh-Jones, "Introduction," in *About the House: Lévi-Strauss and Beyond*, ed. Janet Carsten and Stephen Hugh-Jones (Cambridge: Cambridge University Press, 1995), 1.

17. It seems that Müller was trying to show that building is not, in fact, "an act against nature," as Neil Harris argues. See Neil Harris, *Building Lives: Constructing Rites and Passages* (New Haven: Yale University Press, 1999), 1.

18. For an accessible introduction to this vision of humanitarianism, which also happens to be oriented around the metaphor of shelter, see Rieff, *A Bed*. For an anthropological introduction to the "classical" humanitarian principles, such as neutrality, impartiality, and independence, see Redfield, *Life in Crisis*, chap. 4.

19. Barbara Holub, *Das Bienvenue: Ein Recht Auf Raum Für Alle* (Vienna: Social Design Arts as Urban Innovation, 2016).

20. Stephanie Nolen, "Home, On Demand: Abeer Seikaly's Pop-Up Tents," *Globe and Mail*, November 18, 2015.

21. Kashmira Gander, "The Designers Trying to Help Victims of the Refugee Crisis by Building Apps and Shelters," *Independent*, June 30, 2016; Oliver Wainwright, "Why IKEA's Flatpack Refugee Shelter Won Design of the Year," *Guardian*, January 27, 2017; Rich McEachran, "Exo Units: The Shelters Redefining Emergency Housing," *Guardian*, April 3, 2014.

22. Adam Taylor, "A Dutch Architect's Plan to Put Europe's Refugees on a Man-Made Island near Tunisia," *Washington Post*, June 1, 2016. See also the proposal for a new transnational polity developed under the name Refugia. Robin Cohen and Nicholas Van Hear, *Refugia: Radical Solutions to Mass Displacement* (Abingdon: Routledge, 2020). Other related plans include Egyptian billionaire Naguib Sawiris's intentions to buy a Greek island where refugees can found a new society and the Refugee Nation proposed by Jason Buzi, an American real-estate developer.

23. Interview with Matthieu Mirta, Paris, May 30, 2017.

24. Peter Redfield, "Shacktopia: The Meantime Future of Humanitarian Design," *Social Anthropology / Anthropologie sociale* 30, no. 2 (2022): 16–33.

25. Redfield is comparing these restricted utopias to the more familiar, modernist utopias of economic growth, rising wealth, and a more robust welfare state.

Much of the success of this approach, however, turns on whether or not such products suppress or facilitate effective social change. Scott-Smith, "Humanitarian Neophilia," 2239.

26. As Redfield points out, utopias are always built with a specific frame of reference. Thomas More's 1551 book, which marks the origin of the word, was also a creature of its time, presenting a world of permanent equilibrium, a world that was so perfect that it required no forward trajectory, a static utopia that reflected a premodern ideal of orderly and sealed societies. Modern utopias, in contrast, are oriented instead around the idea of progress. Redfield, "Shacktopia."

27. Interview, Zaoüi.

28. Maryline Baumard, "Camp Humanitaire: L'Etat et Paris en Quête de Compromis," *Le Monde*, June 10, 2016. This tension between the city and the state is an interesting part of this example. Much of the literature on humanitarianism is rather state centric, but the recent expansion of Cities of Sanctuary and the contrasting attitude of mayors such as Hidalgo can illuminate the many fissures within humanitarian politics. For another example, see Jonathan Darling, "A City of Sanctuary: The Relational Re-Imagining of Sheffield's Asylum Politics," *Transactions of the Institute of British Geographers* 35, no. 1 (2010): 125–40.

29. For an influential articulation of this point, see Didier Fassin, "Humanitarianism as a Politics of Life," *Public Culture* 19, no. 3 (2007): 499–520. The relationship between humanitarianism and politics is especially well documented in the case of France. See, e.g., Didier Fassin, "Compassion and Repression: The Moral Economy of Immigration Policies in France," *Cultural Anthropology* 20, no. 3 (2005): 362–87; Ticktin, "Where Ethics and Politics Meet," 33–49; Ticktin, *Casualties of Care.*

30. Tom Scott-Smith, "Humanitarian Dilemmas in a Mobile World," *Refugee Survey Quarterly* 35, no. 2 (2016): 1–21.

31. Défenseur des Droits, *Rapport d'Observation: Démantèlement des Campements et Prise en Charge des Exilés* (Paris: Défenseur des Droits, 2016); UNHCR, *L'Experience des Centres d'Accueil En France* (Paris: UNHCR, 2017).

32. Interview, Mirta.

33. Interview, Mirta.

34. Baumard, "Paris Aura un Camp."

35. Interview, Beller.

36. Maria Hagan, "Contingent Camps: An Ethnographic Study of Contested Encampment in the Northern French and Northern Moroccan Borderlands" (PhD diss., University of Cambridge, 2022).

37. Interview with Caroline Maillary, Paris, May 30, 2017.

38. Interview with Sébastien Thiéry, Paris, June 2, 2017. Haussmann's cleansing of Paris, interestingly, was also about managing migrants—in that case, migrants fleeing rural poverty from the countryside.

39. The distinction between interior and exterior has been a recurring theme in anthropology. In a famous article on the Berber House, Pierre Bourdieu argues that crossing the threshold of the home triggers a change that makes the world turn inside out. One could say something similar about the Yellow Bubble. Upon enter-

ing the bubble, a migrant's relationship to the state went into reverse. Outside, there was relative freedom but a great deal of squalor. Inside, there was relative comfort but a great deal of control and restriction. As they moved from outside to inside, migrants became less visible to Parisians, and they then became dispatched as a political problem. Rendering migrants invisible may not have been the architect's *intention*, but it did, however, become the effect. See Bourdieu, "The Berber House," 98–110.

40. This brings to mind the earlier case of la Cité de Refuge, constructed by Le Corbusier and the Salvation Army under bridges across the Seine. As one architectural commentator asked, "Whose discomfort was thereby relieved?" Was it "the hut dwellers or everyone else's?" Ann Cline, *A Hut of One's Own: Life Outside the Circle of Architecture* (Cambridge: MIT Press, 1997), 123.

41. Interview, Beller.

42. Interview, Zaoüi.

43. Alex Andreou, "Anti-homeless Spikes: 'Sleeping Rough Opened My Eyes to the City's Barbed Cruelty,'" *Guardian*, February 18, 2015; Naomi Smith and Peter Walters, "Desire Lines and Defensive Architecture in Modern Urban Environments," *Urban Studies* 55, no. 13 (2018): 2980–95.

44. Interview, Beller.

45. See chapter 5 and, for a summary, see Candea and Da Col, "Return to Hospitality," S1–S19.

46. Mark Duffield, *Post-humanitarianism: Governing Precarity in the Digital World* (Cambridge: Polity, 2019).

47. Redfield, "Bioexpectations," 157–84; Peter Redfield, "Fluid Technologies: The Bush Pump, the Lifestraw® and Microworlds of Humanitarian Design," *Social Studies of Science* 46, no. 2 (2016): 159–83.

48. Lilie Chouliaraki, "The Theatricality of Humanitarianism: A Critique of Celebrity Advocacy," *Communication and Critical Cultural Studies* 9, no. 1 (2012): 1–21; James Thompson, *Humanitarian Performance: From Disaster Tragedies to Spectacles of War* (London: Seagull Books, 2013).

49. Interview with Antoine Bazin, Paris, June 1, 2017.

50. The worst thing about this "designer solution," she continued, was the way that it "contributes to the idea that soon we will be able to put the bubble away because people will stop arriving. . . . The City Hall created this camp to hide the misery, and that is what this camp serves to do. It hides the misery." Interview, Maillary.

51. For an example of this situation, see Ioanna Kotsioni, "Detention of Migrants and Asylum-Seekers: The Challenge for Humanitarian Actors," *Refugee Survey Quarterly* 35, no. 2 (2016): 41–55.

52. The legal activist was dismissing beauty, but in other contexts, it is common for activists to highlight aesthetic violations and poor design as an affront to human dignity. This is, of course, part of what motivates humanitarian architects in the first place. I am grateful to one of the anonymous reviewers of this manuscript for pointing this out.

53. Esther Ruth Charlesworth describes humanitarian architecture as a "healing gesture," but it can be a harming gesture as well. The Yellow Bubble showed how humanitarian architecture can communicate compassion while simultaneously facilitating control, revealing a far darker side to the new world of benevolent large-scale design. Charlesworth, *Humanitarian Architecture*, 6.

54. Maryline Baumard, "Le Centre Humanitaire Pour Migrants, une Occasion Manquée Pour Anne Hidalgo," *Le Monde*, April 3, 2018.

Conclusion

1. Hannah Arendt, *The Jewish Writings, ed*. Jerome Kohn and Ron Feldman (New York: Schocken Books, 2007), 264. This quotation is from the short essay "We Refugees," which was originally published in 1943 in the Jewish periodical the *Menorah Journal*.

2. For a useful overview of autonomy, see Gerald Dworkin, *The Theory and Practice of Autonomy* (Cambridge: Cambridge University Press, 1988). Definition issues will be developed below.

3. Joseph Raz, *The Morality of Freedom* (Oxford: Clarendon Press, 1986), 154.

4. Fassin, "Humanitarianism," 499–520. See also Peter Redfield, "The Unbearable Lightness of Expats: Double Binds of Humanitarian Mobility," *Cultural Anthropology* 27, no. 2 (2012): 358–82. Adia Benton deepens these arguments about inequality by pointing out the specific dynamics of race. See Adia Benton, "Risky Business: Race, Nonequivalence and the Humanitarian Politics of Life," *Visual Anthropology* 29, no. 2 (2016): 187–203.

5. This point is articulated in Joel Feinberg, *The Moral Limits of the Criminal Law*, vol. 3, *Harm to Self* (Oxford: Oxford University Press, 1986), 27–51. See also Thomas Scanlon, *What We Owe to Each Other* (Cambridge: Belknap Press, 1998), 252–53.

6. Among the rich literature on harms caused by humanitarianism, there tends to be more on large-scale rather than small-scale effects. See, e.g., Terry, *Condemned to Repeat?*

7. For a classic edited collection on the problems with participation in aid, see Bill Cooke and Uma Kothari, eds., *Participation: The New Tyranny?* (London: Zed Books, 2001).

8. This summary draws on Raz, *Morality of Freedom*, 369–99. See also Gerald Dworkin, "Autonomy," in *A Companion to Contemporary Political Philosophy*, ed. Robert Goodin, Philip Pettit, and Thomas Pogge (London: Wiley, 2017), 439–51. Raz articulates three conditions rather than two, the third being mental capacity.

9. For more on cash for shelter, see Catholic Relief Services, *Using Cash for Shelter: An Overview of CRS Programs* (Baltimore: Catholic Relief Services, 2015); ICRC and International Federation of Red Cross and Red Crescent Societies, *Guidelines for Cash Transfer Programming* (Geneva: ICRC and International Federation of Red Cross and Red Crescent Societies, 2007); UNHCR, *An Introduction to Cash-Based Interventions in UNHCR Operations* (Geneva: UNHCR, 2012).

10. I want to make clear that this is an ideal rather than reality because some

people, sadly, cannot find safety in the place they call home. It might also be said that this is a Western ideal as the notion of autonomy certainly emerges from the European intellectual tradition. Yet the integration of cultural practices into the case for autonomy has always been part of the attraction of this idea. There is a gendered aspect to this, too, especially when we consider how control over parts of the home is patterned.

11. For a recent overview of literature on homemaking in relation to forced displacement, see Luce Beeckmans et al., eds. *Making Home(s) in Displacement: Critical Reflections on a Spatial Practice* (Leuven: Leuven University Press, 2022); Boccagni and Bonfanti, *Migration and Domestic Space*; Daniela Giudici, "Home-making and Forced Migration: A Bibliography" (working paper, HOASI, University of Trento, Trento, Italy, 2019).

12. This argument about autonomy is also relevant in relation to domestic-housing policy. See Casey Dawkins, "Autonomy and Housing Policy," *Housing, Theory and Society* 34, no. 4 (2017): 420–38.

13. Interview with Don Weinreich, New York, January 17, 2017.

14. Interview with Tom Newby, Oxford, November 23, 2016.

15. The modernist tradition, in particular, has tended to dismiss and overturn local ways of life by imposing a mistaken universalism and strident set of beliefs about how humans *should* be living rather than reflecting how they *wish* to live their lives. For a classic account, see Scott, *Seeing like a State.*

16. In a different context, this has been described as the "unity of human misery." See Barrington Moore, *Reflections on the Causes of Human Misery and upon Certain Proposals to Eliminate Them* (Boston: Beacon Press, 1972), 1.

17. The most famous articulation of this point appears in John Rawls, *A Theory of Justice* (Oxford: Clarendon Press, 1972).

18. Amartya Sen, *Development as Freedom* (Oxford: Oxford University Press, 1999). Sen's capability approach is an explicit response to the idea of basic needs driving a theory of justice. If we focus on needs, he argues, we fail to reflect people's different priorities and we lose space for freedom. For Sen, the question was not whether the need is met but whether we have the *capability* to meet that need should we choose to do so. John Rawls's theory, in contrast, focuses on the distribution of "primary goods"—which he specifies as rights and liberties, opportunities and powers, income and wealth. These allow people to cover their own basic needs. See also John Rawls, *Political Liberalism* (New York: Columbia University Press, 1993), 180.

19. In some ways, this is the opposite approach to those of Sen and Rawls. Rather than focusing on what we require to meet our own needs (e.g., primary goods or capabilities), these approaches consider why the satisfaction of needs might be important.

20. David Wiggins, in particular, emphasizes tremendous moral force behind the notion of needs, which stimulates action in a way that "capability" cannot. "Given the special force carried by 'need,'" he argues, "we ought to try to grasp some special content that the word possesses in virtue of which that force accrues

to it." See David Wiggins, *Needs, Values, Truth* (Oxford: Oxford University Press, 1987), 6.

21. David Braybrooke, *Meeting Needs* (Princeton: Princeton University Press, 1987), 48–59.

22. David Miller, *Principles of Social Justice* (Cambridge, MA: Harvard University Press, 1999), 203–29.

23. Len Doyal and Ian Gough, *A Theory of Human Need* (Basingstoke: Macmillan, 1991), 49–50.

24. This list of nonmaterial needs comes from Paul Streeten, "Basics Needs: Premises and Promises," *Journal of Policy Modeling* 1, no. 1 (1979): 136–46.

25. Doyal and Gough, *Theory of Human Need*, 47–69. By "autonomy," they were referring to the mental competence to deliberate and the ability to choose from between a range of options—similar to the way I have framed autonomy in this conclusion. See also Lawrence Hamilton, *The Political Philosophy of Needs* (Cambridge: Cambridge University Press, 2003), 12–13, 35–47.

26. Gerard Rosich, *The Contested History of Autonomy: Interpreting European Modernity* (London: Bloomsbury, 2019); Jerome Schneewind, *The Invention of Autonomy: A History of Modern Moral Philosophy* (Cambridge: Cambridge University Press, 1998); Lucas Swaine, "The Origins of Autonomy," *History of Political Thought* 37, no. 2 (2016): 216–37.

27. Paul Guyer, "Kant on the Theory and Practice of Autonomy," *Social Philosophy and Policy* 20, no. 2 (2003): 70–98; Susan Meld Shell, *Kant and the Limits of Autonomy* (Cambridge, MA: Harvard University Press, 2009).

28. John Gray, *Mill on Liberty: A Defence* (London: Routledge, 2013), 54–57, 90–95; Douglas Husak, "Paternalism and Autonomy," *Philosophy and Public Affairs* 10, no. 1 (1981): 27–46. See also Harry Frankfurt, "Freedom of the Will and the Concept of a Person," *Journal of Philosophy* 68, no. 1 (1971): 5–20.

29. W. G. Sebald, *Austerlitz* (New York: Modern Library, 2002), 19.

30. For more on the politics of ephemerality in relation to architecture and the refugee camp, see Anooradha Siddiqi, "Ephemerality," *Comparative Studies of South Asia, Africa and the Middle East* 40, no. 1 (2020): 24–34.

31. Maria Hagan, "The Contingent Camp: Struggling for Shelter in Calais, France," in *Structures of Protection? Rethinking Refugee Shelter*, ed. Tom Scott-Smith and Mark E. Breeze (Oxford: Berghahn Books, 2020), 112.

32. Hicks and Mallet, *Lande*, 24.

33. William Wallis, George Parker, and Lucy Fisher, "First Asylum Seekers Moved to UK's Bibby Stockholm Barge," *Financial Times*, August 8, 2023. The use of ships as refugee accommodation has a long history, with one example—the use of a large boat stationed in the canals of Copenhagen to house refugees from Bosnia and Herzegovina—documented compellingly in the film *Flotel Europa* (dir. Vladimir Tomic, 2015.)

34. Bachelard, *Poetics of Space*, 81–82.

35. Bachelard, *Poetics of Space*, 81.

Bibliography

Aalto, Alvar. "Emergency Housing: Emergency Housing for Refugees and in Solution of Immediate Post-war Housing Problems." *Journal of the Royal Institute of British Architects* 48, no. 7 (1941): 119–21.

Agier, Michel. *The Jungle: Calais's Camps and Migrants*. Medford: Polity, 2018.

Agustín, Óscar García, and Martin Bak Jørgensen. *Solidarity and the 'Refugee Crisis' in Europe*. Basingstoke: Palgrave Macmillan, 2018.

AidEx. "Home." Accessed November 21, 2023. https://www.aid-expo.com.

Albadra, Dima, David Coley, and Jason Hart. "Toward Healthy Housing for the Displaced." *Journal of Architecture* 23, no. 1 (2018): 115–36.

Albadra, Dima, Marika Vellei, David Coley, and Jason Hart. "Thermal Comfort in Desert Refugee Camps: An Interdisciplinary Approach." *Building and Environment* 124 (2017): 460–77.

Alderman, Liz. "Wintry Blast in Greece Imperils Refugees in Crowded Camps." *New York Times*, January 11, 2017.

Amnesty International. *Trapped in Greece: An Avoidable Refugee Crisis*. London: Amnesty International Publications, 2016.

Andersson, Ruben. *No Go World: How Fear Is Redrawing Our Maps and Infecting Our Politics*. Oakland: University of California Press, 2019.

Andreou, Alex. "Anti-homeless Spikes: 'Sleeping Rough Opened My Eyes to the City's Barbed Cruelty.'" *Guardian*, February 18, 2015.

Aravena, Alejandro. *Reporting from the Front: Biennale Architettura 2016, Venice*. 2 vols. Venezia: Marsilio, 2016.

Aravena, Alejandro, and Andrés Iacobelli. *Elemental: Incremental Housing and Participatory Design Manual*. Ostfildern: Hatje Cantz, 2016.

Arendt, Hannah. *The Jewish Writings*. Edited by Jerome Kohn and Ron Feldman. New York: Schocken Books, 2007.

Arsan, Andrew. *Lebanon: A Country in Fragments*. London: Hurst and Company, 2018.

Augé, Marc. *Non-places: Introduction to an Anthropology of Supermodernity*. London: Verso, 1995.

Bachelard, Gaston. *The Poetics of Space*. Boston: Beacon Press, 1969.

Baker, Aryn. "After a Long Delay, Lebanon Finally Says Yes to IKEA Housing for Syrian Refugees." *Time*, December 16, 2013.

Baker, Aryn. "Greek Anarchists Are Finding Space for Refugees in Abandoned Hotels." *Time*, November 3, 2016.

Ban, Shigeru, and Riichi Miyake. *Shigeru Ban: Paper in Architecture*. New York: Rizzoli International Publications, 2009.

Barnett, Michael. *Empire of Humanity: A History of Humanitarianism*. Ithaca: Cornell University Press, 2011.

Baumann, Hanna. "Moving, Containing, Displacing: The Shipping Container as Refugee Shelter." In *Structures of Protection? Rethinking Refugee Shelter*, edited by Tom Scott-Smith and Mark E. Breeze, 15–29. Oxford: Berghahn Books, 2020.

Baumard, Maryline. "Camp Humanitaire: L'Etat et Paris en Quête de Compromis." *Le Monde*, June 10, 2016.

Baumard, Maryline. "Des Villes Refuges Pour Migrants." *Le Monde*, June 20, 2016.

Baumard, Maryline. "Le Centre Humanitaire Pour Migrants, une Occasion Manquée Pour Anne Hidalgo." *Le Monde*, April 3, 2018.

Baumard, Maryline. "Paris Aura un Camp Humanitaire Pour Accueillir les Réfugiés." *Le Monde*, May 31, 2016.

Beazley. "Flat-Packed Refugee Shelter Named Best Design of 2016." News release, Design Museum, London, January 26, 2017. https://www.beazley.com/news/2017/winners_beazley_designs_of_the_year.html.

Beeckmans, Luce, Alessandra Gola, Ashika Singh, and Hilde Heynen, eds. *Making Home(s) in Displacement: Critical Reflections on a Spatial Practice*. Leuven: Leuven University Press, 2022.

Belavilas, Nikos, and Polina Prentou. "The Typologies of Refugees Camps in Greece." Keynote address at Autonoma: International Conference on Urban Autonomy and the Collective City, Athens, Greece, July 1, 2016.

Bender, Felix. "Should Refugees Govern Refugee Camps?" *Critical Review of International Social and Political Philosophy* (2021): 1–24. https://doi.org/10.1080/13698230.2021.1941702.

Benton, Adia. "Risky Business: Race, Nonequivalence and the Humanitarian Politics of Life." *Visual Anthropology* 29, no. 2 (2016): 187–203.

Berger, John. *And Our Faces, My Heart, Brief as Photos*. London: Bloomsbury, 2014.

Betts, Alexander, and Paul Collier. *Refuge: Transforming a Broken Refugee System*. London: Allen Lane, 2017.

Betts, Alexander, Fulya Memisoglu, and Ali Ali. "What Difference Do Mayors Make? The Role of Municipal Authorities in Turkey and Lebanon's Response to Syrian Refugees." *Journal of Refugee Studies* 34, no. 1 (2020): 491–519.

Black, Richard. "Putting Refugees in Camps." *Forced Migration Review*, no. 2 (August 1998): 4–7.

Boano, Camillo, and Francisco Vergara Perucich. "Half-Happy Architecture." *Viceversa* 4 (2016): 59–81.

Boccagni, Paolo. *Migration and the Search for Home: Mapping Domestic Space in Migrants' Everyday Lives*. New York: Palgrave Macmillan, 2017.

Boccagni, Paolo, and Sara Bonfanti. *Migration and Domestic Space: Ethnographies of Home in the Making*. London: Springer, 2023.

Borton, John, and Sarah Collinson. *Responses to Mixed Migration in Europe: Implications for the Humanitarian Sector*. London: Overseas Development Institute, 2017.

Bourdieu, Pierre. "The Berber House or the World Reversed." In *Rules and Meanings: The Anthropology of Everyday Knowledge*, edited by Mary Douglas, 98–110. Harmondsworth: Penguin Education, 1973.

Bradburd, Daniel. *Being There: The Necessity of Fieldwork*. Washington: Smithsonian Institution Press, 1998.

Bradley, Miriam. "Five Shades of Grey: Variants of 'Political' Humanitarianism." *Disasters* 46, no. 4 (2022): 1027–48.

Brand, Stewart. *How Buildings Learn: What Happens after They're Built*. London: Viking, 1994.

Brankamp, Hanno. "Camp Abolition: Ending Carceral Humanitarianism in Kenya (and Beyond)." *Antipode* 54, no. 1 (2022): 106–29.

Braybrooke, David. *Meeting Needs*. Princeton: Princeton University Press, 1987.

Breeze, Mark E. "Towards Better Shelter: Rethinking Humanitarian Sheltering." In *Structures of Protection? Rethinking Refugee Shelter*, edited by Tom Scott-Smith and Mark E. Breeze, 287–300. New York: Berghahn Books, 2020.

Brun, Catherine. "Hospitality: Becoming 'IDPs' and 'Hosts' in Protracted Displacement." *Journal of Refugee Studies* 23, no. 3 (2010): 337–55.

Cabot, Heath. "The Business of Anthropology and the European Refugee Regime." *American Ethnologist* 46, no. 3 (2019): 261–75.

Cabot, Heath. "'Contagious' Solidarity: Reconfiguring Care and Citizenship in Greece's Social Clinics." *Social Anthropology* 24, no. 2 (2016): 152–66.

Cabot, Heath. "The European Refugee Crisis and Humanitarian Citizenship in Greece." *Ethnos* 84, no. 5 (2018): 747–71.

Candea, Matei, and Giovanni Da Col. "The Return to Hospitality." *Journal of the Royal Anthropological Institute* 18 (2012): S1–S19.

Carpi, Estella. *The Politics of Crisis-Making: Forced Displacement and Cultures of Assistance in Lebanon*. Bloomington: Indiana University Press, 2023.

Carpi, Estella. "Winking at Humanitarian Neutrality: The Liminal Politics of the State in Lebanon." *Anthropologica* 61, no. 1 (2019): 83–96.

Carsten, Janet, and Stephen Hugh-Jones, eds. *About the House: Lévi-Strauss and Beyond*. Cambridge: Cambridge University Press, 1995.

Carsten, Janet, and Stephen Hugh-Jones. "Introduction." In *About the House: Lévi-*

Strauss and Beyond, edited by Janet Carsten and Stephen Hugh-Jones, 1–46. Cambridge: Cambridge University Press, 1995.

Cassely, Jean-Laurent. "Le Paris d'Anne Hidalgo: Les Bobos, C'est Fini, Voici les Sosos." *Slate France,* June 28, 2013.

Catholic Relief Services. *Using Cash for Shelter: An Overview of CRS Programs.* Baltimore: Catholic Relief Services, 2015.

Chalcraft, John. *The Invisible Cage: Syrian Migrant Workers in Lebanon.* Stanford: Stanford University Press, 2009.

Charlesworth, Esther Ruth. *Humanitarian Architecture: 15 Stories of Architects Working after Disaster.* London: Routledge, 2014.

Chatty, Dawn. *Displacement and Dispossession in the Modern Middle East.* New York: Cambridge University Press, 2010.

Chatty, Dawn. *Syria: The Making and Unmaking of a Refuge State.* London: Hurst and Company, 2018.

Cheliotis, Leonidas, and Sappho Xenakis. "What's Left? Political Orientation, Economic Conditions and Incarceration in Greece under Syriza-Led Government." *European Journal of Criminology* 18, no. 1 (2021): 74–100.

Chouliaraki, Lilie. "The Theatricality of Humanitarianism: A Critique of Celebrity Advocacy." *Communication and Critical Cultural Studies* 9, no. 1 (2012): 1–21.

Chtouris, Sotiris, and DeMond Miller. "Refugee Flows and Volunteers in the Current Humanitarian Crisis in Greece." *Journal of Applied Security Research* 12, no. 1 (2017): 61–77.

City Plaza. "39 Months City Plaza: The End of an Era, the Beginning of a New One." Accessed May 16, 2022. https://best-hotel-in-europe.eu.

Cline, Ann. *A Hut of One's Own: Life Outside the Circle of Architecture.* Cambridge: MIT Press, 1997.

Cohen, Robin, and Nicholas Van Hear. *Refugia: Radical Solutions to Mass Displacement.* Abingdon: Routledge, 2020.

Collier, Paul. "A Jobs Solution to the Migration Crisis." *World Bank Blogs,* September 9, 2015. https://blogs.worldbank.org/jobs/jobs-solution-migration-crisis.

Collier, Stephen, Jamie Cross, Peter Redfield, and Alice Street, eds. "Little Development Devices / Humanitarian Goods." Special issue, *Limn* 9 (2017).

Collins, Lauren. "Paris's First Official Refugee Shelter." *New Yorker,* November 7, 2016.

Collins, Sam, Tom Corsellis, and Antonella Vitale. *Transitional Shelter: Understanding Shelter from the Emergency through Reconstruction and Beyond.* London: ALNAP, 2010.

Cooke, Bill, and Uma Kothari, eds. *Participation: The New Tyranny?* London: Zed Books, 2001.

Copley, Clare. "Curating Tempelhof: Negotiating the Multiple Histories of Berlin's 'Symbol of Freedom.'" *Urban History* 44, no. 4 (2016): 698–717.

Corsellis, Tom. *Transitional Shelter Guidelines.* Geneva: International Organization for Migration, 2012.

Corsellis, Tom, and Antonella Vitale. *Transitional Settlement: Displaced Populations*. Oxford: Oxfam, 2005.

Crabapple, Molly. "The Attack on Exarchia, an Anarchist Refuge in Athens." *New Yorker*, January 20, 2020.

Crisp, Jeff, and Karen Jacobsen. "Refugee Camps Reconsidered." *Forced Migration Review*, no. 3 (December 1998): 27–30.

Cross, Jamie, and Alice Street. "Anthropology at the Bottom of the Pyramid." *Anthropology Today* 25, no. 4 (2009): 4–9.

Cuny, Frederick. "Refugee Camps and Camp Planning: The State of the Art." *Disasters* 1, no. 2 (1977): 125–43.

Dalal, Ayham. *From Shelters to Dwellings: The Zaatari Refugee Camp*. Bielefeld: Verlag, 2022.

Dalal, Ayham, Amer Darweesh, Philipp Misselwitz, and Anna Steigemann. "Planning the Ideal Refugee Camp? A Critical Interrogation of Recent Planning Innovations in Jordan and Germany." *Urban Planning* 3, no. 4 (2018): 64–78.

Dalal, Ayham, Aline Fraikin, and Antonia Noll. "Appropriating Berlin's Tempohomes." In *Spatial Transformations: Kaleidoscopic Perspectives on the Refiguration of Spaces*, edited by Angela Million, Christian Haid, Ignacio Castillo Ulloa, and Nina Baur, 285–93. London: Routledge, 2022.

Darling, Jonathan. "Becoming Bare Life: Asylum, Hospitality, and the Politics of Encampment." *Environment and Planning D: Society and Space* 27, no. 4 (2009): 649–65.

Darling, Jonathan. "A City of Sanctuary: The Relational Re-Imagining of Sheffield's Asylum Politics." *Transactions of the Institute of British Geographers* 35, no. 1 (2010): 125–40.

Darling, Jonathan. "Forced Migration and the City: Irregularity, Informality, and the Politics of Presence." *Progress in Human Geography* 41, no. 2 (2017): 178–98.

Darwish, Mahmoud. *A River Dies of Thirst*. Translated by Catherine Cobham. New York: Archipelago Books, 2009.

Davis, Ian. *Shelter after Disaster*. Oxford: Oxford Polytechnic Press, 1978.

Davis, Ian. "What Have We Learned from 40 Years' Experience of Disaster Shelter?" *Environmental Hazards* 10, no. 3–4 (2011): 193–212.

Dawkins, Casey. "Autonomy and Housing Policy." *Housing, Theory and Society* 34, no. 4 (2017): 420–38.

De Certeau, Michel. *The Practice of Everyday Life*. Berkley: University of California Press, 1984.

Défenseur des Droits. *Rapport d'Observation: Démantèlement des Campements et Prise en Charge des Exilés*. Paris: Défenseur des Droits, 2016.

Delugan-Meissl, Elke, Sabine Dreher, and Christian Muhr. *Reports and Stories from 'Places for People.'* Venice: Biennale Architettura, 2016.

Derrida, Jacques. *Of Hospitality*. Stanford: Stanford University Press, 2000.

Dessauce, Marc. *The Inflatable Moment: Pneumatics and Protest in 1968*. New York: Princeton Architectural Press, 1999.

DeVictor, Xavier. "How Long Do Refugees Stay in Exile? To Find Out, Beware of Averages." *Development for Peace* (blog). *World Bank Blogs*, December 9, 2019. https://blogs.worldbank.org/dev4peace/2019-update-how-long-do-refugees-stay-exile-find-out-beware-averages.

Diken, Bülent, and Carsten Bagge Laustsen. "The Camp." *Geografiska Annaler Series B-Human Geography* 88, no. 4 (2006): 443–52.

Dimitriadi, Angeliki. *Irregular Afghan Migration to Europe: At the Margins, Looking In*. London: Palgrave Macmillan, 2018.

Donnelley, Paul. "Inside the Abandoned Lebanese Shopping Centre That Is Now Home to More than 1,000 Syrian Refugees." *Daily Mail*, June 18, 2014.

Doraï, Kamel, and Pauline Piraud-Fournet. "From Tent to Makeshift Housing: A Case Study of a Syrian Refugee in Zaatari Camp." In *Refugees as City-Makers*, edited by Mona Fawaz, Ahmad Gharbieh, Mona Harb, and Dounia Salamé, 136–39. Beirut: American University of Beirut, 2018.

Doyal, Len, and Ian Gough. *A Theory of Human Need*. Basingstoke: Macmillan, 1991.

Dualeh, Mohamed. "Letter: Do Refugees Belong in Camps?" *Lancet* 346, no. 8986 (1995): 1369–70.

Duffield, Mark. "Challenging Environments: Danger, Resilience and the Aid Industry." *Security Dialogue* 43, no. 5 (2012): 475–92.

Duffield, Mark. *Post-humanitarianism: Governing Precarity in the Digital World*. Cambridge: Polity, 2019.

Dunn, Elizabeth Cullen. "The Chaos of Humanitarian Aid: Adhocracy in the Republic of Georgia." *Humanity: An International Journal of Human Rights, Humanitarianism, and Development* 3, no. 1 (2012): 1–23.

Dunn, Elizabeth Cullen. *No Path Home: Humanitarian Camps and the Grief of Displacement*. Ithaca: Cornell University Press, 2018.

Dunn, Elizabeth Cullen, and Martin Demant Frederiksen. "Uncanny Valleys: *Unheimlichkeit*, Approximation and the Refugee Camp." *Anthropology Today* 34, no. 6 (2018): 21–24.

Dworkin, Gerald. "Autonomy." In *A Companion to Contemporary Political Philosophy*, edited by Robert Goodin, Philip Pettit, and Thomas Pogge, 439–51. London: Wiley, 2017.

Dworkin, Gerald. *The Theory and Practice of Autonomy*. Cambridge: Cambridge University Press, 1988.

Easthope, Hazel. "A Place Called Home." *Housing, Theory and Society* 21, no. 3 (2004): 128–38.

Edkins, Jenny. "Sovereign Power, Zones of Indistinction, and the Camp." *Alternatives: Local, Global, Political* 25, no. 1 (2000): 3–25.

EOOS. *The Cooked Kitchen: A Poetical Analysis*. Vienna: Springer, 2006.

EOOS. *Meet EOOS*. Pamphlet. Vienna: EOOS, June 2014.

Fassin, Didier. "Compassion and Repression: The Moral Economy of Immigration Policies in France." *Cultural Anthropology* 20, no. 3 (2005): 362–87.

Fassin, Didier. "Humanitarianism as a Politics of Life." *Public Culture* 19, no. 3 (2007): 499–520.

Fawaz, Mona. "Planning and the Refugee Crisis: Informality as a Framework of Analysis and Reflection." *Planning Theory* 16, no. 1 (2016): 99–115.

Fawaz, Mona. "An Unusual Clique of City-Makers: Social Networks in the Production of a Neighborhood in Beirut (1950–75)." *International Journal of Urban and Regional Research* 32, no. 3 (2008): 565–85.

Fawaz, Mona, Ahmad Gharbieh, Mona Harb, and Dounia Salamé, eds. *Refugees as City-Makers*. Beirut: Issam Fares Institute, 2018.

Fechter, Anne-Meike, and Anke Schwittay. "Citizen Aid: Grassroots Interventions in Development and Humanitarianism." *Third World Quarterly* 40, no. 10 (2019): 1769–80.

Feinberg, Joel. *The Moral Limits of the Criminal Law*. Vol. 3, *Harm to Self*. Oxford: Oxford University Press, 1986.

Feldman, Ilana. *Life Lived in Relief: Humanitarian Predicaments and Palestinian Refugee Politics*. Oakland: University of California Press, 2018.

Feldman, Ilana. "What Is a Camp? Legitimate Refugee Lives in Spaces of Long-Term Displacement." *Geoforum* 66 (2015): 244–52.

Fischer, Leandros, and Martin Bak Jørgensen. "'We Are Here to Stay' vs. 'Europe's Best Hotel': Hamburg and Athens as Geographies of Solidarity." *Antipode* 53, no. 4 (2021): 1062–82.

"Flat-Pack Accounting." *Economist*, May 11, 2006. https://www.economist.com/business/2006/05/11/flat-pack-accounting.

Foster, Nick. "Berlin Neighborhood Thrives at Edge of Old Airport." *New York Times*, August 8, 2013.

Frankfurt, Harry. "Freedom of the Will and the Concept of a Person." *Journal of Philosophy* 68, no. 1 (1971): 5–20.

Gander, Kashmira. "The Designers Trying to Help Victims of the Refugee Crisis by Building Apps and Shelters." *Independent*, June 30, 2016.

Garvey, Pauline. *Unpacking IKEA: Swedish Design for the Purchasing Masses*. London: Routledge, 2017.

Gatter, Melissa. "Preserving Order: Narrating Resilience as Threat in Jordan's Azraq Refugee Camp." *Territory, Politics, Governance* 11, no. 4 (2021): 695–711.

Gatter, Melissa. *Time and Power in Azraq Refugee Camp: A Nine-to-Five Emergency*. Cairo: American University in Cairo Press, 2023.

George, Jennifer Ward. "Humanitarian Sheltering: Analysing Global Structures of Aid." PhD diss., University of Cambridge, 2023.

George, Jennifer Ward, Peter Guthrie, and John Orr. "Redefining Shelter: Humanitarian Sheltering." *Disasters* 47, no. 2 (2023): 482–98.

Ghandour-Demiri, Nada, and Petros Passas. "Materiality, Agency and Temporariness in Camps in Greece." In *Material Culture and (Forced) Migration: Materializing the Transient*, edited by Friedemann Neumann, Andrea Lauser, Antonie Fuhse, and Peter Bräunlein, 282–304. London: UCL Press, 2022.

Giudici, Daniela. "Homemaking and Forced Migration: A Bibliography." Working paper, HOASI, University of Trento, Trento, Italy, 2019.

Givoni, Michal. "Beyond the Humanitarian/Political Divide: Witnessing and the Making of Humanitarian Ethics." *Journal of Human Rights* 10, no. 1 (2011): 55–75.

Glasman, Joël. *Humanitarianism and the Quantification of Human Needs: Minimal Humanity.* New York: Routledge, 2020.

Goh, Esther Schroeder. "Structures to Shelter the Mind: Refugee Housing and Mental Wellbeing in Berlin." In *Structures of Protection? Rethinking Refugee Shelter,* edited by Tom Scott-Smith and Mark E. Breeze, 175–84. New York: Berghahn Books, 2020.

Gordon, Robert. *The Rise and Fall of American Growth: The U.S. Standard of Living since the Civil War.* Princeton: Princeton University Press, 2016.

Gray, John. *Mill on Liberty: A Defence.* London: Routledge, 2013.

Green, Sarah, and Patrick Laviolette, eds. "The Other Side of the Crisis: Solidarity Networks in Greece." Special section, *Social Anthropology* 24, no. 2 (May 2016).

Gueguen-Teil, Cannelle, and Irit Katz. "On the Meaning of Shelter: Living in Calais's Camps de la Lande." In *Camps Revisited: Multifaceted Spatialities of a Modern Political Technology,* edited by Irit Katz, Diana Martín, and Claudio Minca, 83–99. London: Rowman and Littlefield, 2018.

Guyer, Paul. "Kant on the Theory and Practice of Autonomy." *Social Philosophy and Policy* 20, no. 2 (2003): 70–98.

Haddad, Simon. "The Origins of Popular Opposition to Palestinian Resettlement in Lebanon." *International Migration Review* 38, no. 2 (2004): 470–92.

Hagan, Maria. "Contingent Camps: An Ethnographic Study of Contested Encampment in the Northern French and Northern Moroccan Borderlands." PhD diss., University of Cambridge, 2022.

Hagan, Maria. "The Contingent Camp: Struggling for Shelter in Calais, France." In *Structures of Protection? Rethinking Refugee Shelter,* edited by Tom Scott-Smith and Mark E. Breeze, 111–22. Oxford: Berghahn Books, 2020.

Hamilton, Lawrence. *The Political Philosophy of Needs.* Cambridge: Cambridge University Press, 2003.

Hardt, Michael, and Antonio Negri. *Empire.* Cambridge, MA: Harvard University Press, 2000.

Harris, Neil. *Building Lives: Constructing Rites and Passages.* New Haven: Yale University Press, 1999.

Hart, Jason, Natalia Paszkiewicz, and Dima Albadra. "Shelter as Home? Syrian Homemaking in Jordanian Refugee Camps." *Human Organization* 77, no. 4 (2018): 371–80.

Heidegger, Martin. *Poetry, Language, Thought.* New York: Harper and Row, 1971.

Herz, Manuel. "Refugee Camps—or—Ideal Cities in Dust and Dirt." In *Urban Transformation,* edited by Ilka Ruby and Andreas Ruby, 276–89. Berlin: Ruby, 2008.

Herzfeld, Michael. "'As in Your Own House': Hospitality, Ethnography, and the Stereotype of Mediterranean Society." In *Honor and Shame and the Unity of the*

Mediterranean, edited by David D. Gilmore, 75–89. Washington, DC: American Anthropological Association, 1987.

Hicks, Dan, and Sarah Mallet. *Lande: The Calais 'Jungle' and Beyond*. Bristol: Bristol University Press, 2019.

Hindman, Heather, and Anne-Meike Fechter, eds. *Inside the Everyday Lives of Development Workers: The Challenges and Futures of Aidland*. Sterling: Kumarian, 2011.

Hoffmann, Sophia. "Humanitarian Security in Jordan's Azraq Camp." *Security Dialogue* 48, no. 2 (2017): 97–112.

Holmes, Seth, and Heide Castañeda. "Representing the 'European Refugee Crisis' in Germany and Beyond: Deservingness and Difference, Life and Death." *American Ethnologist* 43, no. 1 (2016): 12–24.

Holub, Barbara. *Das Bienvenue: Ein Recht Auf Raum Für Alle* (Vienna: Social Design Arts as Urban Innovation, 2016).

Holzberg, Billy. "'Wir Schaffen Das': Hope and Hospitality beyond the Humanitarian Border." *Journal of Sociology* 57, no. 3 (2021): 743–59.

Howard, Jim, and Robert Mister. "Lessons Learnt by Oxfam from Their Experience of Shelter Provision 1970–1978." *Disasters* 3, no. 2 (1979): 136–44.

Howden, Daniel. "Moria: Anti-shelter and the Spectacle of Deterrence." In *Structures of Protection? Rethinking Refugee Shelter*, edited by Tom Scott-Smith and Mark E. Breeze, 57–70. New York: Berghahn Books, 2020.

Howden, Daniel, and Apostolis Fotiadis. "The Refugee Archipelago: The Inside Story of What Went Wrong in Greece." *New Humanitarian*, March 6, 2017.

Howden, Daniel, and Apostolis Fotiadis. "Where Did the Money Go? How Greece Fumbled the Refugee Crisis." *Guardian*, March 9, 2017.

Huggler, Justin. "Berlin Turns Stasi Headquarters into Refugee Shelter." *Daily Telegraph*, November 23, 2015.

Husak, Douglas. "Paternalism and Autonomy." *Philosophy and Public Affairs* 10, no. 1 (1981): 27–46.

Hyndman, Jennifer. *Managing Displacement: Refugees and the Politics of Humanitarianism*. Minneapolis: University of Minnesota Press, 2000.

ICRC and International Federation of Red Cross and Red Crescent Societies. *Guidelines for Cash Transfer Programming*. Geneva: ICRC and International Federation of Red Cross and Red Crescent Societies, 2007.

Ingold, Tim. "Anthropology Contra Ethnography." *HAU: Journal of Ethnographic Theory* 7, no. 1 (2017): 21–26.

Ingold, Tim. "That's Enough About Ethnography!" *HAU: Journal of Ethnographic Theory* 4, no. 1 (2014): 383–95.

Ishkanian, Armine, and Isabel Shutes. "Who Needs the Experts? The Politics and Practices of Alternative Humanitarianism and Its Relationship to NGOs." *Voluntas: International Journal of Voluntary and Nonprofit Organisations* 33 (2021): 397–407.

Jameson, Fredric. *Postmodernism, or, the Cultural Logic of Late Capitalism*. London: Verso, 1991.

Janmyr, Maja. "No Country of Asylum: 'Legitimizing' Lebanon's Rejection of the 1951 Refugee Convention." *International Journal of Refugee Law* 29, no. 3 (2017): 438–65.

Janmyr, Maja. "Precarity in Exile: The Legal Status of Syrian Refugees in Lebanon." *Refugee Survey Quarterly* 35, no. 4 (2016): 58–78.

Janmyr, Maja. "Spaces of Legal Ambiguity: Refugee Camps and Humanitarian Power." *Humanity: An International Journal of Human Rights, Humanitarianism, and Development* 7, no. 3 (2016): 413–27.

Janmyr, Maja, and Are Knudsen. "Introduction: Hybrid Spaces." *Humanity: An International Journal of Human Rights, Humanitarianism, and Development* 7, no. 3 (2016): 391–95.

Jansen, Bram. *Kakuma Refugee Camp: Humanitarian Urbanism in Kenya's Accidental City.* London: Zed Books, 2018.

Jencks, Charles. *The Language of Post-modern Architecture.* London: Academy Editions, 1978.

Katz, Irit. "Between Bare Life and Everyday Life: Spatializing Europe's Migrant Camps." *Architecture_MPS* 12, no. 2 (2017): 1–21

Keenan, Brian. *An Evil Cradling.* London: Vintage, 1993.

Kennedy, Jim, and Charles Parrack. "The History of Three Point Five Square Metres." In *Shelter Projects 2011–2012*, edited by Joseph Ashmore, 109–10. Geneva: IFRC and UNHCR, 2013.

Khalil, Sally Abi. *Lebanon Looking Ahead in Times of Crisis: Taking Stock of the Present to Urgently Build Sustainable Options for the Future.* Beirut: Oxfam, 2015.

Kiddey, Rachael. "Reluctant Refuge: An Activist Archaeological Approach to Alternative Refugee Shelter in Athens (Greece)." *Journal of Refugee Studies* 33, no. 3 (2020): 599–621.

Kikano, Faten, Gabriel Fauveaud, and Gonzalo Lizarralde. "Policies of Exclusion: The Case of Syrian Refugees in Lebanon." *Journal of Refugee Studies* 34, no. 1 (2021): 422–52.

Kingsley, Patrick. "'Prisoners of Europe': The Everyday Humiliation of Refugees Stuck in Greece." *Guardian*, September 6, 2016.

Kleinschmidt, Kilian. "Cities of Tomorrow: From Temporariness to Inclusion." Blox Hub, May 24, 2019. https://bloxhub.org/urban-resilience/cities-of-tomorrow -from-temporariness-to-inclusion.

Knudsen, Are. "Camp, Ghetto, Zinco, Slum: Lebanon's Transitional Zones of Emplacement." *Humanity: An International Journal of Human Rights, Humanitarianism, and Development* 7, no. 3 (2016): 443–57.

Kotronaki, Loukia. "Outside the Doors: Refugee Accommodation Squats and Heterotopy Politics." *South Atlantic Quarterly* 117, no. 4 (2018): 914–24.

Kotronaki, Loukia, Olga Lafazani, and Giorgos Maniatis. "Living Resistance: Experiences from Refugee Housing Squats in Athens." *South Atlantic Quarterly* 117, no. 4 (2018): 892–95.

Kotsioni, Ioanna. "Detention of Migrants and Asylum-Seekers: The Challenge for Humanitarian Actors." *Refugee Survey Quarterly* 35, no. 2 (2016): 41–55.

Lafazani, Olga. "Homeplace Plaza: Challenging the Border between Host and Hosted." *South Atlantic Quarterly* 117, no. 4 (2018): 896–904.

Lafazani, Olga. "Intervention—1.5 Year City Plaza: A Project on the Antipodes of Bordering and Control Policies." Antipode Online, November 13, 2017. https://antipodeonline.org/2017/11/13/intervention-city-plaza/.

Larking, Emma. "Are Refugee Camps Totalitarian?" *Arendt Studies* 2 (2018): 243–52.

Lasswell, Harold. *Politics: Who Gets What, When, How.* New York: Peter Smith, 1950.

Laugier, Marc-Antoine. *An Essay on Architecture; in Which Its True Principles Are Explained, and Invariable Rules Proposed, for Directing the Judgement and Forming the Taste of the Gentleman and the Architect, with Regard to the Different Kinds of Buildings, the Embellishment of Cities.* London: Osborne and Shipton, 1755.

Lischer, Sarah Kenyon. *Dangerous Sanctuaries: Refugee Camps, Civil War, and the Dilemmas of Humanitarian Aid.* Ithaca: Cornell University Press, 2005.

Magnusson, Warren. *Politics of Urbanism: Seeing like a City.* London: Routledge, 2011.

Makdisi, Ussama. "Reconstructing the Nation-State: The Modernity of Sectarianism in Lebanon." *Middle East Report* 200 (1996): 23–30.

Malamud, Randy. "The New Psychogeography of Tempelhof Airport, Once a Nazi Landmark." *The Atlantic*, December 23, 2013.

Malkki, Liisa. *The Need to Help: The Domestic Arts of International Humanitarianism.* Durham: Duke University Press, 2015.

Malkki, Liisa. *Purity and Exile: Violence, Memory and National Cosmology among Hutu Refugees in Tanzania.* Chicago: University of Chicago Press, 1995.

Maniatis, Giorgos. "From a Crisis of Management to Humanitarian Crisis Management." *South Atlantic Quarterly* 117, no. 4 (2018): 905–13.

Margaronis, Maria. "Greece's Haven Hotel." *Crossing Continents.* BBC World Service. BBC Radio 4, April 5, 2018.

Maslow, Abraham. "A Theory of Human Motivation." *Psychological Review* 50 (1943): 370–96.

McClelland, Mac. "How to Build a Perfect Refugee Camp." *New York Times*, February 13, 2014.

McConnachie, Kirsten. "Camps of Containment: A Genealogy of the Refugee Camp." *Humanity: An International Journal of Human Rights, Humanitarianism, and Development* 7, no. 3 (2016): 397–412.

McConnachie, Kirsten. *Governing Refugees: Justice, Order and Legal Pluralism.* Law, Development and Globalization. Abingdon: Routledge, 2014.

McConnachie, Kirsten. "Rethinking the 'Refugee Warrior': The Karen National Union and Refugee Protection on the Thai–Burma Border." *Journal of Human Rights Practice* 4, no. 1 (2012): 30–56.

McEachran, Rich. "Exo Units: The Shelters Redefining Emergency Housing." *Guardian*, April 3, 2014.

McLaughlin, Níall. "Six Pockets of Time." Lecture given at University College London, London, England, March 20, 2019.

Meier, Daniel. "Al-Tawteen: The Implantation Problem as an Idiom of the Palestinian Presence in Post-civil War Lebanon (1989–2005)." *Arab Studies Quarterly* 32, no. 3 (2010): 145–62.

Mendel, Gideon. *Dzhangal*. London: GOST Books, 2017.

Merry, Sally Engle. *The Seductions of Quantification: Measuring Human Rights, Gender Violence, and Sex Trafficking.* Chicago: University of Chicago Press, 2016.

Miller, David. *Principles of Social Justice.* Cambridge, MA: Harvard University Press, 1999.

Mitchell, Jon. "A Fourth Critic of the Enlightenment: Michel De Certeau and the Ethnography of Subjectivity." *Social Anthropology* 15, no. 1 (2007): 89–106.

Moore, Barrington. *Reflections on the Causes of Human Misery and upon Certain Proposals to Eliminate Them.* Boston: Beacon Press, 1972.

Mori, Masahiro. "The Uncanny Valley." Translated by Karl MacDorman and Norri Kageki. *IEEE Robotics and Automation Magazine*, June 2012, 98–100.

Mortland, Carol. "Transforming Refugees in Refugee Camps." *Urban Anthropology* 16, no. 3/4 (1987): 375–404.

Mosse, David, ed. *Adventures in Aidland: The Anthropology of Professional International Development.* Oxford: Berghahn Books, 2011.

Mould, Oli. "The Calais Jungle: A Slum of London's Making." *City* 21, no. 3–4 (2017): 388–404.

Mould, Oli. "The Not-So-Concrete Jungle: Material Precarity in the Calais Refugee Camp." *Cultural Geographies* 25, no. 3 (2018): 393–409.

Mourad, Lama. "Brothers, Workers or Syrians? The Politics of Naming in Lebanese Municipalities." *Journal of Refugee Studies* 34, no. 2 (2021): 1387–99.

Mourad, Lama. "'Standoffish' Policy-Making: Inaction and Change in the Lebanese Response to the Syrian Displacement Crisis." *Middle East Law and Governance* 9, no. 3 (2017): 249–66.

Mudu, Pierpaolo, and Sutapa Chattopadhyay, eds. *Migration, Squatting and Radical Autonomy.* London: Routledge, 2016.

Murphy, Keith. *Swedish Design: An Ethnography.* Ithaca: Cornell University Press, 2015.

Nasrallah, Fida. "Lebanese Perceptions of the Palestinians in Lebanon: Case Studies." *Journal of Refugee Studies* 10, no. 3 (1997): 349–59.

Nolen, Stephanie. "Home, On Demand: Abeer Seikaly's Pop-Up Tents." *Globe and Mail*, November 18, 2015.

Norris, Lucy. "Economies of Moral Fibre? Recycling Charity Clothing into Emergency Aid Blankets." *Journal of Material Culture* 17, no. 4 (2012): 389–404.

NRC (Norwegian Refugee Council). *The Camp Management Toolkit.* Oslo: NRC, 2008.

NRC (Norwegian Refugee Council). *An Evaluation of the NRC Shelter Occupancy Free-of-Charge Modality in Lebanon.* Beirut: NRC, 2018.

Nyers, Peter. *Rethinking Refugees: Beyond States of Emergency.* Global Horizons Series. London: Routledge, 2006.

Oliver, Paul. *Dwellings: The House across the World.* Oxford: Phaidon, 1987.

Oliver, Paul. *Shelter and Society.* New York: Praeger, 1969.

Onishi, Norimitsu. "Lebanon Worries that Housing Will Make Syrian Refugees Stay." *New York Times,* December 11, 2013.

Owens, Patricia. "Reclaiming 'Bare Life': Against Agamben on Refugees." *International Relations* 23, no. 4 (2009): 567–82.

Pande, Amrita. "'The Paper That You Have in Your Hand Is My Freedom': Migrant Domestic Work and the Sponsorship (Kafala) System in Lebanon." *International Migration Review* 47, no. 2 (2013): 414–41.

Pao, Maureen. "New Kind of IKEA Hack: Flat-Packs Head to Refugee Camps." NPR, July 2, 2013. https://www.npr.org/sections/parallels/2013/06/27/196356373/new-kind-of-IKEA-hack-flat-packs-head-to-refugee-camps.

Papanek, Victor. *Design for the Real World: Human Ecology and Social Change.* St. Albans: Paladin, 1974.

Paras, Andrea, and Janice Gross Stein. "Bridging the Sacred and the Profane in Humanitarian Life." In *Sacred Aid: Faith and Humanitarianism,* edited by Michael Barnett and Janice Gross Stein, 211–39. Oxford: Oxford University Press, 2012.

Park, Robert Ezra, and Ralph Turner. *On Social Control and Collective Behavior: Selected Papers.* Chicago: University of Chicago Press, 1967.

Parsloe, Toby. "Arriving through Infrastructures: Berlin's Institutional Shelters for Refugees 2015–2019." PhD diss., University of Cambridge, 2021.

Parsloe, Toby. "From Emergency Shelter to Community Shelter: Berlin's Tempelhof Refugee Camp." In *Structures of Protection? Rethinking Refugee Shelter,* edited by Tom Scott-Smith and Mark E. Breeze, 275–86. New York: Berghahn Books, 2020.

Pascucci, Elisa. "Refugee Shelter in a Logistical World: Designing Goods for Supply-Chain Humanitarianism." *Antipode* 53, no. 1 (2021): 260–78.

Petrakis, Maria. "In Athens, Former Olympic Venues Now Play Host to Refugees." *Los Angeles Times,* November 12, 2015.

Philpott, Colin. *Relics of the Reich: The Buildings the Nazis Left Behind.* Barnsley: Pen and Sword, 2016.

Poll, Zoey. "Bursting the Bubble: A Critical Examination of Hospitable Paris." Master's thesis, University of Oxford, 2017.

Pollock, Susan, and Reinhard Bernbeck. "A Gate to a Darker World: Excavating at the Tempelhof Airport." In *Ethics and the Archaeology of Violence,* edited by Alfredo Gonzalez-Ruibal and Gabriel Moshenska, 137–52. London: Springer, 2015.

Porter, Theodore. *Trust in Numbers: The Pursuit of Objectivity in Science and Public Life.* Princeton: Princeton University Press, 1995.

Quarantelli, Enrico. "Patterns of Sheltering and Housing in US Disasters." *Disaster Prevention and Management: An International Journal* 4, no. 3 (1995): 43–53.

Radford, Talia. "Refugee Camps Are the 'Cities of Tomorrow,' Says Humanitarian Aid Expert." *Dezeen,* November 23, 2015.

Rakopoulos, Theodoros. "Resonance of Solidarity: Meanings of a Local Concept in Anti-austerity Greece." *Journal of Modern Greek Studies* 32, no. 2 (2014): 313–37.

Ramadan, Adam. "Spatialising the Refugee Camp." *Transactions of the Institute of British Geographers* 38, no. 1 (2013): 65–77.

Rancière, Jacques. *Disagreement: Politics and Philosophy*. Translated by Julie Rose. Minneapolis: University of Minnesota Press, 1999.

Rapoport, Amos. *House Form and Culture*. Englewood Cliffs: Prentice Hall, 1969.

Rawls, John. *Political Liberalism*. New York: Columbia University Press, 1993.

Rawls, John. *A Theory of Justice*. Oxford: Clarendon Press, 1972.

Raz, Joseph. *The Morality of Freedom*. Oxford: Clarendon Press, 1986.

REACH. *Al Za'atari Refugee Camp Shelter Assessment*. Geneva: REACH Initiative, 2014.

Redclift, Victoria. "Abjects or Agents? Camps, Contests and the Creation of 'Political Space.'" *Citizenship Studies* 17, no. 3–4 (2013): 308–21.

Redfield, Peter. "Bioexpectations: Life Technologies as Humanitarian Goods." *Public Culture* 24, no. 1 (2012): 157–84.

Redfield, Peter. "Fluid Technologies: The Bush Pump, the Lifestraw® and Microworlds of Humanitarian Design." *Social Studies of Science* 46, no. 2 (2016): 159–83.

Redfield, Peter. *Life in Crisis: The Ethical Journey of Doctors without Borders*. Oakland: University of California Press, 2013.

Redfield, Peter. "Shacktopia: The Meantime Future of Humanitarian Design." *Social Anthropology / Anthropologie sociale* 30, no. 2 (2022): 16–33.

Redfield, Peter. "The Unbearable Lightness of Expats: Double Binds of Humanitarian Mobility." *Cultural Anthropology* 27, no. 2 (2012): 358–82.

Rieff, David. *A Bed for the Night: Humanitarianism in Crisis*. London: Vintage, 2002.

Rosich, Gerard. *The Contested History of Autonomy: Interpreting European Modernity*. London: Bloomsbury, 2019.

Roth, Silke. *The Paradoxes of Aid Work: Passionate Professionals*. London: Routledge, 2015.

Rozakou, Katerina. "Crafting the Volunteer: Voluntary Associations and the Reformation of Sociality." *Journal of Modern Greek Studies* 34, no. 1 (2016): 79–102.

Rozakou, Katerina. "Solidarity #Humanitarianism: The Blurred Boundaries of Humanitarianism in Greece." *Etnofoor* 29, no. 2 (2017): 99–104.

Rudofsky, Bernard. *Architecture without Architects: A Short Introduction to Nonpedigreed Architecture*. Albuquerque: University of New Mexico Press, 1964.

Rygiel, Kim. "Politicizing Camps: Forging Transgressive Citizenships in and through Transit." *Citizenship Studies* 16, no. 5–6 (2012): 807–25.

Rygiel, Kim, Feyzi Baban, and Suzan Ilcan. "The Syrian Refugee Crisis: The EU-Turkey 'Deal' and Temporary Protection." *Global Social Policy* 16, no. 3 (2016): 315–20.

Sandri, Elisa. "'Volunteer Humanitarianism': Volunteers and Humanitarian Aid in the Jungle Refugee Camp of Calais." *Journal of Ethnic and Migration Studies* 44, no. 1 (2018): 65–80.

Sanyal, Romola. "A No-Camp Policy: Interrogating Informal Settlements in Lebanon." *Geoforum* 84 (2017): 117–25.

Sayigh, Yezid. *Armed Struggle and the Search for State: The Palestinian National Movement 1949–1993.* Oxford: Clarendon Press, 1997.

Scanlon, Thomas. *What We Owe to Each Other.* Cambridge: Belknap Press, 1998.

Schmal, Peter Cachola, Oliver Elser, and Anna Scheuermann. *Making Heimat: Germany, Arrival Country.* Berlin: Hatje Cantz Verlag, 2016.

Schneewind, Jerome. *The Invention of Autonomy: A History of Modern Moral Philosophy.* Cambridge: Cambridge University Press, 1998.

Schurade, Svenja. "Writing a History of the 'Long Summer of Migration.'" *Journal Blog. Public Anthropologist,* August 3, 2021. https://publicanthropologist.cmi .no/2021/08/03/writing-a-history-of-the-long-summer-of-migration-reflections -on-activist-academic-practices/.

Scott, James. *Seeing like a State: How Certain Schemes to Improve the Human Condition Have Failed.* London: Yale University Press, 1998.

Scott-Smith, Tom. "Beyond the Boxes: Refugee Shelter and the Humanitarian Politics of Life." *American Ethnologist* 46, no. 4 (2019): 509–21.

Scott-Smith, Tom. "The Humanitarian-Architect Divide." *Forced Migration Review* 55 (June 2017): 67–68.

Scott-Smith, Tom. "Humanitarian Dilemmas in a Mobile World." *Refugee Survey Quarterly* 35, no. 2 (2016): 1–21.

Scott-Smith, Tom. "Humanitarian Neophilia: The 'Innovation Turn' and Its Implications." *Third World Quarterly* 37, no. 12 (2016): 2229–51.

Scott-Smith, Tom. *On an Empty Stomach: Two Hundred Years of Hunger Relief.* Ithaca: Cornell University Press, 2020.

Scott-Smith, Tom. "Paradoxes of Resilience: A Review of the World Disasters Report 2016." *Development and Change* 49, no. 2 (2018): 662–77.

Scott-Smith, Tom. "Places for People: Architecture, Building, and Humanitarian Innovation." *Journal of Humanitarian Affairs* 1, no. 3 (2019): 14–22.

Scott-Smith, Tom. "Places of Partial Protection: Refugee Shelter since 2015." In *Structures of Protection? Rethinking Refugee Shelter,* edited by Tom Scott-Smith and Mark E. Breeze, 1–12. Oxford: Berghahn Books, 2020.

Scott-Smith, Tom. "Sticky Technologies: Plumpy'nut®, Emergency Feeding and the Viscosity of Humanitarian Design." *Social Studies of Science* 48, no. 1 (2018): 3–24.

Sebald, W. G. *Austerlitz.* New York: Modern Library, 2002.

Sen, Amartya. *Development as Freedom.* Oxford: Oxford University Press, 1999.

Serntedakis, Giorgos. "'Solidarity' for Strangers: A Case Study of 'Solidarity' Initiatives in Lesvos." *Etnofoor* 29, no. 2 (2017): 83–98.

Shell, Susan Meld. *Kant and the Limits of Autonomy.* Cambridge, MA: Harvard University Press, 2009.

Shryock, Andrew. "Breaking Hospitality Apart: Bad Hosts, Bad Guests, and the Problem of Sovereignty." *Journal of the Royal Anthropological Institute* 18, no. s1 (2012): S20–S33.

Shryock, Andrew. "Thinking about Hospitality, with Derrida, Kant, and the Balga Bedouin." *Anthropos* 103, no. 2 (2008): 405–21.

Siddiqi, Anooradha. "Ephemerality." *Comparative Studies of South Asia, Africa and the Middle East* 40, no. 1 (2020): 24–34.

Sigona, Nando. "Campzenship: Reimagining the Camp as a Social and Political Space." *Citizenship Studies* 19, no. 1 (2015): 1–15.

Sinclair, Cameron, and Kate Stohr, eds. *Design like You Give a Damn: Architectural Responses to Humanitarian Crises.* London: Thames and Hudson, 2006.

Skran, Claudena, and Evan Easton-Calabria. "Old Concepts Making New History: Refugee Self-Reliance, Livelihoods and the 'Refugee Entrepreneur.'" *Journal of Refugee Studies* 33, no. 1 (2020): 1–21.

Slim, Hugo. "Relief Agencies and Moral Standing in War: Principles of Humanity, Neutrality, Impartiality and Solidarity." *Development in Practice* 7, no. 4 (1997): 342–52.

Smale, Alison. "Tempelhof Airport, Once a Lifeline for Berliners, Reprises Role for Refugees." *New York Times*, February 10, 2016.

Smith, Helena. "Greece: Severe Weather Places Refugees at Risk and Government Under Fire." *Guardian*, January 10, 2017.

Smith, Naomi, and Peter Walters. "Desire Lines and Defensive Architecture in Modern Urban Environments." *Urban Studies* 55, no. 13 (2018): 2980–95.

Soederberg, Susanne. "Governing Global Displacement in Austerity Urbanism: The Case of Berlin's Refugee Housing Crisis." *Development and Change* 50, no. 4 (2019): 923–47.

Sphere Project. *The Sphere Handbook: Humanitarian Charter and Minimum Standards in Humanitarian Response.* 4th ed. Rugby: Sphere Association, 2018.

Starzmann, Maria Theresia. "Excavating Tempelhof Airfield: Objects of Memory and the Politics of Absence." *Rethinking History* 18, no. 2 (2014): 211–29.

Stinson, Liz. "IKEA Develops a Smart Flat-Pack Shelter for Disaster Refugees." *Wired*, July 10, 2013.

Streeten, Paul. "Basics Needs: Premises and Promises." *Journal of Policy Modeling* 1, no. 1 (1979): 136–46.

Strik, Tineke. *Refugees at Risk in Greece.* Strasbourg: Council of Europe, 2016.

Swaine, Lucas. "The Origins of Autonomy." *History of Political Thought* 37, no. 2 (2016): 216–37.

Taylor, Adam. "A Dutch Architect's Plan to Put Europe's Refugees on a Man-Made Island near Tunisia." *Washington Post*, June 1, 2016.

Taylor, Alan. "France Dismantles 'the Jungle' in Calais." *The Atlantic*, October 26, 2016.

Terry, Fiona. *Condemned to Repeat? The Paradox of Humanitarian Action.* London: Cornell University Press, 2002.

Theodossopoulos, Dimitrios. "Philanthropy or Solidarity? Ethical Dilemmas about

Humanitarianism in Crisis-Afflicted Greece." *Social Anthropology* 24, no. 2 (2016): 167–84.

Thies, Jochen, Ian Cooke, and MaryBeth Friedrich. *Hitler's Plans for Global Domination: Nazi Architecture and Ultimate War Aims*. New York: Berghahn Books, 2012.

Thompson, James. *Humanitarian Performance: From Disaster Tragedies to Spectacles of War*. London: Seagull Books, 2013.

Thornhill, Teresa. *Hara Hotel: A Tale of Syrian Refugees in Greece*. London: Verso, 2018.

Ticktin, Miriam. "Calais: Containment Politics in the 'Jungle.'" *Funambulist Magazine* 5 (2016): 29–33.

Ticktin, Miriam. *Casualties of Care: Immigration and the Politics of Humanitarianism in France*. Berkeley: University of California Press, 2011.

Ticktin, Miriam. "Where Ethics and Politics Meet: The Violence of Humanitarianism in France." *American Ethnologist* 33, no. 1 (2006): 33–49.

Trachtenberg, Marvin. *Building-in-Time: From Giotto to Alberti and Modern Oblivion*. New Haven: Yale University Press, 2010.

Trauner, Florian, and Jocelyn Turton. "'Welcome Culture': The Emergence and Transformation of a Public Debate on Migration." *Austrian Journal of Political Science* 46, no. 1 (2017): 33–43.

Turam, Berna. "Refugees in Borderlands: Safe Places versus Securitization in Athens, Greece." *Journal of Urban Affairs* 43, no. 6 (2021): 756–80.

Turner, John. "Housing as a Verb." In *Freedom to Build: Dweller Control of the Housing Process*, edited by John Turner and Robert Fichter, 148–75. New York: Macmillan Press, 1972.

Turner, John, and Robert Fichter, eds. *Freedom to Build: Dweller Control of the Housing Process*. New York: Macmillan Press, 1972.

Turner, Lewis. "Explaining the (Non-)Encampment of Syrian Refugees: Security, Class and the Labour Market in Lebanon and Jordan." *Mediterranean Politics* 20, no. 3 (2015): 386–404.

Turner, Paul. "Romanticism, Rationalism, and the Domino System." In *The Open Hand: Essays on Le Corbusier*, edited by Russell Walden, 14–41. Cambridge: MIT Press, 1977.

Turner, Simon. *Politics of Innocence: Hutu Identity, Conflict, and Camp Life*. Studies in Forced Migration. Oxford: Berghahn Books, 2010.

Turner, Simon. "What Is a Refugee Camp? Explorations of the Limits and Effects of the Camp." *Journal of Refugee Studies* 29, no. 2 (2015): 139–48.

UNDRO (United Nations Disaster Relief Coordinator). *Shelter after Disaster: Guidelines for Assistance*. Geneva: Office of the UNDRO, 1982.

UN-Habitat. *Multilingual Glossary of Human Settlements Terms*. Nairobi: United Nations Centre for Human Settlements, 1992.

UNHCR (United Nations High Commissioner for Refugees). *Guideline for Collective Shelter and Small Shelter Units in Lebanon*. Beirut: UNHCR, 2012.

UNHCR (United Nations High Commissioner for Refugees). *Handbook for Emergencies*. 3rd ed. Geneva: UNHCR, 2007.

UNHCR (United Nations High Commissioner for Refugees). *An Introduction to Cash-Based Interventions in UNHCR Operations*. Geneva: UNHCR, 2012.

UNHCR (United Nations High Commissioner for Refugees). *L'Experience des Centres d'Accueil En France*. Paris: UNHCR, 2017.

UNHCR (United Nations High Commissioner for Refugees). *Policy on Alternatives to Camps*. Geneva: UNHCR, 2014.

UNHCR (United Nations High Commissioner for Refugees). *Shelter Design Catalogue*. Geneva: UNHCR, 2016.

UNHCR (United Nations High Commissioner for Refugees). "Shelter Typologies." Accessed January 16, 2024. https://data.unhcr.org/en/documents/download/62289.

United Nations. *Lebanon Crisis Response Plan 2017–2020*. Beirut: United Nations, 2019.

University of Oxford. "Shelter without Shelter." Refugee Studies Centre. Accessed November 26, 2023. https://www.rsc.ox.ac.uk/shelter-without-shelter.

Van den Berghe, Annabell. "These Refugees Escaped War. Now They're Freezing in Greece's Migrant Camps." *Washington Post*, January 28, 2017.

van der Borght, Stefaan, and Mit Philips. "Letter: Do Refugees Belong in Camps?" *Lancet* 346, no. 8979 (1995): 907–8.

Vandevoordt, Robin. "Subversive Humanitarianism: Rethinking Refugee Solidarity through Grass-Roots Initiatives." *Refugee Survey Quarterly* 38, no. 3 (2019): 245–65.

Vellinga, Marcel. "The End of the Vernacular: Anthropology and the Architecture of the Other." *Etnofoor* 23, no. 1 (2011): 171–92.

Wainwright, Oliver. "IKEA Brings Flatpack Innovation to Emergency Refugee Shelters." *Guardian*, July 2, 2013.

Wainwright, Oliver. "Why IKEA's Flatpack Refugee Shelter Won Design of the Year." *Guardian*, January 27, 2017.

Wallis, William, George Parker, and Lucy Fisher. "First Asylum Seekers Moved to UK's Bibby Stockholm Barge." *Financial Times*, August 8, 2023.

Walzer, Michael. *Spheres of Justice: A Defence of Pluralism and Equality*. Oxford: Robertson, 1983.

Warner, Marina. "Report: Bearer-Beings and Stories in Transit / Storie in Transito." *Marvels and Tales* 31, no. 1 (2017): 149–61.

Weiss, Thomas. "Principles, Politics, and Humanitarian Action." *Ethics and International Affairs* 13, no. 1 (1999): 1–22.

White, Benjamin Thomas. "17 Years in a Refugee Camp: On the Trail of a Dodgy Statistic." *Singular Things* (blog), July 4, 2015. https://singularthings.wordpress.com/2015/07/04/17-years-in-a-refugee-camp-on-the-trail-of-a-dodgy-statistic/.

Wiggins, David. *Needs, Values, Truth*. Oxford: Oxford University Press, 1987.

Windel, Friederike, Arita Balaram, and Krystal M. Perkins. "Discourses of the *Willkommenskultur* (Welcoming Culture) in Germany." *Critical Discourse Studies* 19, no. 1 (2022): 93–116.

Wirth, Louis. "Urbanism as a Way of Life." *American Journal of Sociology* 44, no. 1 (1938): 1–24.

Wong, Liliane. *Adaptive Reuse: Extending the Lives of Buildings.* Basel: Birkhäuser, 2016.

Yassin, Nasser, Tarek Osseiran, Rima Rassi, and Marwa Boustani. *No Place to Stay? Reflections on the Syrian Refugee Shelter Policy in Lebanon.* Beirut: UN-Habitat, 2015.

Young, Holly. "Life in the Aluminium Whale: A Study of Berlin's ICC Shelter." In *Structures of Protection? Rethinking Refugee Shelter,* edited by Tom Scott-Smith and Mark E. Breeze, 163–73. New York: Berghahn Books, 2020.

Zolberg, Aristide, Sergio Aguayo, and Astri Suhrke. *Escape from Violence: Conflict and the Refugee Crisis in the Developing World.* Oxford: Oxford University Press, 1989.

Index

Page numbers in italics denote figures, and endnotes are indicated by "n" followed by the endnote number.

The authorized representative in the EU for product safety and compliance is:
Mare Nostrum Group
B.V Doelen 72
4831 GR Breda
The Netherlands

www.ingramcontent.com/pod-product-compliance
Lightning Source LLC
Chambersburg PA
CBHW020855270326
41928CB00006B/714

* 9 7 8 1 5 0 3 6 4 0 2 8 3 *